Praise for

SAVING BOBBY

"I am sitting on the back porch of our condo bawling. I just finished *Saving Bobby* and I am filled with a belief that this 349-page book is the bravest thing I have ever seen in print. As Renée Hodges made it so clear in the end and was so apparent in each page, this is her story and maybe her eventual salvation. This process has brought Hodges to her darkest places and she found her salvation there. This sounds simple but I know how really hard that is. No one wants to do that. But she did."

—William H. Davis, MD, Orthopedic Surgeon,
Medical Director, OrthoCarolina Foot & Ankle Institute

"As an orthopaedic surgeon, I can say that we have faced the perfect storm in unwittingly facilitating opioid addiction in our patients. . . . This has created an environment where the downstream catastrophe of opioid addiction has not been prioritized or even really thought much about. Renée Hodges has now given us a very loud, clear wakeup call that we must heed. . . . One has to ponder the tremendous good fortune and massive effort required to shepherd Bobby through the process of recovery."

—Claude T. Moorman, III, MD, executive director, Duke
Sports Sciences Institute and Head Team Physician, Duke
Athletics

"If you have a recovering substance abuser in your life or even if you don't, this is an engaging read and a page turner. A truly inspiring look at a young man who was on a downward spiral until he found the right person to help him."
—Linsey L. Hughes, Executive in Residence,
Duke Financial Economics Center

"Renée Hodges spent a courageous year on the front lines of opiate addiction by taking in her struggling nephew, Bobby. Her story of his addiction odyssey is an all-too-common and silent experience in modern America. This story . . . exposes how difficult addiction can be, how it can be found anywhere—rich or poor—and ultimately how it may be overcome. Hodges's story grips the reader from the very first page. Out of her experience with her nephew comes an immensely moving and ultimately uplifting portrait of one American family as it confronts—and surmounts—addiction and fear."
—Mimi Lukens, Senior Lecturer at Law, Duke Law School

"Hodges bravely shares the events leading to Bobby's addiction and places them in context—letting us see family behaviors and cultural patterns that contributed to the challenge. She confronts the stigma of shame surrounding addiction—in a real and personal way. The book is also a love story: a story of a woman who refuses to do the convenient thing and give up on her nephew. Its message provides encouragement for the many families that are involved in this same struggle."
—Ruth Caccavale, Founder,
Bull City Book Club, Durham, North Carolina

"Start to tell anyone the premise behind Renée Hodges's remarkable book, and odds are they'll stop you before you get two sentences out. Their faces betray stunned recognition—'That's what happened to my brother's youngest daughter'; 'Oh dear heaven, you could be talking about my oldest son'; 'My best friend's son died from an overdose when he was twenty, she's never been the same'—because this story, though it is so poignantly Bobby and Renée's story, belongs to us all. None of us has gone untouched by this tragic, life-altering epidemic. *Saving Bobby* strikes a chord in all of us: drawn by the larger picture of a frightening epidemic, we are caught in the gripping drama of the personal. This is a book you cannot put down. This is a story you cannot forget—nor should you."

—Dee Mason, journalist, author, playwright,
and public speaker

SAVING
BOBBY

SAVING
BOBBY

HEROES AND HEROIN
IN ONE SMALL COMMUNITY

BY

RENEE HODGES

SHE WRITES PRESS

Published 2018
Printed in the United States of America
ISBN: 978-1631523755 pbk
ISBN: 978-1-63152-376-2 ebk

Library of Congress Control Number: 2017957045

For information, address:
She Writes Press
1563 Solano Ave #546
Berkeley, CA 94707

Book design by Stacey Aaronson

She Writes Press is a division of SparkPoint Studio, LLC.

This work is a memoir. It reflects my experiences and memories as
accurately as possible. Some of the names in this book have been changed
to respect the privacy of those in my stories. While I have used emails and
texts to construct this story, this book was written mostly from memory. I
lean toward the dramatic and see life in Technicolor, but I have shared this
story as honestly and to the best of my ability as possible.

From Renée:

To Bobby, the most courageous man I know.
To my wonderful husband and children. You are my heart.
To Anne, love for now and eternity.
To Mary, one day.

From Bobby:

To Mom and Dad, Aunt Née and Uncle Will.
To Jeff.

To loving communities everywhere—especially ours.

History repeats itself, first as tragedy, second as farce.

Paraphrased from Karl Marx

And the day came when the risk to remain tight in a bud was more painful than the risk it took to blossom.

Anaïs Nin

PREFACE

I didn't go into my nephew Bobby's recovery with any professional experience, but it just stood to reason that if I wanted to help my loved one, I should surround him with an atmosphere of full disclosure and transparency, a supportive place where he could not hide or be hidden. Only later did I realize how many try to conceal their family's struggle with addiction, isolating themselves and causing undue stress and shame. Addiction is not a parenting failure or something to be embarrassed about. Secrecy, cover-ups, excuses, and denial do not help an addict—or a recovery. This hiding subtly reinforces that the addiction is a secret and therefore shameful. Being truthful from the get-go also avoids the awkwardness of that inevitable moment when the addiction is discovered by friends.

If the addict thinks his supporters, family, and friends are concealing his addiction out of shame, he will internalize that shame, and it will become one more roadblock on the way to recovery. Addiction plus shame is a horrible combination.

For the addict, it may be that hiding or ignoring addiction also gives the disease more power. The more secretive we are about our addiction, or that of family or friends, the easier it is for the addict to shirk accountability or for an enabler to continue the cycle of enabling.

As much as I would like to pretend there is no addiction in my family, there is. This is the simple truth. Addiction is a disease and, like breast cancer or heart disease, it can run in families. Pretending otherwise will not make it go away.

For years, I watched as my family hid from the stark reality of addiction. If we don't say it, it ain't true. If you can't see it, we don't have to face it. Excuses, avoidance, and denial. My family, like millions of other families, felt that talking about addiction openly would be airing our dirty laundry, but I never bought into it. All those years of secrecy had simply allowed succeeding generations to be blindsided by their vulnerability to addiction.

Secrets make you sick, my friend. Reach out and find your community—whether you are the caregiver, the recoverer, or the next-door neighbor.

There can be no denying: the best way to help those that are recovering is to recognize that we are all in this together.

PART ONE

Painkillers Are a Gateway to Heroin

In medicine, oxycodone is known as an opioid analgesic, a powerful painkiller prescribed to patients with acute or chronic pain. On the streets, it's known as heroin in a pill. . . . The truth is heroin is little more than a natural form of oxycodone. It has the same effect on the brain and, for addicts, satisfies the same urge. The big difference is that these days heroin is often more available, more potent and, above all, cheaper.[1]

NIH: National Institute on Drug Abuse

Because prescription opioids are similar to, and act on the same brain systems affected by, heroin and morphine, they present an intrinsic abuse and addiction liability, particularly if they are used for non-medical purposes.

Nearly half of young people who inject heroin surveyed in three recent studies reported abusing prescription opioids before starting to use heroin. Some individuals reported taking up heroin because it is cheaper and easier to obtain than prescription opioids.[2]

---

[1] Mariana van Zeller, "Painkillers are a gateway to heroin," CNN, June 23, 2011, http://www.cnn.com/2011/OPINION/06/23/ zeller.oxycodone.heroin/
Note: Mariana van Zeller won a 2009 Peabody Award for her documentary on prescription drug abuse and pill trafficking.

[2] NIDA (2014). Heroin. Retrieved November 16, 2016, from https://www.drugabuse.gov/publications/drugfacts/ heroin

FDA.gov

Opioids—so named because they are synthetic versions of opium—are narcotics that work by changing the way the brain perceives pain. They are available in forms that include pills, liquids, and skin patches. Commonly prescribed opioids: OxyContin, Percocet, Percodan, hydrocodone, Lortab, Vicodin, (Fentanyl).

T-MINUS EIGHT WEEKS ONE DAY

From: Renée Hodges
Subject: Thomas Howard
Date: January 2, 2013, at 3:07 p.m.
To: Mary Costello, psychologist

Hi Mary,

My best friend, Anne Howard, needs some professional advice, someone to tell her what to do to help her son, Thomas, who has relapsed again. Please recommend drug counselors for Anne, not Thomas. Mary, the situation is really bad, so it would need to be someone who could help her with the legal steps for commitment as Thomas is not a minor and he will not go to rehab voluntarily. If he doesn't get help soon, I'm so afraid he won't live out the year.

Thanks, Renée

T-MINUS FOUR WEEKS

BOBBY

When my brother, John, called me for help, I knew the situation must be serious. Although John and I have a genial relationship, I was not a confidant of his, nor had he talked to me about his son's problems in the past.

I knew Bobby was being treated for an addiction to pain medication, which his doctor had initially prescribed for debilitating back pain while Bobby was in college, almost eight years earlier. It wasn't widely known at that time—2005—that opioids were so highly addictive. So by the time Bobby graduated from college in 2009, he was a full-blown prescription addict. His parents had no idea the extent of Bobby's usage until after he graduated. He overdosed at an LSU football game and became unresponsive. John immediately whisked him away to a drug and rehab hospital in Nevada. Fast forward to January 2013 when Bobby was released once again from another of a growing list of rehabilitation centers. This time he was placed in a halfway house in Florida. The last I'd heard, he'd been searching for a job. Then I got the phone call from John saying things had quickly gone downhill.

What John told me broke my heart. Bobby had left the halfway house and was sleeping in a park, telling his dad how he was tired and that he didn't know if he could continue with life for much longer. Bobby felt he was in too much pain to work and that his counselor was not being sympathetic. And he was very angry.

I am a compulsive problem solver. I instinctively try to find solutions to other people's sticky problems. At the least,

I am a good listener. Because John and I had not been close in many years, I was surprised by the rawness of my brother's voice on the phone; the hurt and desperation were audible. My compulsion to solve this problem heated to a boil.

My brain began to whirl and I tried to look at Bobby's situation from a different angle. It seemed so simple at the time: back problems led to drug problems. Even when Bobby was clean, the back problems were still there, so he continued to have drug problems. Fix the back, fix the problem. See? How simple was that?

I suggested that Bobby come to Duke University Medical Center, located in Durham, North Carolina, for a complete physical. They have a Concierge Medicine service where a flat fee entitled patients to a full year of care.

My brother agreed with this approach. He told me that he had been thinking the same thing: address the physical problem first and then the emotional recovery would follow.

I added, "Call Bobby and tell him to hang in there. I'll set him up ASAP. Don't worry, we will get to the bottom of this."

T-MINUS THREE WEEKS

MAKING PLANS

From: John Redford
Subject: Bobby R
Date: February 10, 2013, at 9:08 p.m.
To: Renée Hodges

Renée,

We are picking Bobby up from the halfway house in Florida and bringing him home to Louisiana until we can fly into Durham and get the medical part figured out. Didn't think it wise for him to have any significant downtime while waiting to hear from Duke as we need to stay structured with him and have him busy. It's not my first choice as I would like to have him come straight to Durham but it works. We also won't have to worry about his truck being stuck in Florida. We're going to be busy pulling together medical records for him in the event he needs to go through the Duke hospital system. Thanks for your love and support. This should buy us all a little time.

John

Duke University Medical Center is one of the top research hospitals in the world. Surely, with good medical care, a resolution would be found.

I was not new to young men in trouble. My best friend Anne's son, Thomas, just three years older than Bobby, had been living on the edge for most of his adult life. Addicted to drugs from his teens, thirty-one-year-old Thomas had overdosed more than once, on each occasion miraculously discovered in time to spend weeks in ICU only to be released, rehabbed, and relapsed. Thomas lived with Anne just down the street, and I was as invested in Thomas's efforts at recovery as I planned to be for Bobby's. My dream was for the two boys, clean and sober, to become best friends and productive citizens.

I called Duke the next morning, ready to start work on the solution. I have so much belief in that hospital, and I was thrilled when Bobby agreed to be seen, to come out of the park, to try again. John and Bobby flew up for their first appointment exactly one week later.

T-MINUS TWO WEEKS

February 17

ARRIVAL

Bobby and John arrived at my house late Sunday night, the night before Bobby's first doctor's appointment. They stumbled in, fatigued from their flight from Louisiana and the stress of the past weeks. I hugged first John and then Bobby, who trailed a bit behind, shoulders stooped in his winter coat, quiet and unreadable. He kept his hands to his sides, allowing me the pleasure of embrace, but rigidly, not reciprocating. It had been several years since I had seen Bobby, and I was surprised by the marked change in his appearance and demeanor. He used to be handsome and thin, six foot three and a gentle and charismatic boy, with a smile on his face and joke on his tongue. Now he looked defeated.

Taking his coat, I noticed he had put on weight, his polo shirt pulled snugly across his thick chest and tucked haphazardly into his beltless khaki pants. He had grown his hair to his shoulders, sandy blond locks slicked back with gel, making him look younger than his twenty-eight years.

He was the kid I remembered, but something was off. I contemplated this until I nearly snapped my fingers in recognition: his youthful innocence was gone. I didn't yet comprehend what had taken its place.

In the fifteen minutes we spent downstairs catching up, Bobby mumbled a mannerly "Thank you," but otherwise he was sullen and uncommunicative, an invisible barrier erected, unseen but definitely felt.

After my husband, Will, showed them to their upstairs

rooms, Bobby quickly excused himself and disappeared. From my perch in the kitchen, I could just barely see him in the shadows created by the floodlight in the backyard, an orange glow from his cigarette bobbing and weaving like a drunken firefly as he befriended the dogs, the tip brightening every time he took a long pull. I wondered when he started smoking and what else I didn't know about my nephew.

DR. PATE

The next morning, worried they might get lost, I drove John and Bobby to their first appointment.

The concierge section of Duke University Medical Center is not in the hospital. The waiting room looks like it could be the waiting room for any large corporation. Concierge Medicine is a great idea for someone who has a lot of specific doctoring needs; it's open to anyone who can pay the fee up front. John and I decided Bobby needed to contract with an internist, someone who would give him a thorough workup given his extensive list of physical symptoms.

The waiting room was inviting and tastefully decorated with nice potted trees and a pile of magazines laid neatly across the cocktail table in perfect lines. The only giveaway that we were in a medical office was the nurse behind the check-in counter, wearing a monochromatic scrub outfit with an attached picture ID hanging around her neck, turned backward in a new security policy.

Short, dark-haired, and dark-skinned, Dr. Pate was reserved and very businesslike. I first met him with both John and Bobby in the lobby. After the introductions, I took my seat and did not go with them to the exam room.

For several hours I sat quietly and impatiently, imagining what sort of intrusive questions a doctor might ask a new patient, one that was a habitual drug user—"How long have you had this back pain? What is your family history? Have you ever had unprotected sex?"—with Bobby unflinchingly answering all questions, suggestions, or directions under his father's watchful eye. "Yes, sir," "No, sir," and "I don't think, sir."

Bobby had written out a list of his ailments for Dr. Pate which John shared with me just before his appointment. Reading them, I thought we were not a minute too soon getting Bobby in to see the doctor.

1. *Throwing up: When I wake up in the mornings, I throw up. I do not force myself, it just happens. If I throw up too much in one day, I begin to see small traces of blood. This has been going on for six years now.*

2. *Back pain: I have pain in my lower-mid back every day. It affects my mood and activity level. I have become very depressed because the current medication does not work. I cannot walk more than half a mile without sitting down because of the pain. If I bend down too long or too many times, my back hurts. I have been to several back doctors and did a several-months-long stint at a pain clinic. The last chiropractor I went to said I was too inflamed for him to work on me. I struggle with this every day. My back pain is the center of my problems because I feel it leads to my depression. It hurts so badly, and complaining does nothing. When people ask me, I just say I am fine, when the truth is, on a typical day the pain is a six on a scale of one to ten. If I do anything that causes me to strain myself, it is a nine. I reserve ten for being unable to move. This has been going on for eight years now.*

3. *Migraines, Headaches: In the past I would have one or two a month, and they were debilitating to the point I could not get out of bed. I have had at least one migraine each of the past two weeks. My tear ducts open up and I release a large amount of tears. I sweat a great deal; my head pounds to the point I cannot think or move. Over-the-counter pain medication does not work at all. Sometimes if I strain too much, it feels like something pops in the right side of my brain and a piercing pain comes upon me that lasts for hours. Then for the next week if I bend down or strain myself, the pain comes back in rhythm with my heartbeats. This has been going on for six years now.*

4. *Depression: I suffer greatly from depression. Sometimes, I have no desire to do anything productive and do not even want to talk. It affects the people around me, especially my mom and dad. It feels like there is a hole in my heart and there is no getting out of the pain I am in. This has been going on since the age of twelve.*

5. *Anxiety: Sometimes I have horrible panic attacks when I am in public. I get light-headed and feel the need to go back to my house and lie in bed. These are brought on by things like people wanting to socialize with me, or thinking about having to do something that involves people I care about, or someone yelling at me and showing anger or taking the alpha-male stance with me. When these panic attacks happen, I have to go be by myself. I will re-create the situation in my head and think about what I should have said or done for hours. This has been going on for eight years now.*

6. *Bowel movements: Most of my bowel movements are diarrhea, and in the mornings I can see my medication go straight through me and into the toilet. When I get nervous, I frequently feel the urge to urinate, but I do not produce a great amount of urine. This has been noticeable for a couple of years now.*

7. *Numbing of the hands: Sometimes for no reason, my hands become numb and tingle for hours at a time. I have noticed this for the past two years.*

My husband, Will, agreed that having Bobby seen at Duke and letting him stay with us for a period of time was the right thing to do, but stressed that it would only be for a few weeks. I alerted our longtime housekeeper, Annie Walters, that Bobby would be staying with us for a short while, just until he got on his feet. Our three children were older and out of the house—Rachel, recently graduated from college and gainfully employed in Nashville; William, a senior getting his engineering degree; and the baby, Katherine, in her freshman year in college. Will and I had enjoyed exactly one semester of no children at home, and my husband was getting very comfortable with the concept of empty-nesting.

John and Bobby spent five days with us while Bobby was being assessed by his new doctor. After the initial appointment at Duke, I went about my daily life—I was busy getting ready for a sailing trip that Will and I had been invited to go on the following week—and John took the medical reins. For the rest of the week, John accompanied Bobby to follow-up appointments and tests. Dr. Pate was very thorough, and we understood that it would take time before there would be any diagnosis.

It became apparent that Bobby's back pain was exacerbated by the long days of waiting and tests. He spent a lot of time in his room or in front of the television, and Will and I were unable to have a very personal conversation with him. I was greatly encouraged when the four of us met Anne for dinner. Bobby and Anne seemed to make a connection immediately: both Anne and Bobby smoked and everyone knows the best place to make friends is in the smokers' section, that small hidden area where strangers are thrust together by their love of tobacco. I know. I used to be one of them.

———

JEFF GEORGI

It was during this time, the third week in February 2013, that Bobby first met his drug counselor, Jeff Georgi, a man who would impact Bobby's life in miraculous ways. Although Bobby's treatment at Duke was focused on the back pain and his other symptoms, we all felt it important that Bobby had access to an addiction professional, as well as a medical doctor, especially since he had not yet been able to stay clean after leaving rehab.

I also sought guidance and placed myself squarely in the capable hands of another psychologist, Mary Costello, who would be my guide and hold my hand for the next sixteen months—thereby saving my sanity and maybe even my marriage. Mary and I had a nice history together as I had periodically sought out her advice during my years of raising children, whenever I was particularly feeling the stress of marriage and family or life in general. Seeking professional guidance just made sense to me, and she had proven herself an invaluable resource over the years. I had also talked with her several times about how to help Anne help Thomas. It was natural that I would reach out to her now that Bobby would be seeking treatment in Durham.

On Friday, February 22, the day before Will and I were to leave for our sailing trip, John and Bobby flew back to Louisiana to pack Bobby up for his move to North Carolina. We all agreed that Bobby would drive his truck and arrive in Durham on Monday, March 4, at which point I would take over directing Bobby's medical care. I promised Bobby's parents that Will and I were fine hosting Bobby while he was awaiting the results from his extensive physical. All of us were excited to pursue a diagnosis and treatment for Bobby's chronic pain.

I also realized that Louisiana was poison for Bobby's fragile recovery, a place where pushers and enabling friends tracked him like GPS. I didn't realize until much later that Bobby had nowhere else to go.

Will and I expected Bobby's stay with us to be brief. He would soon find a job and an apartment or halfway house and stand on his own. We just needed to help him over the hump. So I put Bobby out of my mind and continued to try on swimsuits, hoping to find one that was truly a miracle suit.

Back in Louisiana, Bobby began packing his few belongings. He would drive himself the sixteen hours to Durham, and arrive just after we got back from sailing. He would have a little time to settle before the next week, which would be filled with follow-up doctors' appointments. After that we'd tackle his living and employment situation.

We had a game plan.

T-MINUS ONE DAY

March 2

DISEMBARKING TORTOLA BVI

After the first few days in beautiful Tortola, I didn't think about email or text messages, or kids for that matter. Being on a sailboat, albeit a catamaran with four couples, is about as relaxing and fun as a trip can get—no wireless, no television, no intrusion from the outside world. It could be habit forming.

We had on board several seasoned sailors, and Will and I were newly graduated from a Sailing 101 course we took the previous summer on a whim, empty nesters looking for activities to share. I might have graduated, but I was really a flunky, as I had to cheat a little by writing "port" on my left hand and "starboard" on my right. I'm afraid I will never be anything but the deck swabber.

It amazes me how close you become to your shipmates in just one week. Maybe it's the wide expanse of open sea where horizon and ocean become one, or maybe it is the wind fingering your face or the burning sun on your back that draws sailors together. It could be that eight of us were crammed on a thrusting roller coaster the size of a postage stamp. Whatever it is, sailing just makes for more vulnerability and deeper friendships: we went from friends to great friends in the span of seven days. Thank God, as I soon realized I would need them all by my side.

Disembarking at the Moorings' dock, the last port of call early on Saturday, March 2, was downright depressing. The week went so quickly that it felt like we had just trimmed the sails for the first time and now we had to clean out the galley.

"Back to reality." Lillian Branch looked at me with the same expression I knew I had on my face.

"Best trip ever," I replied, returning the ugly grimace.

Lillian, Anne Howard, and I all live in the same neighborhood. She is a character. She is scattered but together, intelligent and down-to-earth. She soaks up life like a roll of Bounty paper towels, and when she smiles, her dimples are contagious and you can't help yourself and must smile back. Lillian tells it like it is and really, what you see is what you get. She has undertaken several successful professions in the span of a few decades. Her current career is as a licensed marriage and family therapist, working with individuals, couples, and families.

Putting on our shore shoes, Lillian and I made a beeline to the Moorings' land showers and restrooms. Realizing we had not been in contact with the world for a week, we both grabbed our phones and pressed the on button before our feet hit the pier.

I knew something was unusual as soon as I entered my password. Texts and emails began pinging like popcorn, the sounds abrasive after the peace of being unplugged for a week.

"I sure was missed," I laughed to Lillian.

I started scrolling through my inbox, and then I saw an email thread with "Food for Anne Howard" in the subject line, sent from a church friend.

I think deep down I had a premonition about the email before I even read it because my hands were shaking as I tapped the phone, trying to pull up the message. It was a long thread and the first message I read was about a prayer service for Thomas at a church that another close friend attended.

"Lillian, Lillian!" I found it difficult to hold my phone. "I don't understand this email." She stopped walking and stood next to me.

I pushed down the hysteria. "Why would they be praying for Thomas at Whitehall Presbyterian Church? That isn't his church. I can't seem to get to the bottom of this email. Why is there food? Oh my God, do you think something happened to Anne? Or Thomas?" I shoved my phone at her as if it was a burning coal. "Can you find it? I can't find it." My mind couldn't come to terms with the reality that was starting to sink in. I could see by Lillian's face that she was concerned for my mental state. Thank God she was a therapist. How fortunate for me that with all her different careers she chose that profession and not a dog groomer or cake baker?

"Renée, settle down. Let's sit over here." She sat and I continued to pace and babble. "Can you make sense of it? I don't know what's happened." But I knew. And I paced until Lillian confirmed it. Thomas Howard was dead—found dead in his bedroom by his mother.

The searing pain in my heart was so bad that I put my hand on my chest to stop it. No tears yet, just the face of agony and disbelief and a million other emotions that twisted and turned my eyes and mouth into a cartoonish figure. "Damn, damn, fuck." I save this last word for when I really mean business. I rarely use it, but that was as good a time as any I would ever have.

I looked at Lillian, and she softly put her arms around me to comfort me, tenderly pushing my hair, bleached blond by the sun, out of my eyes. Her compassion opened the floodgate. It washed me down, convulsing and uncontrollable. I was not thinking straight. I have never lost a child, but I felt as though it was my fault that my best friend had lost hers. My fault.

I would become angry eventually, but it would be at myself or at those closest to Thomas for not being able to save him. At that moment, on that beautiful sun-drenched island, all I could think was, *Thomas can't be dead. No, no, no. We should have saved him.* He was a man-child, only thirty-one, close to Bobby's age, who was coming to stay with me in two days. They were going to recover together, take strength from their friendship and shared struggle. But Thomas was gone. Dead of an overdose. Fuck.

Lillian stuck to me like maple syrup and she was just as sweet. She had started to babble too, but it was psychobabble. She exhorted me to call upon my faith. "Do you have a God you believe in? Can you pray right now? Will that help you?"

I wanted to pray, but I have always been on shaky ground when it comes to faith. I truly, with all my heart, want to believe in a higher being, and most of the time I am a very faithful Christian, except when I am a questioner.

So, I wanted to call on Jesus, but all I could do was wonder why Jesus would take that poor tormented boy. Why did Thomas have to die when he had so much to live for?

I frantically placed a call to Anne. A mutual friend of ours answered the phone, and when she heard my voice, she passed the receiver over.

"Hello?" I heard the tears my best friend had been shedding in her weak voice.

"Anne?"

It was too much for both of us. We broke down in unison, sobbing, our sorrow welded together by our love and loss of Thomas.

"Renée, how did you hear? I told everyone not to call you because you were on the boat, that I needed to be the one to tell you." Even in her pain and grief, she thought of me.

As I bit my lip, I tasted the salty mixture of my tears and the cool sea air. I had difficulty talking, breathing, and I was at a loss for words. It is an unusual day when I am at a loss for words. "We just got off the boat and I checked my cell phone and I was confused because I was sent an email for food for you and I couldn't figure out why you needed food . . ." Okay. I was still babbling.

I saw Will rounding the corner in full stride. I hadn't even noticed that Lillian had left my side to alert the others.

He encircled me with his arms, and I quietly shook and sobbed on his shoulder as I listened to Anne impart the details of finding Thomas aspirated, not breathing, heart stopped on the floor of his childhood room.

The ferry ride and flight home from Tortola were a blur. My friends were wonderful and more than once I caught them looking at me with long faces full of sympathy. Then they would pat my hand or my head, constantly and politely asking if they could get me something, anything. My friends had the burden of being too close to someone who had been touched by death.

ZERO DAYS

Sunday, March 3 at 2:14 a.m.

PHONE CALL

God, I was tired. I began the day on a beautiful sailboat in the British Virgin Islands and ended the day in North Carolina, holding the hand of my wonderful friend as I shared her grief.

I collapsed into an exhausted sleep, a repose so deep that when the phone rang, I could not get my eyes to open and brain to turn on for a few seconds. It was instinct that drew my palm to my bedside table, searching by touch for the cause of disruption. Fumbling, I finally lifted the receiver to my ear, struggled up on one elbow, eyes still shut.

"Hello?" I said, so low and soft that I cleared my throat and repeated it with more emphasis. "Hello?"

"Aunt Née, Aunt Née, help me. Please God help me."

I was instantly wide awake but terribly confused. I bolted straight up in bed and turned on the bedside lamp in one swoop.

"Who is this?" I demanded.

The voice on the other end was shrill, terrified; I did not recognize my own nephew. "Aunt Née, it's Bobby. I don't know what is happening to me. Help me, please help me."

Will was still peacefully asleep, blissfully unaware of anything as he slept with a set of earphones, listening to the radio all night. I swear I could be murdered next to him and he would wake in the morning and ask me if I wanted coffee.

I began beating on my husband's back, slapping so hard that there would be outlines of my hand on him for several days. Will turned over, dazed and bewildered, dead tired from our long, emotional day.

24

"Will, wake up," I covered the receiver and pleaded. "Something is wrong with Bobby."

I was afraid. My hands shook and my heart pounded, but my brain switched to autopilot, and as my nerves steadied, I pulled myself together, finding calm in the middle of a crisis. I took a deep breath and uncovered the receiver. Soothingly I said, "Bobby, you must calm down. I cannot help you if I cannot hear you. Where are you now?"

I glanced at the digital clock. Two fourteen in the morning. Will was sitting up and had turned on his bedside lamp. I gave him charade hand signals, telling him that Bobby was on the phone and there was a problem. Will waited and watched as I probed Bobby for more information.

"Bobby. Where. Are. You?" I tried the stern, direct approach.

"I don't know. I don't know where I am. I can't remember anything. I can't remember how I got here. I'm so scared, Aunt Née. And they keep beating on my truck, beating on my windows and calling my name . . ."

I thought I heard him crying; I definitely heard men in the background banging on his windows and calling his name. It was a muffled cacophony and I felt chilled.

"Look around you. What do you see?"

"Darkness. Old apartment buildings. A chain-link fence."

"Can you start your truck? Good. Start it and then floor it. Get out of wherever you are as fast as you can. Go, Bobby, go now!"

I heard the squeal of tires as he peeled out.

When he spoke into the phone again, I barked orders, "Pull into the first 7-Eleven you can find. Look for street signs. Look for anything that might help us find you."

"There isn't anything, Aunt Née, no street signs. And the

Pak-A-Sak is closed, barred up. I am by myself. There are no people."

Think, Renée, think. I was totally rattled at that point. I could hear Bobby trying to calm down by talking to himself. Clearly, he was terrified.

"Keep driving. Do you have a GPS?"

"Only on my phone but I have to stop to switch over to it."

"Do not break contact with me. Do not stop the truck. Do you hear me? Do not break contact. Keep driving." I didn't know what was going on, but I thought the last thing he should do was stop.

Seconds later he came to a street sign and read it to us. It was a sign to I-75. I breathed a huge sigh of relief as he followed it and entered the on-ramp. We could guide him from there.

Next to me Will was furiously working iMaps and he turned to me in shock. "He's in Atlanta. I think he is in a bad section of Atlanta."

Will picked up the phone and followed his progress until he passed through Atlanta and into a northern suburb. Will directed him to the nearest hotel, but Bobby admitted he was without cash or credit cards; his wallet had gone missing. We gave our credit card number and waited until he was in his room with the door locked before we let him hang up.

"The first thing you will do tomorrow morning, before you even brush your teeth, is you will call me."

Wearily, he softly responded, "Yes, ma'am. Thank you, Aunt Née and Uncle Will. Thank you."

———

BOBBY'S ARRIVAL II

Sunday, March 3 at 10:45 p.m., Durham, North Carolina

Bobby arrived late Sunday night, after checking out of the Atlanta hotel, and driving to Durham. I called him several times during the day, concerned by our wake-up call the night before, but I never broached the subject because disturbingly Bobby could only drive an hour or so at a time before having to pull over and take a catnap. What should have been a six-hour trip became a ten-hour trip.

Before he arrived, I called his drug counselor, Jeff Georgi, and told him about the late night phone call. When Jeff said he would call Bobby, I felt relief; I was strung tightly, having spent the day at Anne's home, and it was hard to focus on anything else.

I flew out of the house that night when I heard the approaching rattle of a loose muffler. The white, flatbed truck slowly, ever so slowly, maneuvered out of the darkness and into the light of the garage, inching along like a turtle, uncertain whether to proceed or not. Bobby stepped down from the runner; he grabbed a gym bag from the back steel container attached to the deck, slinging it over his shoulder. His appearance was disconcerting. Just a little over a week ago he had been dressed like a frat boy, polo shirt and khaki pants, hair slicked back. As if seeing him for the first time, I suddenly realized he was fat—no, more like swollen, blown up like a pool float, his neck flesh squeezed out over the dingy, dirty-white wife beater he was wearing, pulled so tightly across his barreled chest that one could count the number of chest hairs through the thin material. Baggy, extra-long gym shorts

27

and expensive-looking sneakers completed his apparel. The March night was brisk, but the chill didn't seem to faze him. His unkempt hair was raggedly long, jagged like a rock outcropping, possibly from an angry self-cut when his bangs became too unruly for him and he impulsively took a swipe at them with some dull scissors. A strong whiff of stale cigarette smoke assaulted my nostrils, reminding me of walking by the smokers' room in the airport as a customer enters or exits.

His Tar Heel-blue eyes, always startling in their brilliancy, were pointed to the ground, hidden behind his hair, hiding the pain in his eyes from the world—if he couldn't see us, we wouldn't be able to see him. He rolled his slightly hunched shoulders as he shuffled his tall frame inside, eyes always on the floor, hair softly swishing across his forehead. Even as I stopped him and directly asked him questions, he didn't raise his head to meet my gaze. His monotone, monosyllabic answers were even more troubling than his appearance. "I'm tired. I am going up to bed," he mumbled and turned on his heel to journey up the back stairs to the bedroom he had stayed in before. I listened as he pounded each step loudly, carrying an unknown and heavy burden in his feet. I listened until the door softly closed. Tomorrow, I assured myself, tomorrow Bobby and I would connect.

THE FIRST FEW DAYS

Monday, March 4

MARY COSTELLO

I was surprised to find myself wide awake at six o'clock in the morning. I am hardly ever up at that time, but that morning I was drinking coffee with the rising sun. I had previously scheduled a nine-thirty session with psychologist Mary Costello to help me prepare for Bobby's planned arrival, not knowing the houseguest would already be snug in his bed upstairs.

Mary would become my guidepost while Bobby was living with us, reassuring when I was doubtful, stern when I was overly ambitious, compassionate when I cried. Even now I can't believe how fortunate it was I had scheduled this appointment, picking the date weeks ago for this of all mornings, three days after Thomas had passed away and one day after Bobby appeared at my doorstep in such a shocking state.

"Hey, Renée." Mary's voice was soft and upbeat. She motioned to me from the waiting room, habitually running a tad behind. "Sorry, I'm running late," she confessed. I smiled. I am never bothered by this ritual as I know she is healing the world and I am willing to wait my turn.

As a child and family psychologist for over three decades, Mary is still at the top of her game, and I am awed and inspired when I think of the way in which she has dedicated her life to helping others. I cannot imagine the things she has witnessed or heard—or how many people she has helped.

The first thing one notices when meeting her is the wildness in her hair, a true juxtaposition to her calm demeanor.

Rivulets of curls spring down and around, and I imagine her waking up every morning to a new day of smoothing and brushing, a never-ending struggle to tame the lion's mane. Regularly she runs her fingers through it, catching and pulling the curls to their full extent, and then letting go as they spring back to their permanently erratic yet gorgeous state.

She opened the door to her office and stood aside, ushering me in like she was inviting me to share tea instead of my innermost secrets. The stresses of her career do not show on her face. She looks years younger than the three diplomas hanging on her office wall proclaim her to be. Big deep brown eyes, not black, but dark chocolate—so dark that it is hard to find her pupils when she looks into my eyes and I find it difficult to lock on hers. If I do hold her gaze for too long, I feel her penetrating right through my exterior into the deepest parts of my being. I know she is looking for a truth, maybe dark, maybe honest. So I usually flush and cringe, thinking she might find something I don't even know is in there. And I look out the window.

I tremble sometimes with the deepness of our sessions, with the vulnerability of it all. I try to be funny and cavalier, sometimes evasive, but she's good. Damn. She's really good. I know she'll find it—whatever it is—whatever I'm trying to hide from myself, from her, from the world. And when she does find a little something, she is patient and she waits, carefully mulling over the words she might use, twitching her mouth in a rabbit-like motion, slowly pulling me in, closer and closer until I realize she has been leading me all along to some amazing self-discovery. It is painful and beautiful and very, very powerful.

Our initial sessions must have been a surprise to Mary. My lack of boundaries and minimal knowledge regarding the unwritten rules of therapy made for some interesting first sessions.

"Mary, how ya doing? What did you do this weekend? Do you have kids? Where do you live?"

Looking back, I asked her some ridiculously personal questions. My God, she probably bought a lifetime supply of pepper spray and installed an "Intruder, leave the premises!" alarm system. It only took me a few sessions to realize that she never answered any of my personal inquiries, instead redirecting them to questions about myself, or pretending she didn't hear me and, as we grew more comfortable together, just plain ignoring me.

The one-sided nature of therapy is odd and unusual. For the months Bobby lived with me, I weekly splayed myself wide open, pondering life-and-death dilemmas one day and my navel the next. Even after years of knowing her, I still can't tell you anything concrete about her; I don't know where she lives or the names of her pets, her favorite color or restaurant. But what I can tell you is that by now, I may know more about her than I do about some of my friends.

It is somewhat of a game with me these days, pushing the boundaries with her. A bit of a dance. Deep down, I believe she knows that I need to trust she will keep her boundaries as well as mine. I grew up in a family that never learned about boundaries, and it has defined me in ways I am only just discovering. Conversely, no matter how far I push the envelope, Mary is solid. Rock steady. It is so comforting and safe.

She holds a certain power over me: this is the by-product of good therapy. She is like a magnet, drawing me each time to my now-familiar little chair, pulling me to the same familiar corner office on the second floor. More than once I have laughed and joked that she was my addiction. How alluring to have an hour dedicated to talking only about yourself? Having someone who just wants what's good for you, who listens to your problems, nodding with empathy, who imparts her knowledge, wisdom, and experience to help you find your way in life, or, in this particular case, someone to help me find a way to help Bobby. Yes, there is so much truth in the statement that I might become addicted to Monday mornings in her office. I might have to talk to my psychologist about that one.

But that particular Monday morning with Mary, I felt shell-shocked. My body and brain were not working in conjunction, and when I talked, I felt as if someone else was speaking. Mary and I had discussed Thomas and his addiction many times, most recently via email several weeks before he died, when I pleaded for names of drug counselors for Anne.

My written words will haunt me the rest of my life: "If Thomas doesn't get help now, he will be dead within the year." I didn't know that horse had already left the barn.

I jumped into the facts immediately: leaving the sailboat, finding out Thomas died, Bobby's strange phone call and even stranger arrival to Durham. My voice wavered at times, but I was steadfast. I knew I couldn't let in one ounce of feeling or I would melt on Mary's floor. She listened, and as she imparted advice, I let her gradually lead me where I needed to go, relishing that someone else with professional experience was helping me find clarity. Like a visually impaired person relies on a Seeing Eye dog to guide them, I was dependent on Mary to help me find my way.

ANNE AND THOMAS HOWARD

Bobby was still asleep when I arrived home from Mary's. I checked in with our housekeeper, Annie Walters, and told her to text me when he woke up. I was going to spend the rest of the morning with Anne at her home down the street. I didn't know if I would be a comfort to Anne, but I felt I must be with her. While there, I kept busy answering the phone, preparing lists, organizing the endless food arrivals.

Anne was the first person I met when Will and I moved to Durham nearly twenty-five years ago. Anne, at sixty-five now, is eleven years older than me, but age has never been a factor for us. We were kindred spirits from the beginning, and she quickly became the family I was missing in this area, the older sister I always wanted.

There is an unseen pull between Anne and me. First, I am a bit damaged. Not in the Hannibal-Lecter-serial-killer way, nor enough for Nurse Ratched to check me in, but in real ways, deep ways. God blessed and cursed me with the capacity to feel things so deeply that my highs are gold medal–winning euphoria and my lows will bring me to my knees. Only my husband sees the real dizzying zig and zag of my empathic inner workings. He knows to hold my hand while we are watching *Lassie* reruns, for one never knows when Lassie gets herself into a fix. He also knows that I have X-ray vision; I can see into the recesses of your soul.

I have this theory, maybe from some long-lost magazine article or perhaps the hidden corners of a deranged mind, but I like it. I think we were all part of tribes before we walked upright and began wearing clothes. Separate tribes, created and closely wound together by commonality. "Ugh, me like kiwi. Ugh, me do too. Ugh, me like your water buffalo sarong. Ugh, me like yours too. Ugh, me like Mogo. Ugh, me slept with him last night." Chemistry is born.

Although the human race has scattered across the world, I can still find my tribal sister or brother at a black-tie cocktail party or a monster truck rally. The pull is almost instantaneous—magnetic, Gorilla Glue strong. I hear a belly laugh and a snort, and zing—my long-lost cave sister! I watch a young teenager on the dance floor and zing—I've found a long-lost cousin! I meet old and young, black or white, educated or not, male or female, and I feel the chemistry. But not with everyone. A wet, limp handshake makes me think, *He must be from that tribe across the valley.*

Anne is from my tribe. We have chemistry and we have shared many things on many levels through the years: weddings, deaths of parents and close friends, highs and lows. But sharing the death of her child feels like it is not real. How do you share something when you are numb and can't feel it?

Anne and I are also polar opposites in many ways. It is hard to get Anne to be serious about much as she will laugh when she is happy, and laugh when she is in slight discomfort, a trait I dearly wish I possessed. If Anne were to drop a bowl of chili on her floor, shattering one of her best china pieces, the gooey mess exploding toward the ceiling and her coiffed hair, her newest fashionable shoes covered, pinto beans mingling on her just-cleaned carpet, she would look at me and say "Shee-itt," in her Southern drawl, and then shrug her shoulders. "Oh, we-ll." And then she would laugh. I can't repeat what I would do.

In instances of great emotional difficulty, she doesn't laugh but rather hides—compartmentalizing grief and pain somewhere even I can't reach. Anne learned this early as she was the daughter of an alcoholic mother, and she has been pushing away and hiding from pain for decades.

My mother is the hider in my family, also the daughter of an alcoholic, and I have searched futilely for the key to these locked areas all my life. I suppose that is why Anne and I are so close; I am still on the search for locked closets and I am a dog on a hunt. I can't see something but I smell it, and I won't give up until I root it out, dig it up, and sink my teeth into it. Whatever, wherever it is, I have some driving need to confront it. I know it is out there—still locked and hidden.

On that day Anne was subdued and weepy, but she could not sit still. She pulled out pictures and old scrapbooks and told Thomas stories in the present tense. Is there some unwritten rule about when one talks about the deceased in the past tense? I knew Anne had been mentally preparing for this for a long time, preparing for the day she would wake up and Thomas, her only son, would not.

Thomas had struggled with drug use since he was in his teens. Although he had had several near fatal overdoses and several month-long stints in rehab plus many months fighting to stay clean, the allure of the fabricated high was just too much for him. At the age of thirty-one, with so much life yet to live, Thomas had succumbed to his disease, here, in this house, directly above where I was standing. I balled my fists and pushed this thought somewhere else. It was too much for me to think about just then.

Anne's home was full. Her daughter and sisters had rallied to be with her. There were decisions to be made. I had done all I could do for the time being. I kissed and hugged her and promised to come by later.

When I arrived home late that afternoon, I took Mary's advice from our session that morning and called Jeff

Georgi, Bobby's drug rehab counselor. This was the second call in two days asking him how to handle the delicate situation of Bobby's arrival while I was struggling with my own pain from Thomas's death.

Jeff said, frankly, I was to be honest and truthful and not hold back. So that was what I did.

When Bobby and his father had been with us in February, I'd invited Anne out to dinner. Anne had shared some of Thomas's history with Bobby, including his last overdose and recovery. Although Bobby had never met Thomas, he and Anne quickly bonded through their mutual struggles with drug addiction and, I suspect, their predilection for cigarettes. I think they came from the same tribe also.

I caught Bobby as he was sleepily going outside to have a smoke, still wearing the clothes he'd obviously slept in. "Thomas Howard OD'd on Friday night. He didn't make it."

"He died?" His head whipped up.

My voice cracked. "Yes, Thomas is dead. You have arrived into a house that is grieving and in turmoil. You know how close we are to Ms. Anne and Thomas. They have been our family since we moved here." I could see the shock on his face.

"I want to be able to take care of you properly, but I'm afraid I have to take care of Ms. Anne right now. I can't think straight and I am struggling myself."

We sat in silence for a minute or so. It was a comfortable silence, both of us deep in our own thoughts.

The funeral was in a few days. I wanted to drill home that Thomas had died of a drug overdose, so I told Bobby he had a choice to make: he could choose not to attend the funeral, or he could choose to go and be a support to us and to see firsthand what drug addiction does to a family.

He didn't take long to think about it. After taking the

cigarette break I hijacked earlier, he returned with his decision. "Aunt Née, I think I want to go to the funeral to support you and Ms. Anne."

Good answer, Bobby. I almost smiled.

———

From: Renée Hodges
Subject: update
Date: Monday, March 4, 2013, at 11:30 p.m.
To: Mary Costello

Mary,

No need to respond to this. I just think if I write to you it helps me sort things out and I might be able to get to sleep. And things are going so fast that it helps me to know we are on the same page. So here's today's update and it's a doozy.

This afternoon, after seeing you this morning, I called John, Bobby's father, to tell him about Bobby's escapades and his confusing phone call from Atlanta Saturday night. John told me this: last week before Will and I arrived home from sailing, Bobby was packing to come to Durham, but on Friday, he allegedly stole his father's prescription of Lortab, an opioid pain medication, which went unused and forgotten after John's rotator cuff surgery in January. John, a recovering alcoholic, went pill-free after the surgery, but the physician gave him a prescription anyway. (Geez! What is with these doctors?)

John found out the bottle was missing and confronted Bobby. They had a huge argument, and afterward Bobby decided to leave his house for good. He jumped in his truck and started driving from Louisiana to Durham on Friday night (Bobby's twenty-ninth birthday) instead of our agreed upon Sunday start! John didn't tell me about the fight nor the alleged taking of Lortab until this morning. I'll need to address this lack of communication with John at some point, but for now I just let it go.

I also called Jeff Georgi, Bobby's addiction counselor, as you suggested. Jeff said many things, but the one that sticks with me is that Bobby is high risk, whatever that means. Jeff also said that it is highly probable that Bobby is using again. I'm willing to do just about anything because I didn't get the feeling that Jeff thought Bobby was going to make it. He didn't say that, of course, but it was what my ears were hearing.

Anne is holding up and is surrounded by lots of love and lots of family and friends. I am holding up as well, but I'm awfully close to the side of the cliff. Writing it all out seems to calm me and let me step back a few paces. Thanks and good night.

Renée

———

THOMAS

Tuesday, March 5

A wake was held the next night. I was invited to go early to be with the family members. This meant a lot to me as I have been very close to Anne for many years, by her side throughout her troubles with Thomas's addiction. Will did not attend the wake. Not because he wasn't close to the Howards but because he is not good with anything to do with death. I know and accept this. I sometimes laugh and tell Annie, our housekeeper, to make sure I have a decent funeral, one that goes on for several days, to mourn and celebrate me properly. Otherwise, I'll still be warm when Will buries me. And that's the truth.

The main hall of the funeral home was decorated with institutional maroon carpet meant for many thousands of footsteps and wallpaper carefully selected to soothe and lessen anxiety. It was not doing its job.

The undertakers stood at the door to welcome the hesitant guests; they wore identical uniforms—dark suits, subdued ties, and somber faces—and spoke their hellos softly as if they too shared your grief or were afraid to disturb the dead. They directed me to the correct room, nicely furnished in faux antique furniture and overstuffed sofas, dotted intermittently with easels of flowers, picked by the florist for this one day, to also go to their grave. I have an aversion to a spray, that stand of plucked flowers that signifies the condolences and grief of friends or family of the deceased. They make me sad. There were easels of sprays everywhere.

I signed the registry and began hugging Thomas's family members. I know them well. Even though Anne was several years divorced from Thomas's father, we were all there for one horrible reason, which pulled us closer together.

We gathered to pray with Reverend David Bowen, the pastor of Anne's church. We held hands in a circle, and I stood next to Anne and held her securely, my arm around her waist, just to make sure she knew she was not alone. Thomas was her only son and he loved his mother so much. There is no proof, but it is my belief that he came home to die, tired of the fight and finally giving in to his demons and torment.

Before Thomas made his final trip home, he'd been living in a halfway house. There he had befriended the house supervisor, a middle-aged African American man and recovered alcoholic named J.R. He had been mostly illiterate, and it was Thomas who taught him to read better. J.R. made a speech that brought us all to tears, telling us it was because of Thomas that he could read from Ephesians that night.

Thomas was always trying to help people in need—even when it was Thomas who needed the most help. J.R.'s speech was a special moment. It helped us to know that Thomas's heart was in the right place even when the cravings became too much for him.

———

FUNERAL

Wednesday, March 6, 1:30 p.m.

I didn't see Anne before the church service the following day. She had offered me a seat with the family, but I declined, feeling I needed to be close to Will and Bobby.

The sun was shining and it was pleasantly warm for an early March day. I opened the car door in the church parking lot, stood, and looked up at the sky. I took my sunglasses off and squinted. I was not looking for anything; I just needed to feel the sun and heat on my face.

I suddenly felt weary and apprehensive. Damn it, I was on the verge of crying, and I hadn't even made it to the front steps. Bobby finished his cigarette in the parking lot. Although I had long since sworn off smoking, I now wished I had brought some Nicorette gum for myself.

Will, Bobby, and I went together, arm in arm, safety in numbers, into the Church of the Good Shepherd.

There was music playing in the background, beautiful on another day, mournful today. I thanked the usher for the program with Thomas's picture on the cover looking out at me, forevermore one-dimensional.

I glued my eyes to the reddish-purple carpet, so immaculately vacuumed that I followed the tracks down the center aisle. I sensed people I knew, close friends and acquaintances on either side, but I could not meet their eyes for fear my knees would give way.

Will steered us to the very back pew of the first section, already half-full with Anne's oldest and dearest friends. This was where we belonged. With Will squeezed in on one side of me, and Bobby on the other, I tried to relax.

We were early for the funeral, so I was able to slowly look around and comprehend my surroundings, a lens coming into focus.

The Church of the Good Shepherd was fairly new, more utilitarian and functional than ornate. I missed the stained glass windows of the Catholic churches I'd sporadically attended throughout my marriage. The sanctuary was contemporary, with a high, high ceiling and stained wood rafters and awkward cutouts for skylights where a simple wooden cross hangs so that the sun's rays will spotlight it at just the right time of day. I had attended this church on many occasions to hear my good friend Pastor David Bowen, a tall, lanky guy, nearing sixty, and known for his bow ties and rousing sermons. But that day's sermon was going to be different.

There, in front of the stark altar, was a coffin: beautiful and black and polished so keenly that I could see the reflection of guests in its shine. A spray of flowers had been lovingly placed on top.

The family began to file in. I saw Anne first. Escorted by her daughter, she was tight-lipped and drawn, but she moved with purpose and quickly took her seat of honor in the first pew.

It was Thomas's father who undid me. I could hear his wails of grief before I saw him. He had a brother on either side, gripping his arms, holding him up, urging him down the center aisle toward the coffin of his only son. Half dragged, half carried. I turned away when I saw his tortured face. I could still hear his sobs and then realized I could hear mine as well.

Will took my left hand in both of his and squeezed it hard for reassurance, our sorrow flowing as one through our warm touch.

I realized that Bobby hadn't moved, not one little muscle. He was sitting erect but looking down at his hands. He was so still I wasn't sure he was breathing.

This was the moment of the funeral I remember so well. With my nose running, tears pouring like rain, I took my free hand and reached out for Bobby's, grasping it and squeezing it as tightly as Will was squeezing mine. The three of us became linked, and I gently closed my eyes and prayed inside my head, *God, please, please. Please help us. Please help us all.*

WALKING THE HALLS

I could hear him again, the nightly squeaking of the floorboards as Bobby paced back and forth, back and forth. To the window, to the bathroom, the pattern changing as he crossed the Turkish runner in the hall.

"Holy hell, what time is it?" I said to no one. Although Will would wake during the worst of Bobby's nightmares, his headphone habit meant he seldom heard Bobby's nightly treks.

Two, three, sometimes four or five o'clock in the morning. Okay. He was coming down the stairs now. *Beep, beep.*

This beep signaled that the back door was open, and I could mentally see him as he exited the screen porch and pulled a cig from his shorts pocket. I turned over and dozed, but I never really got back to sleep. The moment the door signal beeped again, I was wide awake, and I heard him slowly, ploddingly, make his way upstairs. Gently, he opened and shut the bedroom door and all was quiet again. Until the next night.

―――――

FOLLOW-UP WITH DR. PATE

Thursday, March 7, 9:00 a.m.

If there is one thing I have learned in my years of seeking medical treatment for myself and my children, it is that even when the brain is willing, if a doctor is giving you a report on yourself, it is hard to take in all that he or she is telling you. Your thoughts seem to hit pause, and the play button is not hit again until that moment when the doctor asks, "Do you have any questions for me?" So I decided I would go with Bobby to his follow-up appointment with Dr. Pate.

"I'll bring my notebook and take good notes for you so that you don't have to worry about writing it down. If you are here to stay in Durham and Uncle Will and I are to take care of you while you are healing, it is as important for us to know your physical condition as it is for you."

This was a big deal. Bobby had yet to open up emotionally to us, and I was very much in the dark about his physical ailments except for the list he supplied his father before his first doctor's appointment. I knew he was in physical pain. I could see it in his eyes, in the way he walked, and by his constant complaints. But he was also in emotional pain.

Since Bobby's initial visit to Duke the third week in February, Dr. Pate had ordered every test except math for him, filling vial after vial of blood, leaving no stone unturned. Today, after the cumulative weeks of X-rays, labs, specialty testing of upper and lower GI, and ahead of a colonoscopy scheduled to be performed the next morning, Dr. Pate was ready to sit down and talk.

Surprisingly, Bobby put up no resistance to my suggestion to tag along. He shrugged his shoulders with a *do what you have to do because I don't care* response. I didn't know what to expect, but I had thought he would put up more opposition to his ole, meddling aunt getting this deep into his business. I would come to realize that he had not had any type of privacy in a few years.

Bobby was called back, and I drummed my fingers on the armchair, waiting to see if I would be given permission to join him.

After fifteen minutes, which seemed like the slowest fifteen minutes ever, I approached the nurse.

"Umm, my nephew is being seen by Dr. Pate, and I would like to join him, please, to hear his follow-up report."

The nurse looked at me with the sweetest smile on her face, but I knew she was thinking, *Geez, give the kid a break.*

"One moment please." She picked up the phone, never taking her eyes off me.

"Okay. You can go back now."

Except for the number on the door, the examination room was identical to every other room I had seen at Duke: checkerboard tile floor perfectly laid in a one-foot-by-one-foot grid, faux cherry cabinets with silver metal hand pulls, pleather black examination table with a white paper roll pulled and end torn, the prerequisite sink and Steris antibacterial soap, small desk, and a computer with a picture of the Duke University chapel as its screen saver.

Bobby looked up sheepishly as I joined the party. "I forgot" is all he said. I believed him. He didn't seem to care that I was there. He didn't seem to care about anything much at all.

Dr. Pate extended his hand and I introduced myself. I sat and pulled my spiral notebook from my purse to ask for a quick synopsis of what they had already covered.

There were still some tests to be taken, but Dr. Pate confirmed that all the tests on Bobby had come back negative so far. At his recommendation, Bobby was to check out the Duke Wellness Center and set up times to work one-on-one with a physical therapist and trainer. Lastly, Bobby was to book a session with the nutritionist on staff in Dr. Pate's office. I was very happy about this appointment as I was sure that if Bobby felt better, well, he would feel better. Working out and eating more nutritiously would be a great start. Dr. Pate was also going to begin reducing the multiple mood-altering medications Bobby was taking, and I brightened significantly at this news.

Dr. Pate finally explained that he was very interested in pain and pain management and that there was an excellent program available through the concierge service, if Bobby would like to check it out. This was a viable option, but Bobby had already spent significant time over the last years attending pain clinics to no avail. His pain was a conundrum. Dr. Pate could not yet find a structural reason for it, and until we diagnosed what was causing the pain, I was afraid we would be hamsters on a wheel, spinning and spinning exhaustively and never going anywhere.

I had been so busy asking questions and writing in my little notebook that I failed to connect that Dr. Pate's nurse was one of Anne's close friends, a proud member of an all-single ladies group who called themselves "the hens." I had been aware of this fun social group for a while, but I had only first met this particular hen the previous day at Anne's house after the funeral. (Was that just the previous day? It felt like weeks ago.) It had been a brief introduction, and I hadn't recognized her without her black dress on. I would find out much later that she too had a personal family connection to addiction and that the interest and softness she showed Bobby was an empathy born of experience.

———

HOUSE KEY AND PAINTBALL

That afternoon, after I dropped Bobby off at home, I went to Anne's house to check on her. After my visit, I made an unscheduled stop at Home Depot. I searched for a while through the unknown territory of tools and sheet metal—foreign objects all. These kinds of stores make me uncomfortable and I avoid them. I think it is because I don't understand how to use 99 percent of the items in a home improvement store and I dislike not knowing things. I persevered until I found what I had come for. Keys. Not just regular keys. Duke Blue Devil template keys. I took my house key off the chain and handed it to the salesperson. "Please make one Duke Blue Devil key copy." After the key was handed over, I gleefully stuffed it in my pocket. *A special key for a special person*, I thought.

Having a house key in your pocket is like a security blanket; it offers reassurance and emotional support. It means you have a place to call home, a roof over your head. Somewhere you can always go. I wanted Bobby to feel he was not alone, that Will and I were taking him in as our immediate family, and we were totally behind him. It was difficult in so many ways. Bobby was emotionally detached. I believed the concoction of prescribed meds he had been taking was deadening his ability to feel emotion. Even if he were not taking these mood-altering drugs, I could see that he had a passive-aggressive side and it manifested itself in unresponsiveness. Either way, whether by prescription or deliberately, I was having trouble connecting with him.

I was determined that I would trust him until he gave me reason not to. But I also needed to vigilantly keep temptations out of his way.

When he and his father came in February for the initial evaluation, I realized then that I knew next to nothing about taking care of someone with an opioid addiction history. Mary gave me several pieces of advice in our session the day before Will and I left on our sailing trip, the day John and Bobby flew back to Louisiana to pack up. "You have to take precautions," she said. "Not just for your protection but for Bobby's." I knew she was right, but I felt a little hypocritical starting this process as if he were a convict.

However, as soon as I got home from Mary's office that day, I set aside packing for the sailing trip and I followed her advice. I cleaned out every medicine cabinet, finding pills prescribed in the prehistoric era, some so old the pills had melted into each other, leaving a white or blue glob in the bottom of the amber pill bottle.

I looked in every cupboard and drawer. I threw away old boxes of sinus medicine simply because they contained pseudoephedrine. The meds I deemed safe or necessary were housed in a cosmetic bag, zipped and stored under my bathroom sink. I felt a little guilty (all right, a lot guilty) that the first week Bobby had been in my home he could have found a ten-year supply of free, albeit nasty-looking drugs mere yards from where he slept. Shame on me.

I brought the tall kitchen garbage bag full of my discards to my local pharmacy "take-back" program (the green way of discarding pills), and it almost took two people to haul it up and over the countertop.

What a revelation it was to me to see how many old, expired prescription and nonprescription drugs I had stockpiled over the years, and I wouldn't even consider myself a hoarder.

When Bobby moved in after our sailing trip, I told him honestly upon arrival, "I promise you that there are no opium-based drugs in this household. There are no stimulants or benzos in any cabinet or drawer. You won't find so much as a stimulating vitamin. I want to save you the trouble if you should decide you want to go looking for something."

Get it all out there, up front, I said to myself. *No room for misinterpretation.* But the fact was, I didn't tell him everything. I didn't mention that I had taken everything of value—silverware, jewelry, electronics, money, checkbooks—and locked it all in the storage closet, setting the alarm. As a final thought, on Will's suggestion, we locked and alarmed the hunting closet where Will kept his array of hunting rifles, shotguns, and ammo. I did want to trust that Bobby would not hurt himself or—God forbid—anyone else, but I also knew he was very sick. I had to be smart. I needed to be sure my family was safe. The memory of Thomas overdosing in his own home was a fresh reminder that I could not control every situation.

Bobby wasn't with us a week before I felt sure I had done the right thing.

He had grown up hunting, as had my husband, my son, my daughters, my brother and father, and my father's father, and so on. Many women in the family hunted as well. I have known men who will put on a business suit with a camo hunting jacket and pants zipped right over it. Rise at daybreak, duck hunt, be at work at 8:00 a.m., duck gumbo that night. That was my South and that was just what we did in Louisiana.

So, I was excited when Bobby found the old dusty paintball guns in the garage and asked to use them. They had given a lot of innocent pleasure to many kids—including my own. But when I checked Bobby's Facebook page that evening, I became disturbed by a video he'd posted. Using his cell phone, he'd recorded himself shooting the paintball gun on the automatic setting, spraying hundreds of paintballs, moving the gun back and forth, back and forth, back and forth in the direction of some geese lucky enough to be too far away. The video itself was not disturbing. What upset me was the absolute and total glee registered on his face, and his high-pitched, almost hysterical laugh. This coming from someone who hadn't expressed a single emotion since arriving.

For the first time I had serious doubts about what I had gotten myself into.

From: Renée Hodges
Subject: 3/7 update to self
Date: Thursday, March 7, 2013, at 10:44 p.m.
To: Self

Today was a pretty good day. Although Bobby walked the halls again last night, when I met him at his doctor's office for the final update, he seemed to be in good spirits. He is smiling more, and just his physical stance seems to have less tension than usual. The nightmares are what hurt and scare me. Shrill screams, garbled words, the agony I hear in his voice. These are nightly and I do not go up to his room. He is afraid to sleep, I know. I'm not sure, but I believe these demons are part of his depression, part of his healing process.

He even went online last night and talked with a young lady. How nice that he might make a friend.

I am going to trust him until he loses my trust. So far, he has been honest and forthright and I have been the same. I have told him I will not enable him and I will support and facilitate his recovery, but I will not put up with drug use under my roof.

Lord, I hope I can hold to my word. He doesn't have anywhere else to go.

I think of Thomas all the time and my heart is so heavy with grief. Surely, surely, Bobby will pull through. Please, God.

Email to my brother, John, and sister-in-law, Jill, Bobby's parents.

From: Renée Hodges
Subject: things
Date: Friday, March 8, 2013, at 8:23 a.m.
To: Jill Redford, John Redford

Dear Jill and John,

Several things: first, Bobby is a delight. Just the few days he has been here he is opening like a spring flower, ever so slowly, petal by petal. He is terribly vulnerable and I have been firm but very lenient at the same time.

This week was difficult. Bobby went with me to Thomas's funeral and it was a very emotional service, as you might imagine, but it was a hopeful one also.

He opened up a bit after that. He promised me he will never use in

*my house while he is staying with me. I know, I know. But it was
still nice to hear him say it.*

*He confessed to me he had several unsupervised hours after
Thomas's service where he considered running away to find some
drugs but that he decided to play with the dogs instead. I made him
call his counselor Jeff Georgi yesterday because he had a very
rough day, maybe the aftermath of the funeral, and he left a
message for him saying he needed to talk with him. As of now I
don't know if they have talked. Before going to bed though, Bobby
said he was feeling a little better. He also said he wants to talk to
David Bowen, the preacher at the funeral. I have emailed the Right
Reverend and they are going to set up a time to have coffee.*

*It concerns me that Bobby is getting calls and texts from people he
shouldn't be. He asked me to have his cell number changed. He
should handle this himself, but he will undergo medical procedures
all day today and will have no time.*

*He is very bright and capable and I am quite hopeful—even though
I realize it is very early in the honeymoon.*

Love, Renée

COLONOSCOPY

Friday, March 8, 11:30 a.m.

We had to drive a little further but were able to do the
colonoscopy today instead of waiting several weeks. It was a
good trade-off.

Bobby had complained of stomach problems for months,

if not years: diarrhea, nausea, vomiting. He told me he could not keep food down, and if he did, it always went straight through him. So Dr. Pate had ordered this awkward procedure, Bobby's first, and I would be his driver to and from the appointment.

The GPS barked, "You have arrived at your destination," and I looked at a newly built satellite office somewhere near the airport. I was able to pull right to the front door. Instead of opening his car door, Bobby complained of back pain and pushed the shotgun seat so far backward it would make a passenger in Delta first class jealous.

"Our lucky day." I smiled and patted Bobby on the hand, trying to act nonchalant and happy, focusing on our good parking karma even though I knew he was about to go through the most dreaded of all medical procedures.

It was hard to know what he was thinking. We had chatted on the way about nothing in particular. I am not a good chit-chatter; small talk is not my gift. I can do it for a few minutes, but then I switch on the radio.

It had been half a decade since I'd had my first colonoscopy, and I was sympathetic to his reluctance. I gave him permission to smoke in my van. What harm could it do? It might even help with the sweat sock, locker room smell left over from years of carrying my kids' athletic equipment.

Yesterday he had come to me with the prep instructions and we'd jumped into action. No nuts, seeds, stringy foods, or red Jell-O. I'm sure it is for the safety of the physician as well as false positives.

I'd given him directions to the local pharmacy to buy the necessary supplies, but he had hesitated. "I don't have any money," he'd confessed, solemn and embarrassed. I belatedly realized he had no way to get money either, as his wallet with debit card had been stolen in Atlanta. I gave him a few bills and made a mental note to address this issue in the very near future.

After Bobby put out his cigarette, he checked in at the clinic and received a clipboard of forms to fill out. I pretended to give him his privacy, but secretly watched as he checked lots of boxes and wrote many answers. He listed current medications and they took up half the page. I reminded him to make a special note that no pain medications should be administered at any point in the procedure because of his prior abuse.

Finally, he was called back. I gave him a half wave and settled in for the duration of the examination.

It was several hours before he was led out of the back room, much longer than the usual time required. A nurse firmly held his elbow; he was pale and shaking his head with a frown of disgust.

"Are you all right?" My heart beat a bit faster.

"It didn't take," he replied coldly.

"What didn't take?"

"The anesthesia. They couldn't put me to sleep. I was awake the whole time."

I stopped short and turned to the attentive nurse, fleetingly thinking that she was too slight to hold Bobby up if he fainted, and asked, "What?"

The nurse spoke in her best neutral, professional voice. "I have never seen this before. Bobby must have an extremely high tolerance to drugs, so high that we couldn't safely get him to sleep. I'm afraid he was awake and talking throughout the procedure."

I heard from Bobby later that this nice nurse had stayed by his side, holding his hand, until it was over. Upon learning about his move to North Carolina to start a new life, she shared that she too had an addicted son. When Bobby was leaving the recovery room, she slipped him a twenty-dollar bill.

I don't know if she gave it to him because she was proud of him, because he had told her he had no money to even buy colonoscopy drugs, or because she identified with him through his addictive history and her son's situation. Whatever the reason, Bobby will never forget her kindness and neither will I.

Throughout his stay in Durham, we would come in contact with others who had similar addiction problems in their families. Friends and strangers alike stepped out of the shadows of their hidden secret to share their successes and their pain with us, to go the extra mile to show grace and empathy.

But at that moment I was standing next to the kind nurse, shocked by her admission that the anesthesia had not worked. Bobby had broken off from us by this time and was heading to the exit. If it were me, I would have been running.

ONE WEEK

From: Renée Hodges
Subject: Update
Date: Sunday, March 10, 2013, at 5:08 p.m.
To: self

What a whirlwind my life has been these past few days. My sweet Katherine came home from college on Thursday night to be with me; I think she was worried about me.

Bobby ran errands for me in barter for gas for his truck. I sent him to the grocery store for chili-makings and then to the pet store for dog food and bones. He also helped Will treat the ponds with chemicals. He is willing to do whatever I ask of him, and I have really appreciated this.

We invited some close friends, Ally and Peter and Anne and her sister Beth, to watch the annual Duke-Carolina basketball game on TV Saturday evening. We had wings and chili, and Peter had a long talk with Bobby, confessing his son's past addiction and giving Bobby his number in case there was anything Peter could do for him, even just going to lunch.

Anne and Bobby snuck off to smoke several times, and Anne did some bonding with Bobby. I don't know how he felt about this as he doesn't show much emotion, but I know Anne needed to put her arms around him and tell him not to go down the same path as Thomas. I hope it isn't too much for him to shoulder.

Anne had previously mentioned that she and her sister were going to her church Sunday, the one where Reverend Bowen preaches, so Bobby and I decided to go this morning too. It was nice to see a lot of young people there, but the sermon was long and too cerebral, *without speaking to the heart, in my humble opinion. We'll see where going to church takes us.*

I am trying to figure out a schedule for him. That is my main goal. I am feeling drained but so hopeful. One week and counting!

MONEY

From: Renée Hodges
Subject: spending money for Bobby
Date: Monday, March 11, 2013, 9:49 a.m.
To: John Redford, Jill Redford

Hi Jill and John,

Bobby needs some money put into his account. He will be getting a part-time job as soon as Jeff gives him the okay, quite possibly, within the next few weeks. But he needs money until then. He is overdrawn by seven dollars at his Louisiana bank and has no debit card or credit card. The money you gave him before he started his trip is gone, much of it stolen in Atlanta.

If you tell me how much you are going to give him, each week I will ask him to account to me for what he has spent. I know he owes me for Duke Health and Wellness. He begins treatment there today. I can't remember how much that was, but I'll ask him for the exact amount.

He has prescriptions to pick up and he needs gas in his truck. Also, his muffler is hanging off, a remnant from his trip here.

I have given him money to take a girl he found on Match.com on a date and to pick up some things from the pharmacy. He doesn't have many needs, but he does have them.

Let me know how you want to handle this.

He is starting to open up. He has even laughed a few times. Katherine came home and we played tennis for several hours on Saturday; he only complained of his back a little!

We are getting him counseling and working on part-time jobs and taking some classes.

Much love, Renée

From: John Redford
Subject: spending money for Bobby
Date: Monday, March 11, 2013, at 9:55 a.m.
To: Renée Hodges

Hi Renée,
What would you say he needs in his account, and I'll have my secretary Debbie do it today. Also Debbie needs account info.

From: Jill Redford
Subject: spending money for Bobby
Date: Monday, March 11, 2013, at 10:18 a.m.
To: Renée Hodges

Hey, Renée,

I love you for helping with all this! Please contact Debbie at the office. I will ask John to give her the okay for medical and spending money. I think Debbie canceled his card after it was stolen too. I will try to find out what you guys want to do with that.

Unlike Bobby, his sister, and my kids, John and I did not grow up with money. Our family was "military poor," and one of my favorite stories is how my dad secretly borrowed money from the Red Cross to pay the hospital bill when I was born. My mother didn't find this out for many years. I believe it was only seventy-five dollars in 1959 as family lore goes, but to them at the time, it was a fortune. Bobby, his sister, and my children were different; they were all born into upper-income families. My children have never had to worry if the car might break down or hope our lights and electricity would not be turned off before payday. We had breakfast on the table every morning and multiple shoes for all of my children—even a pair of cleats or two.

We have enough money to take vacations that require a passport and to belong to a private club where our children can swim or play golf and take tennis lessons. I have the choice to shop at Neiman Marcus or Stein Mart (although I have a lasting fondness for the latter). Most importantly, we have a medical insurance policy. My children have never wanted for anything. We are living the American dream.

Warning on back of package: having money can be harmful to your health.

There are many great things about having a wad of Benjamin Franklins in your back pocket, as I just listed. What is not discussed is the way money can change a person, a family, a friend. How it can breed jealousy in others, selfishness within, and ultimately, engender entitlement—if one is not very, very careful.

Jeff Georgi had used the word "entitled" about Bobby, and I needed to understand why. He explained to me that when addicts have a sense of entitlement coupled with shame, it makes it that much more difficult for them to kick their habits.

I lay awake that night, with new thoughts swirling around in my head. What exactly did entitlement have to do with addiction? Couldn't anyone feel that way—entitled, that is, rich or poor—not just Bobby? I turned and fluffed my pillow. I had to think about what Jeff said to me, to dig deeper. Picking up my phone, holding it so the bright screen didn't shine on Will, I looked up the definition of "entitlement" in Merriam-Webster's Dictionary:

```
Entitlement:

: the condition of having a right to have, do,
or get something

: the feeling or belief that you deserve to be
given something (such as special privileges)

: a type of financial help provided by the
government for members of a particular group
```

I turned off and put down my phone. What makes a person feel entitled? I was confused. Having money does entitle one to certain things like fancy cars or membership in certain select organizations. But entitlement is also the belief that you should be treated specially, have a special privilege, or that you deserve or have an inherent right to these special privileges. Hmmm, I have money so I should be seated in the best seats, even though you and I paid the same amount? Maybe.

I turned over on my left side, away from Will, knees pulled to my chin. I opened my eyes and stared into nothingness. It is not a question of how much is in your bank account: you can be broke and still believe you are owed something, deserving of special privileges or exceptions. Bobby was a great example of an entitled person. In his short life, he had never really had to struggle for anything. If he wanted something, someone just gave it to him. So "entitlement" is a way of thinking. Damn that's harsh.

I turned over the other way, wiggling some extra space from the dead weight on my right.

"Entitled" is an overworked word today, and its connotations are usually derogatory; it can be used to characterize most everyone—except maybe Mother Teresa and Pope Francis. Jeff thought Bobby might feel entitled. To my knowledge, Bobby had never learned the value of money, and I knew this was confirmed by some of his choices. He wore expensive tennis shoes like designer jewelry. He ate out at fast-food restaurants whenever he had a spare buck instead of grocery shopping and stretching his wallet, but then he would find himself broke and not understand why. He was used to the best, to upgrades, to orchestra seating.

None of this made him a bad person. Delusional, maybe. But not a bad person. Most people that act entitled, rich or poor, don't know they are acting this way. Some act out of insecurities, needing to feel in control. Some are born into entitlement, following the example of their parents. Some people are just arrogant jerks, God bless 'em.

And for some people, addiction *is* the entitlement. "My mother died when I was three." "My stepfather abused me." "I've been laid off." "I've worked hard all my life." Fill in the excuse and finish the sentence with, ". . . so what's it to you if I have a few too many drinks, or smoke, or use?" For these people, they feel entitled to dull the pain with their substance of choice.

The more I tossed, sheets mummy-wrapped around my legs, the more I realized "entitled" is a word that can be used many different ways. Untangling myself, I pledged to figure out why Jeff felt so strongly about Bobby being entitled.

I have been privileged my entire adult life. I have a hard-working husband, and there is no getting around the fact that materially, we are blessed. But success and wealth are not shields against problems. Although with addiction, eventually it will all come down to the checkbook: when you've gone through your money, you still need your fix.

If one is an addict and poor and there isn't enough to eat and no shelter, no money for a drink or hit, desperation sets in pretty quickly. Choices must be made. Will you quit using and find a job—or make money any way possible, including prostituting yourself or selling drugs? Why not just steal? Drugs have the same physical effect on the rich or the poor, but poor people are more likely to end up homeless, in jail, and eventually in a pine coffin six feet under a tad faster than rich people.

If one has money, an addicted lifestyle is a bit easier—for a little while. The curse of being an addict with a roll in your wallet and a trust fund in the bank is that it lulls you into a false sense of security, and then there's entitlement. Need a hit? No problem. I'm not addicted because I have money!

No one can tell me what I am or what I can do. I'll just cut you off or move away, because I have money and I can. As long as I have money, I can continue to use and not face problems or the consequences of my actions. I can always buy the next drink, or the next pill, even if I have to fly to Rio to get it.

Like a super PAC for a presidential candidate, money can keep you in the game longer. It is only after you drain your savings account and run up your cards and your family cuts you off and you have a second or third mortgage—i.e., when you are poor—that you have to face the truth that you are addicted. At the basest level I believe all alcoholics and addicts are alike, rich or poor, male or female, black or white, mother or son, president or sanitation worker. Without intervention, every one of them will end up homeless, in jail, or dead; it is just a matter of when the money runs out.

Bobby had come to us as an addicted and entitled rich kid gone broke. He had sold or pawned everything he had ever owned or cared about—except his truck and some radio-controlled (RC) toy cars, a rich kid's hobby. But he loved those toy cars. When he was released from his year-long stint in a Texas rehab facility several years ago, his father told him he had to get a job and a hobby. Happily, he was hired as a car salesman, but where he got the money for his expensive toy RC cars, I'll never know. He arrived in North Carolina with five or six of them, big kid Matchbox cars with engines and remote controls. They were fast and fun and I could see why he would enjoy playing with them. But they cost upward of $400 to $500 per car. For someone with little or no income, he had chosen a damned expensive hobby.

———

LONELINESS

Tuesday, March 12

Today Bobby confided that he was having a hard time not using. I was greatly relieved he trusted me enough to tell me. Still I was stressed thinking about how close he was to falling off the wagon again, just when I thought he was settling in nicely. Maybe he had too much time on his hands with nothing to do but think.

It was obvious that he was very, very lonely. His whole social world was built around my two dogs, Annie the housekeeper, and Will and me. That afternoon, I spent extra time reaching out to some young people around his age, possible contacts or friends for Bobby. I believed if he could find just one friend to join him for lunch or watch a movie with, it would be transforming. This is what I have always told my kids: make one friend and then you are not alone.

Several kids I contacted had responded positively, and I had set Bobby up to meet them. He had already gone out on a few dates with girls he had met on the Internet. Will and I encouraged this, always making sure he had a little extra money to take the date to coffee or a movie, slipping him a few bucks for running an errand for us.

I crossed my fingers every time he left to pick up a date as it was a social challenge for him. Although Bobby wanted— desperately wanted—a friend, he didn't really know how to make connections with people. With his head hung and shoulders stooped, he preferred quiet to conversation.

I knew he was still too medicated to feel much, if any, emotion, but he was smart enough to know that he had lost many of the last years of his life due to addiction and that he did not have a lot in common with his age group. How would he answer those first awkward questions when getting to know another person? "What do you do?" "Ummm, I am trying to stay alive." "Why did you move to North Carolina?" "Because I have a back problem and I have trouble sitting up for any length of time." "Shall we split a bottle of wine?" "No, you go ahead. Addicts shouldn't drink because it lowers our defenses. But I make a fine designated driver."

Bobby would have to relearn how to relate to others, to have a give-and-take relationship. He had lived in an addict's bubble for a long time, one filled with drug-induced highs and lows, excruciating detoxifications, stints in rehabilitation centers, and then repeat.

Most kids his age were working full-time and almost all of them met out at bars. Even going to dinner with a Match.com date had its pitfalls since drinking alcohol is the norm and several of his dates did not understand his sobriety—and he chose not to enlighten them. He and I talked a little bit about his loneliness and what loneliness means to different people. I told him that one can be lonely in an elevator crowded with people—or in a marriage bed with a spouse sleeping inches away. One could also be happy on a deserted island or living solo in a space station. He would only find his peace and contentedness when he started to love himself, and could be happy by himself, with himself. Having hundreds of friends would not fill the emptiness.

I confessed that I had struggled with this same concept, and that it had taken me years to understand myself better and why I felt this way. I had a need to be needed and a hard time with the word "no." I have always felt the best about myself when I am helping someone else, connecting to another. When I was thirty years old and my father suddenly died, I realized it was he who gave me my self-esteem. Without my father, I felt abandoned and lost. I had never cut the umbilical cord and when death severed it for me, I fell apart.

I looked to my mother and family to give me that same kind of connection but, of course, they could not. Maturity, children, love of spouse have all helped me. We are all searching to fill voids in our life and I can safely say Bobby is not alone in this quest.

He is smart—both book and street smart. He is funny. He is kind. But, as I talked with him that night, I realized he was mired somewhere deep where I couldn't reach. Sometimes I looked at him and he seemed so sad. I asked him what he was thinking, and he said his mother hadn't called him. Had he called her? He said no, that he thought she should call him. Ah, I reminded him, the phone is a two-way street. I surreptitiously texted his mom and asked that she call him. He was on the verge of tears when he hung up with her. God, he was miserably lonely.

One night I brought Bobby to watch Will's tennis match. Afterward Bobby met the men on Will's team. Several immediately offered him work doing odd jobs, and another just made him feel special. I marveled at how easy Will's friends made it look, and wondered whether they realized that their kindness and attention meant the world to a very insecure young man.

Bobby's initial reaction to the kindness of strangers was positive but not lasting. He fell into a deep gloom when he returned home. I think acts of kindness made him feel unworthy, as if he didn't deserve them.

So, I kept telling him how cute he was and that he was a people magnet when he smiled. I just wished he could see himself from the outside and believe that he was a lovely young man. We can be told but hearing it is not enough. With shame-based problems, you might be a saint, but you can never believe it; there is a constant battle with your self-esteem. If I could look into his eyes for just a minute, I was certain this was what I would see, but he could not hold my gaze for that long.

———

MEDICINE

Wednesday, March 13

It was around a week and a half after Thomas's death and Bobby's arrival on my doorstep when I finally began to let my mind process the enormity of what had transpired in just a few short days. I couldn't get that image of Anne out of my head, beating on Thomas's door, screaming his name, and getting no answer. Finally forcing the door, and finding her son. Eyes open but unseeing, blue face covered in his own vomit, empty syringe just feet away. The thought of Anne finding her son dead of an overdose was haunting.

I had another unnerving thought. What if something were to happen to Bobby, God forbid, or if I were to ever find him unresponsive upstairs? I knew I was ill-equipped to cope with such a trauma. Damn, damn, damn. Could the same thing happen here in my home? Could I go up and knock and hear nothing? I kept transposing Thomas's image with one of Bobby, the image of Thomas lying on the floor, so vivid in my mind I could almost smell the scent of death in the air. What would I do? I needed a plan, just in case. I could feel the immediacy of my panic. Fortunately, planning has always been how I keep that panic at bay.

Okay, what would I tell the paramedics? I asked myself. Male. Duh. Twenty-nine years old, but just barely, having turned while we were on our sailing trip right before coming to Durham. Drug addicted since his college days. Yes, it was OxyContin, but it was for his back problems. And he was a good kid. You see, it was not his fault—addiction and alcoholism run in our family. It tortured and tormented my brother.

It buried my grandfather and uncle. Mercy, Bobby was only taking what the doctor ordered after all.

I bit my fingernail in two as these thoughts ran through my head. Damn. I just had my nails done. I placed another finger in my mouth.

I knew I had to find out what prescription drugs and dosages Bobby was taking—just in case.

I needed and desperately wanted him to trust me and my gut kept telling me that I was too intrusive, that I didn't know him well enough to just ask him about his prescriptions, that medication is as personal as hygiene. The last thing I wanted to do was make him feel embarrassed and ashamed. But I really felt I needed to know. If he needed medical attention, this information could mean the difference between life and death.

I made a last-minute and very spontaneous decision to show Bobby my own meds. I figured if we both did show-and-tell with each other, the embarrassment would be mutual. I had no idea that this shared surrender of privacy was the beginning of the deep connection I was seeking; what I felt could ultimately save his life.

I sprang into action. "Hey, Bobby. Can I come up and talk to you for a second? Are you busy?"

With my head pinging like an old-fashioned pinball machine, I wended my way up the stairway to the guest bedroom, the room that was still decorated with my daughter's hand-me-down bedroom set, complete with pink headboard and Pepto-Bismol–pink curtains.

I knocked on his door and was grateful for his muffled response. "Come in."

The room was dark, pink drapes closed tightly. Bobby was tucked, fully dressed, in the fetal position under my beautiful white satin bedspread—a Christmas surprise from my husband many years ago. I realized suddenly that giving him a key was only the first step to making him feel at home; we needed to make his room his own.

It was midafternoon, but it could have been midnight. Flipping on the light, and watching Bobby's dazed expression as he groggily sat up and squinted his eyes to acclimate, I held my breath and made my move.

"I want to show you something. I want you to know that many people must take prescription drugs for all sorts of reasons and there is nothing wrong with it. We are fortunate we live in a time that there are medications that, when used as directed"—I emphasized this point—"can be miracle workers. I want to share with you what medications I am taking and tell you why."

I held up the little plastic box I was clutching. It housed my week's supply of pills, each day separate and marked with a letter pertaining to that day of the week. I was surprised at just how uncomfortable I felt showing him my meds.

"Okay." He didn't seem that interested even though I felt like I was standing there naked. Weird.

For a while, he stayed mute and unresponsive, eyes glazed and downcast. Still I persevered and I was actually able to act like I showed off my meds regularly to everyone who came to the front door. "Mr. UPS man, here is my Singulair. I need it because I smoked for twenty years and now there are times I can't breathe. Mr. Yardman and crew, here, look at my light blue pill. I use it because I have bad nightmares where I thrash and scream and this little pill is better than Ambien. Mr. Mailman, thanks for the letter and here, look at my atenolol—two baby white pills I take to keep my heart in musical rhythm." Truly, if someone looked at these few pills and the multiple vitamins I take, they would think I was an elderly person—or (haha) a junkie. Bobby eventually warmed up to the situation, or else he just felt bad that I was so exposed. Eventually, he hauled out a massive accumulation of amber bottles, pulling a gallon-sized Ziploc bag from his bedside drawer.

Whoa. He was taking half the alphabet in pills—a total of thirteen different medications in all shapes, sizes, and dosages. I recognized a few of them immediately: several over-the-counter sinus meds; Flexeril, a muscle relaxer; Cymbalta, a med that treats nerve pain and depression; Prozac, an antidepressant; Trazodone, a sleeping aid and antidepressant; Doxepin, an antianxiety and sleep aid; Neurontin, used for nerve pain and as a mood stabilizer; Etodolac, a nonsteroidal anti-inflammatory drug.

It was the prescriptions I later looked up that stopped me cold in my tracks. Abilify, Haloperidol, and Seroquel—all aggressive antipsychotic meds. For about an hour we sprawled across his bed, Bobby up on his elbows and me cross-legged, leaning back on the upholstered pink headboard. We'd look at the bottle, read the prescription name, and laugh when we became tongue-tied and neither of us could pronounce it.

"What is this color? Look how pretty!" *God that was a stupid thing to say.* "See . . . I have a cute blue pill too." *Renée, you are an imbecile.* "Look at mine" *Jeez, what was I doing?* Against the white of the comforter, our multicolored pills looked like a grand mix of jelly beans.

I took note of the amazing amount of medicine Bobby had been prescribed, appalled because I knew that it was prescription medicine that had gotten him into this hell in the first place.

With the help of Dr. Pate, *this* was going to change. There was no way all these prescriptions—high-powered and mood-altering drugs—could be doing him good.

And, good Lord, I needed to do something about that emasculating bedspread.

———

DEAR FRIENDS

From: Renée Hodges
Subject: My nephew has moved to town! Do you need some errands run? Lightbulbs changed, dogs walked?
Date: Thursday, March 14, 2013, at 10:30 a.m.
To: Friends listserv

Dear friends,

My nephew Bobby Redford, my brother's son, moved to Durham recently and is living with me at the moment. Long term, he is looking for a job, or possibly school, but until then he needs some money! Please keep him in mind if you want your dog walked or brought to the vet (great with dogs!), lawn mowed, lightbulbs changed, milk and bread from the store, etc. Returns? Packages mailed? Mailings done. He is willing to do most anything, except really heavy lifting. And anything you pay him will be greatly appreciated.

If you do have an errand for Bobby, I'd like for you to know more about him. He is twenty-nine and a very smart, kind, handsome, young man who was sent to a Texas Hospital Scoliosis Center when he was twenty-one. He became addicted to the medicine that was prescribed for his back pain and has struggled with opioid substance abuse since.

He has a college degree from University of Louisiana at Lafayette. He has been clean now for a while, and is looking for a fresh, new start. He moved here for a complete evaluation at Duke University Medical Center, and I am delighted to say he loves this area. Everyone he has met has been so nice to him, and I am greatly encouraged.

He has his own vehicle. All you have to do is call him on his cell, or at my house (since cell service is limited inside my house). Please think of Bobby first when you need something done. And if you have a young man or woman around his age who might show him around town, would you let me know so they can meet? It does take a village . . .

Best, Renée

Reaching out to my friends had been an easy decision. In fact, I never really questioned it. I simply decided to be open and honest about Bobby's disease from the very beginning. There was no hiding under a bushel, no secrets, no denial—from any of us.

When Bobby arrived in Durham, I was ready to join his fight, but intuitively I knew I couldn't go it alone. I couldn't deny or avoid what was happening in our household and in our lives. I couldn't pretend that he was healthy and just visiting his aunt and uncle to get a fresh start in a new town. I wasn't going to have the burden of lying to myself, and I sure wasn't going to lie to my friends and family. Anyway, what would have been the point of that? Bobby had a disease and he needed everyone's support, love, and understanding—not the devastating impact of silence or the hurtful and sad avoidance of cover-up. Lying, manipulation, spinning, evasion, and deception are already a part of the addictive process. I didn't want it to be a part of the recovery process too.

Although I can now see what a powerful choice openness

was and what a difference it made not only in his recovery but in my ability to support him, back then, it really wasn't a conscious decision. It just happened. I enlisted the aid of my family and friends, opening up to them and seeking their advice. They, in turn, kept him accountable and watched his back. I trusted a professional to guide me when I wavered or questioned. From the very beginning, I leaned on others, trusting that sharing this monumental situation would be the right thing to do. I opened the door wide and invited everyone into our lives and it was wonderful. We were lessening the shame and we were giving him a support system. These friends and family members, as well as professionals, provided us with everything from an encouraging word to the promise of accountability.

And because we were open and vulnerable, the most amazing thing happened, an unexpected bonus. Others started to unburden and disclose, sharing their hidden stories. People I had known for years shared stories I had never suspected. In the store or on my cell phone I could hear the relief in their voices as many opened their memory hamper, and shared their addiction secrets with me, for maybe the very first time.

Why did I become a confidant? I believe it is because others saw us refuse to attach shame to our situation, and then witnessed the liberation and healthy outlook that came with being open and vulnerable. They saw someone to whom they could relate, someone in whom they could confide without fear of judgment. And it felt good to open up, to feel less alone and share their own stories with someone who had empathy and a willing ear.

This emboldened me. Every time someone stopped to ask how they could help us, I felt stronger. When friends called to tell me about their child's struggles with OxyContin, or other legal opioids—or heroin—I felt less alone. I also became more and more frustrated with the knowledge that prescription opioids and their addictive qualities are destroying so many real people, not just people in another state or city or another part of town. I'm talking about people here in my own neighborhood—a gated affluent neighborhood, where we all wave to each other on the street.

Why didn't I know this? Why hadn't I seen this? Where had I been? Having Bobby in my home made me an automatic member of a private club—and only now could I share stories of another's addicted family member or friend.

When someone finally decides to seek treatment, only then does he understand that addiction, like a tattoo, always leaves a permanent scar. This is the mark of shame—the disfiguring of the whole family indelibly inked by a misunderstood disease.

I saw the shame in some of their eyes, the deep sadness and resignation as they confessed their terrible secrets. I heard the fear and the weariness in their voices. They all just needed someone who might understand and who would listen without judgment.

As more and more people told me their brave and sad stories, I realized we are all in this together. As I say too often, it takes a village. We had helped create this small and strong village by telling our story and allowing others to tell theirs. Addiction is a disease and it cannot be hidden away like a colony of lepers on an isolated island, shameful and out of sight. We all must take heroin and opioid addiction out of the closet, bring it out in the open, and fight it together— head-on. This is the only way we are going to help our most precious possessions—our loved ones.

DAILY PLANNER

When Bobby came to stay with us, I discovered several surprising things in the first weeks. One was that he did not have a calendar of any sort, did not use his smart phone, did not use a date book, and did not check his emails. He was not organized, and he was used to others telling him where to be, what to do, and how to act. Organization was something with which I could definitely help.

When I told him it was his responsibility to keep up with his doctors' and workout appointments, and that he should start using his phone calendar, he became alarmed.

His response cemented what I was learning: Bobby was behind in many ways. When I asked about his lack of responsibility in an early counseling session, Jeff was blunt and informative, explaining that there is a close link between addiction and emotional immaturity. Former addicts often find it hard to deal with the normal challenges of life. When faced with problems, they feel unable to cope. This creates a psychological state known as "learned helplessness." Bobby's scared response made me reassess my command, and I gently provided him with a few ideas to get started.

"There are paper desk planners at Office Depot. Why don't you go there and buy one—a big one." He looked calmer at this suggestion. "We can sit down together every Sunday evening and I'll help you plot out your week."

Thus Sunday evenings became our together time. While an early dinner simmered on the stovetop, Bobby and I would sit down at the kitchen table, its black marble reflecting our determined faces, and we would cover many important topics.

"Let's start with what you did last week," I would lead

him. "How many AA meetings did you attend? Which meeting did you like best? What was the demographic of each meeting? Are there any kids your age?"

It took several weeks before Bobby started to attend AA meetings regularly. During his first week in Durham, he didn't leave his bedroom except to go to doctors' appointments or to smoke. I encouraged him to attend Narc Anon meetings and he scoffed at the thought. Not deterred, I prodded him gently at least once a day on the accountability that AA or Narc Anon would give him.

Finally, he turned to me, laser-like stare cutting deeply, and lectured, "Aunt Née, if I wanted to buy drugs, Narc Anon is where I would go to get contacts. Every drug addict knows that. I feel safer going to AA right now. I'm not strong enough to go to NA."

I was shocked and never mentioned Narc Anon to him again. It seemed inconceivable to me that there might be risk involved in going to a support group meeting, that there were pushers out there lurking in even the most reputable of places. But then, there are pushers in our schools and . . .

Until Bobby felt ready, I was glad he would continue going to AA meetings instead.

On Sunday evenings I would ask him if he had seen his counselor or physician, if he had worked out at the Wellness Center, or, in some cases, if he had done anything at all.

I also found that sitting down together was helpful in assessing his emotional state. I would ask him if there had been anything from the week that he found difficult or upsetting. And I would listen to him. Really listen. I would take mental notes and try to discuss even the smallest issue. Bobby was a mystery, and, as with all good mysteries, one cannot discount a single clue.

Comments that sounded offhand tended not to be trivial at all. The first few Sundays I was forced to prompt him by asking any question that might elicit a response: "How is your urge to use? How was your back this past week? Have you had any contact with your father?"

I had expressly forbidden any contact between Bobby and his father after their argument the night Bobby left to come to Durham until I could get a grasp on his triggers. John was also recovering, having been sober since Bobby was eighteen years old. Like superwoman, I wanted to protect my brother too. Unfortunately, I have no super powers; so temporarily banning contact between the boys was the best protection I knew.

Next, I would ask Bobby to list several things or events he felt good about that had occurred in the past week. "The dogs like me," and "I'm alive . . ."—long pause as if he was un-sure this was a good thing—". . . with a roof over my head," were the two positive comments that first Sunday we sat down. I took them, and inwardly smiled at the progress he was making. I was starting to feel he really could do this.

At the end of each Sunday meeting, we would set a goal for the upcoming week and write it in big letters across the first day of that week on the calendar. It would be a daily re-minder—for both of us. Get out of bed before noon. Attend one more AA meeting than last week. Cut down on the soft drinks. These meager goals seemed monumental in the mo-ment; I kept reminding myself that with one foot in front of the other soon enough we would reach the beach.

Bobby and I would eventually grow these conversations to include things like girls and future plans, but in the first weeks it was difficult to get him to even acknowledge my presence.

It took several months before he began to enjoy sched-uling himself, although I was a believer from the first meeting. The weekly planning session was better than Prozac to lessen my anxiety; it gave me a semblance of order and a yardstick to gauge progress. I knew where he was supposed to be at all times and what he was thinking. It gave him a safe avenue to talk about his accomplishments and struggles, while always looking to the next week. And it rekindled his lost feeling of independence, something he had long since forgotten.

Wrapping up our conversation, Bobby would always place his schedule by the overstuffed chair he had claimed as his own in the family room, within reaching distance at all times.

And then he would set the table for me.

REMOTE

Thursday, March 14

Almost two weeks had passed since Bobby's arrival, and I was working on the computer when he knocked on my bedroom door. He entered and remained standing awkwardly, feeling he needed my permission to sit or talk.

"What can I do for you?" I inquired, putting aside the computer.

"I wanted to see if you would help me buy a new remote."

"I'm not sure I understand?"

Bobby explained that a remote for his toy cars had ei-ther been lost or stolen while he was in Atlanta. He didn't remember.

"How much is it?"

"Around four hundred dollars, but I could get a used one online for a little less."

I waited a second to reply, really because I was momentarily without words. Asking for $400 for a toy when he couldn't put gas in his truck and didn't have enough money for the co-pay for his colonoscopy drugs? *Think, Renée, think.*

"Isn't that a lot of money to be spending on a remote control?"

Bobby answered honestly, "The car is no good without it."

I just went for it. "I cannot in good conscience give you four hundred dollars for a remote. I know you are used to having money, but you do not have it anymore."

I then gently explained to him that this was not what his "allowance" should be used for. I would find him some errand work amongst my friends while he looked to find a cheaper version on eBay or elsewhere. After he earned the money for the remote, he might understand just how expensive that remote really was, and he could choose to spend his hard-earned money on gas, a date, or a remote control if he still wanted it.

"I will also ask your uncle Will to come up with a financial plan so you can A) make some money of your own, and B) be accountable for your own finances."

I decided to come clean with him. "I have never been good with money. Your grandfather and grandmother never taught us the value of nor gave us the responsibility for money, not me and not your dad. I overdrew my account almost every month I was in college. I had multiple overdraft notices, but because Dad was on the board of the local bank in our small town, all overdraft fees were waived and he just put some more money in my account." Revelation! I had been an entitled college student and I didn't even know it.

What I didn't tell Bobby was that even after marrying

Will, I still do not balance my checkbook regularly. It drives Will crazy, but I keep way more in my account each month than I would ever spend; I am pretty frugal and I know a ballpark figure of what I have in the bank at all times and, just in case, I have overdraft protection. I did learn some things from my dad. You could say I am entitled because I don't balance my checkbook each month, but really I don't think so. I think I am just plain lazy.

"You are a grown man now," I said, "and starting today, you are going to learn to be fiscally responsible." Do as I say, not as I do.

Will blew his top when he heard that Bobby had asked me for $400. He couldn't understand that Bobby has never been held accountable for any money, ever. Period. Oh boy!

From: Renée Hodges
Subject: 3/15 update
Date: Friday, March 15, 2013, at 12:09 a.m.
To: Mary Costello

Dear Mary,

I go all day thinking about what is going on in my mind and by the time I have a moment to write, well, it just sort of slips away. I am solid for the moment, but I am starting to fray at the edges. Just a little, but I can tell. It has more to do with trying to balance life with Will, my wonderful husband who I think is a bit jealous having to give up his newly earned empty nest. I blame myself, as I have taken on Bobby as almost a full-time job and Will doesn't seem to get it.

Now, Will is always so nice to Bobby, and I know he knows that this is what we need to be doing, but he can be inflexible and unsympathetic when it comes to some daily issues. He can also be quite judgmental and has difficulty looking beneath the surface.

Part of my job is to make Bobby understand how precious money is and how hard it is to come by, something my extended family has never learned. And I'm determined to help Bobby learn, just like Will and I have taught our other kids.

————

WILL AND RENÉE

I bring much of the anxiety to our marriage. Maybe it is some dysfunctional gene I inherited, but probably it is because I am wired like an accordion. When I think, my thoughts are not static but are full of movement, folding like bellows, in and out, pushed and pulled, fluid and full of motion. My thoughts are generally musical, but sometimes I am just another reed blower.

Will is the stable, linear thinker in the family. He is firm concrete, solid and faithful, and I am potter's clay, pliable and ever evolving. Will prefers the analytical to the emotional, although he can also be boisterous and loud or soft and gentle. He looks at life from a completely different angle than I do, but put us together and together we see every view.

Will knows that I am an emotional over-thinker, especially when the lights are finally turned off for the night and I become restless with the vividness of my own imagination. He rolls over and puts the Will-clamp on me, spooning, while throwing his long arms over me, a straitjacket, securing not only my squirmy body but my mind as well. Usually it takes only a few minutes before I settle down, and I feel safe and sound, tightly bound up by the man I love.

While watching TV together before bed, we are puppies in a litter, snuggled so closely that if one moves, the other must move also. Always our hands are clasped together and Will absently rubs my palm with his thumb.

And there is the foot. The foot is the ultimate field test in our relationship. If I wander too far toward the edge of the bed at any time, sleeping or not, Will splays his foot out seeking, resting his toes softly where they find smooth leg, an assurance that I am still there, that I haven't disappeared in the night. And when I feel his foot resting on me, I don't have to think about it—I know all is well with us. After thirty-two years of marriage, Will's habits are comfortingly predictable.

When it is too quiet in our bedroom, I can feel the distance between us. I can smell it and see it. I am alone in the bed, and yet I am not. When there is a literal abyss with the white of the sheets insurmountable between us, I know something is off. I am unnerved.

That was how I found our bed in the second week of Bobby's stay. Will had moved so far to the outer edge of the mattress that I was afraid he'd slide off. The amount of space between us was like the North Sea, wide, frigid, and unnavigable without a lot of courage and a life jacket.

I had been so obsessed with helping Bobby that I was totally spent and had failed to take notice of Will's feelings about our houseguest. It is hard to pour from an empty pitcher.

I realized that Bobby's problems were so much deeper and darker than I'd imagined and that I might not have the strength to continue. I needed Will to stand with me or I could not go on. I didn't have the energy to do battle with both Bobby and Will flanking me on either side.

"Will." I patted him on the back, as he had already turned over to go to bed, earphones on to aid his sleeping. I was afraid of having this conversation, and my voice was already starting to crack. "Will, can we talk for a moment before you sleep?"

He rolled over and slowly began pulling himself to a sitting position while turning on the bedside light, all in a continuous motion. As he took out his earphones, my bravado quickly faded. I spit it out so fast that I wasn't sure Will understood what I was saying.

"Will, please don't make me choose." I nearly squeaked as I said it.

"Choose?" he replied in confusion.

"Yes. Please don't make me choose between you and Bobby." I pushed the words out of my dry mouth. "I'm asking you. Please. If you make me choose between you and Bobby, I would choose you. You know I would."

Damn. Where did that tear come from? I brushed the traitor off my cheek.

"But then I don't think I would ever be able to forgive myself if something happened to Bobby."

There was the dreaded silence before he emitted a long sigh.

"I'm not comfortable with Bobby in the house," Will confessed. He then pondered for a moment, eyes closed, head leaning back on the upholstered headboard. "I don't feel like he is engaging and interacting with me. We don't have any type of relationship and zero communication. I'm not convinced this is the right place for him to be. I'm not sure he belongs here."

I snuggled closer to him, and his arm drew down over my shoulders as he pulled me tightly to his chest.

"I know," I said. "I'm not sure either. But it has only been two weeks. I can see little cracks happening in him, small positive signs. Can we just give it a few more weeks please? I see something in him. I really do. And, for heaven's sake, Will, what else do I have to do but play tennis? I believe I can help this boy. I feel I can make a difference and"—I pause and draw a breath—"he has nowhere else to go. No one else will take him in."

"Maybe. But it still irks me about the four hundred dollars he wanted for the remote. Even though we didn't give it to him, I can't believe he even asked for it."

I contemplated this. "Will, think about it. He doesn't have the vaguest idea about the value of money. If he needs something, he just calls the secretary at his dad's office. You can help him. You can teach him . . . just like you did with our own kids. You did a remarkable job with them. I know he can learn from you."

Will didn't say anything else but he didn't have to. My ear was lying directly over his heart and I could hear it thumping. As difficult as it was to juggle Will and Bobby, I was so very glad I wasn't in this alone.

The next day I heard their two voices in Will's office as I passed by. When Bobby came down the stairs a bit later, he was carrying a piece of paper, which he handed to me. I read it slowly and breathed a sigh of relief. They had communicated and come up with a money plan.

I typed up Bobby's scrawl and printed a copy for him to refer back to when needed.

Money Rules:

1. *Every Sunday, Bobby will get paid for the previous week.*

2. *He will earn ten dollars per day for every day he works out at least an hour.*

3. *He will earn ten dollars per AA meeting he attends up to seven.*

4. *He will earn ten dollars per meeting with his counselor, Jeff.*

5. *If Bobby misses any one of the five workouts, five AA meetings, or a counseling session without a good reason, he will pay Will ten dollars for each missed meeting.*

6. *The basis for this weekly Sunday payment is that Bobby will receive base funding for his basic needs. Anything extra must be earned and paid for by Bobby.*

7. *For work around the house that Will needs done, Will pays fifteen dollars an hour, the same as he paid William, Rachel, and Katherine.*

8. *For every dollar Bobby earns away from the house, Will will pay 50 percent more if it is below ten dollars, up to fifteen dollars per hour.*

With this agreement, Bobby is to continue to be substance-free, keep to his schedule, be responsible for his finances, and think about nutrition.
We love you.

I added this last part, "We love you," for encouragement. Every chance I got I tried to tell him he was loved.

With this system in place, Bobby could make over $200 a week, sometimes more, if he applied himself. God bless Will.

As I handed Bobby the printed money agreement, I verbally added, "You will need to transfer your checking account to North Carolina and order new checks. You will need to get a debit card." I do know about checks and a debit card.

"I don't have a checking account of my own."

"Okay. Well, then, you need to open one up."

He looked embarrassed. "I have never opened up a checking account."

This confession concerned me. I was realizing that Bobby had had less instruction in money management than I had thought. I opened my first account when I went off to college at eighteen. Perhaps it should be mandatory for all high school students to go to their local bank and open and keep up with a personal checking account, even if there are only a few dollars deposited.

"There's a first time for everyone. I can help guide you. You'll be in the money in no time."

TWELVE DAYS

JEFF GEORGI'S OFFICE

Sometimes things occur and you get a feeling that the event cannot be an accident or you have been there before or you know that person from somewhere, even if you have never met. Things just click. You might be thinking of a friend you haven't talked to in a few years when the phone rings and you hear her voice on the other end. Or you share a special day with your best friend and go to the local nail salon and out of literally a thousand colors of nail polish, you both select the same color.

Reverend Bowen's wife corrects me when I say "coincidental." She says coincidences and weirdly improbable occurrences are all providential, set out by God. I want to think that is the case, that God has scripted my life. When I have deep doubts, I think about the coincidence in the following story; the odds that these events could happen the way they happened and at the same time makes this story come as close to providential proof in my life as humanly or divinely possible.

Upon first meeting Jeff Georgi, Bobby's substance abuse counselor, I did not know what to expect. I had talked to Jeff on the phone several times before finally meeting him in his office with Bobby. I had been familiar with "Jeff the husband" for many years, as his wife, Becky, was my oldest daughter's school counselor and advisor for four years, but I had never met Jeff the professional. I knew Jeff did something with addiction, but I wasn't sure what it was and I had no idea he was exactly what I—well, Bobby—needed right then. All I knew was that Becky had a long history of working with kids and I needed a direction. So when it was decided Bobby was to come to Durham, I asked her for advice on addiction counselors for Bobby. I look back and see another providential stroke that, when I shared, opening up and asking for help, the right person entered my life at the right time.

Jeff is an extremely busy and bright man. He has been practicing psychotherapy with a focus on substance abuse and families for more than thirty years. He holds a fistful of professional licenses, including clinical addiction specialist, certified clinical supervisor, and licensed professional counselor. For two decades, Jeff served as the clinical director of the Duke Addictions Program. Jeff only sees a handful of patients privately as he is much in demand, lecturing and think-tanking around the country. When he agreed to counsel Bobby, I felt like the most blessed person in the world. Divinely inspired, for sure!

When Bobby first started the counseling, he met with Jeff twice a week, and I accompanied him to every counseling session for about a month. There is a little thing called patient-doctor confidentiality, so for the first several appointments, I patiently sat in the waiting room reading old magazine articles on Kim Kardashian until the session was almost over. Then I was called in to join Bobby and Jeff during the last ten minutes. These ten minutes were for me to ask questions regarding how to care for my nephew. This, I guess, was not considered confidential. I found it awkwardly reassuring to talk about how to care for Bobby with him present.

"Jeff, can you give me direction as to how best to help Bobby?" I'd plead.

His answers were straightforward. Bobby was not ready

to engage the world. It would be awhile before he could work or go to school. We should focus on AA meetings, fitness workouts, and doctors' appointments. He should not be left alone. Jeff and Bobby thanked us for giving Bobby another opportunity. Period.

The first time I accompanied Bobby to his session and was invited in for the last few minutes, I was surprised and delighted when Jeff pulled a plastic cup from a cabinet drawer and handed it to Bobby. He instructed Bobby, "Down the hall and to the right."

When we were alone, Jeff explained that Bobby would take a drug test every session starting today. "I have told him that it is not because I don't trust him. It is because if he is going to do the work, if he is going to fight to stay clean, this is the proof and it is a celebration every time the test comes back negative."

Wow. Just those few words taught me a valuable lesson. Any situation can turn into a positive depending on how you view it. Jeff looked at a drug test in a unique way, and from here on out I vowed to try and do the same with other not so pleasant events I knew we would face. I'm not always successful, but Jeff's outlook is a keeper.

Two weeks passed before Bobby signed the disclosure agreement enabling me to have access to any information he imparted during these counseling sessions with Jeff. I felt it was singularly important for me to know what was going on in Bobby's head, especially if Jeff felt I needed to know. I did not feel I could help Bobby if I couldn't connect with him, and the only way to connect was to know what he was thinking. Jeff would only share what he felt was important for me to know: emotional status and drug-testing updates. The bones of what they talked about were between them, and it was important for Bobby to know he could trust Jeff to be able to open up to him.

On March 15, twelve days after his arrival and the first day Bobby signed the privacy agreement, I was invited to the early morning session after only fifteen minutes of reading about the Duggars in the waiting room.

Seated on the far side of the office, my back to the window and face to the door, I was uncomfortable, nervous with expectation. I was flying without a compass and counted on Jeff to be my instrument panel. I had to put my trust in him.

Bobby sat to my left, on a sofa as far away from me as possible. Jeff sat in an upholstered, staid wooden armchair, positioned to form a perfect triangle between the three of us. I felt there was a little too much room between us all, like the office should have been smaller, or the furniture pulled closer to create more intimacy. No one else seemed to care.

Jeff started by leaning forward, catching and looking directly into Bobby's eyes—a hard task, as Bobby was torn between looking at Jeff and at his shoelaces. Without blinking or moving an inch, Jeff said, "Bobby, do you want to tell your Aunt Renée some things?" It was posed as a question, but the demand was in the delivery.

Bobby sat motionless, not breathing. Was I doing the same?

He began with, "Aunt Née, you don't know how sick I was . . ." He continued with a litany of short stories, one by one, emotionless delivery but each vignette leaving me speechless.

I must stop and pat myself on the back right now because on that day I sat rigid, never showing shock while he spoke; throughout the entire monologue I acted like I was hearing Bobby recite a grocery list. It is very difficult to shock me, and to this day I don't know if I was more surprised by Bobby's past or by the fact that no one told me about any of it before he came to live with me. Surely, John or Jill should have mentioned some of his history before now. Maybe they thought I knew? But with everything shrouded in secrecy, how could I?

In that first session I attended with the privacy agreement signed, Bobby confessed to being an alcohol abuser. In college, he would crack a beer in the morning and drink it in the shower. Man, I was even more shocked! When Bobby arrived and we asked him if we should put up the alcohol and not drink around him, he told us that alcohol didn't really bother him.

I began to sweat. Will and I had been drinking around Bobby since he arrived two weeks ago, and we had left the booze in the bar in plain drinking sight. Aunt of the Year, here.

Bobby continued in a barely audible voice and told me he was not just an OxyContin abuser. Although his addiction to Oxy was first, he had since used every street drug, including coke, meth, and "needles," which was code for heroin, the big H. Bobby would take any prescription drug he could buy and he was not picky. At one point, he was spending upward of $200 a day on any drug he could get his hands on. He pawned everything he owned, including his expensive watch, his tools and toolbox, anything with value. He squandered his trust fund.

I could not believe that this was the first time I had heard about his alcohol problem as well as the illegal drug use problem. I was sweating because this meant a tectonic shift in the aid we provided, and an even bigger shift in the lifestyle of our family. Selfishly I thought, *No wine with dinner? No cocktail hour? No mojito on the terrace?* Could I do it? Would Will do it? I was definitely panicking.

First the earthquake, then the tsunami: Bobby confessed that he never thought he would arrive here in Durham two weeks ago. In fact, he had never intended to make it. He had tried to kill himself while he was in Atlanta.

"Go on," Jeff softly encouraged Bobby.

After having the argument with his father over taking his prescription opioid, Bobby had immediately packed and left Louisiana to drive to North Carolina. He made the plan to buy and use any drug, every drug, he could get along I-20. And he did. He was suicidal.

Silence.

Let me get this straight, I thought. *He left his home to drive here and never expected to arrive on my doorstep. The same night that Thomas Howard lost his life to the same damn drugs, Bobby was trying to end his life too? You have to be fucking kidding me.*

Up until that moment, I'd been able to feign detachment, but it became too much effort. With tears running down my face and my voice quivering, I said: "Bobby, is this when you called me from Atlanta and didn't know where you were? Is this why you were so confused and disoriented?"

"Yes, ma'am."

The tears were flowing in earnest and my nose had started to run. Jeff silently put a box of tissues next to my seat. I pulled one.

Softly, I said, "Bobby, it's okay. It's going to be okay." Was I telling him this or trying to talk myself into a sense of okay-ness?

"If you are still alive, there is a reason. I believe there must be a reason. God must have a purpose for you." Voice cracking, nasal from my stopped-up nose, I was finding it hard to think. I was in over my head and I half expected Jeff to tell me as much. But Jeff didn't say anything. He was simply facilitating the conversation. I floundered, a hooked fish in the bottom of a boat.

Bobby looked up and our eyes met. I could see that he did not want to hurt me, that he now was carrying this burden of guilt too.

He shook his head in resignation. "Yes, there must be a reason, Aunt Née, because I did everything I could to not be alive."

Impulsively I jumped up, crossed the carpet quickly, and did the only thing I knew to do. I put my arms around him. Bobby hung his head in shame. And I made a nice wet spot on the front of his T-shirt.

"Oh, Bobby. Oh, Bobby." I didn't know what else to say. I took a seat next to him on the sofa and held his hand. The same night Thomas died, the very same night, Bobby could have died too. God, you must have a plan if you took one boy and left the other. What are the stinking odds that this could happen? Surely, this could not be a coincidence.

In closing, Jeff applauded Will's and my efforts on Bobby's behalf, but he was also stern (and I'm not sure if it was for Bobby's benefit or mine) when he said that Bobby's recovery had to be Bobby's recovery—that Will and I were only there to support and facilitate.

Okay, I'd heard that before. I nodded to Jeff in acceptance, but after what I'd just heard, I believed that Bobby's recovery was now my job too. Those damn blurred boundaries.

From: Renée Hodges
Subject: Update on Jeff Georgi's office visit
Date: Friday, March 15, 2013, at 10:06 p.m.
To: Mary Costello

*First, I just love Jeff Georgi. He really does get it! He is going to
meet Bobby at the Duke Wellness Center every morning to hold
him accountable for going. He gave out his personal cell phone
number and told Bobby to call him anytime, day or night. He said I
could call him too. Ha Ha. His wife, Becky, should watch out! And
he has won Bobby's trust and my eternal gratitude. Yay, Jeff!*

*We talked about a job search, or school. Apparently, the lethal
combination of drugs Bobby took on his long trip to Durham will
take time to get out of his system, and for his body and brain to
bounce back. Bobby has been so tired every day, and Jeff said this
should get better as his body gets healthier and puts time and
distance between Bobby's last massive drug use. I am to give Bobby
several more weeks to fully recover.*

*Haven't heard from John or Jill in a few days. Just as well. I am
really tired.*

Update to self:

From: Renée Hodges
Subject: 3/15 update
Date: Friday, March 15, 2013, at 11:27 p.m.
To: self

*I am in a place I don't know how I got to or how to get out of.
Bobby has been opening up and talking to us, but Will seems to be
putting up more hurdles than I can jump. Bobby told us this morning
that he is thinking that he doesn't know why he is still alive.*

He is very depressed and I am realizing I might not be able to help him. I am realizing he might not make it. I am struggling with this truth.

Will is uncomfortable with all of it. As much as I thought he might buy in, I'm not sure he gets it on a deeper level. I am torn between continuing to help Bobby and balancing Will. It makes me so angry with Will, with myself.

————

DARKNESS

Saturday

The day after seeing Jeff was a rough one for Bobby. He was very low in the morning, and I couldn't seem to reach or make a connection with him. He told me he was still having trouble not using. He thought about it too much.

He said he'd had nightmares about using the night before. These nightmares stain him like black tar, sticky, unwanted, and tough to shake. As I lay in bed, I could hear him screaming late in the night, horrible and high-pitched, unintelligible words. I squeezed my eyes tighter and put my pillow over my head to ward off my feelings of helplessness.

When we finally sat down to talk a bit about his confession in Jeff's office the day before, Bobby told me he had been thinking about why he was alive and if he even wanted to continue to live. "I just wish I cared, Aunt Née."

I gave him the standard "one day at a time" response. I pointed out that he was much loved by us and he had already come a long way. I also told him he had dug a deep, deep hole, so it might take a little more time; but if he just kept crawling upward, he would start to see the light. I warned it wouldn't happen overnight and he should not put a time limit on it.

As we sat together, I googled the definition of depression. My heart beat faster and I admitted to myself that I was way out of my league because I don't understand it. Although I have struggled with highs and lows in my own life, the depth of Bobby's despair was far beyond my own experience. I wanted to fix his sadness, to wave the magic wand and have him feel happiness and thankfulness for being alive, but all I ever saw was the top of his head or the empty look where I could see all the way down to his barren insides.

So, I did what I could do. I kept telling Bobby how much I loved him, how he was beautiful inside and out, and that I was there for him.

I went to the higher power, and I used and manipulated God to work in my favor. "There must be a reason you are alive and Thomas is dead. It can't be a coincidence. It just can't. Look to God for your purpose, trust in Him. He is here for you. We are here for you."

After I told him this, I decided I was just a wee bit hypocritical and that we needed to go back to church together. Since I wasn't a "regular" at any particular church, I decided we would go to the Reverend Bowen's service as Bobby seemed to have made a connection with him.

It had been two weeks since Bobby arrived and I felt like it had been two months. I somehow summoned the energy each morning to put on my cheerleading face for the day, but it was getting more and more difficult. When I retired in the evening, it was all I could do to take my clothes off and crawl in bed.

I was up in the middle of the night, tossing and turning,

listening with half an ear to him pace once again, and I came up with an idea. Because he still had a major desire to use drugs and he had told me he was depressed most all the time, I asked him to write down some things in the hope he could see the blessings in his life.

I asked him to write:

Things I am grateful for
Things I look forward to
Things that have changed since March 3 when I arrived
    in Durham

No surprise that I cried when I read them.

Things I am grateful for:

GOD
Second chance
Warm water
Family
Dad being sober
Roux and Saint (the puppies)
Days I do not feel sick or hurt
Happiness when able
Mom
People who talk to me
My R.C. cars
Hands and legs
Running truck
Nice teeth
Insurance
Opportunity to travel

Hunting farm
Freedom
Nice clothes
Relationships
Ability to stay sober
No felonies
Fresh food
Grandpa, chance to meet him
Heaven or the idea of H.
Spirituality
Not dying

Things to look forward to:

Living
Heaven
Stable and enjoyable job
Earning a living
Taking care of family as they have done for me
Losing more weight
Making my family proud
One year of sobriety
Helping others
Exploring different countries
Learning new things
Falling in love
Starting a family
Having children
Better connection with God
A best friend
Feeling hopeful/useful
Good books

Changes in my life since March 3:

Reconnecting a little with family
Better relationship with my Higher Power
Learning new things
Feeling loved again
Not placing blame on others
My actions affect others
New information about my health
Enjoying living a little more
Branching out away from Louisiana

TWO WEEKS

From: Renée Hodges
Subject: Update
Date: Sunday, March 17, 2013, at 11:46 p.m.
To: Mary Costello

I am tired. Plumb worn out. Today was cold and rainy off and on. Bobby and I went to Reverend Bowen's church again, for the 10:45 service. An associate minister was preaching and my thoughts turned to the negative quickly. But OMG—pun intended—the lesson was on the Battle for the Heart! I felt like the minister had a laser aimed directly at Bobby, that it was a private service for him. I kept looking out of the corner of my eye, positioning the sermon program so that I could look at it and at Bobby at the same time. Did I see tears? I prayed fervently that God would help him with his inner struggles, save his life, direct him and direct me. I was even a bit peeved at the minister that he didn't give me enough quiet time to get all my requests heard.

After church, Will and I had some discussions about Bobby while he was out. I just can't hear anything right now, especially when Will talks. Everything he says comes out like an attack on Bobby or me. Although he could tiptoe, he chooses to march and it makes me anxious and defensive, even when the march is really the most productive step. I am a raw nerve.

Mary, you don't have to read these emails if you don't want to because I see you tomorrow. Writing this out helps me immensely and helps me to get to sleep.

Best, Renée

Update to self:

From: Renée Hodges
Subject: Update to self, 3/17
Date: Sunday, March 17, 2013, at 11:54 p.m.
To: self

Bobby woke up this morning and went to AA before church. He seemed content for most of the day. At around 7:30 p.m. he decided to go to a second AA meeting at a different place. He did not like the speaker at this one.

His mom and dad called while he was gone. I hadn't heard from them in a while, and I was frank and honest, telling them that Bobby never intended to make it to NC but that he was hanging in there. I tried to bring them up to date.

Bobby came in from his meeting while I was talking, and he changed phones to speak to them. Afterward he went straight upstairs to bed. I don't know if talking to his mom makes him upset, but I need to find out.

High points: Bobby was humming to himself in the car today. He is somewhat working out and he is attending AA meetings.

Low points: He is very withdrawn and depressed at times and I can't seem to connect with him.

GOLDEN RULES

Within a couple weeks of Bobby's arrival, I realized that he and I needed to come to an understanding, the proverbial meeting of the minds—although I wasn't sure his mind was functioning very well at the moment, having just learned about his adventure in Atlanta. I peeked into the family room to find him in his favorite overstuffed chair, slumped with his leg swung loosely over the arm, clicking through channels on cable. Over the next months I would realize that the History Channel or any channel to do with sports cars were Bobby's favorite for viewing. He can hear a rattle in my car that I secretly suspect is a phantom and he can tick off three possible issues. And he is never wrong. I'm positive that he could be called in as an automotive expert witness if needed. He also spent hours watching WWII and Vietnam documentaries on TV, and I was thrilled that we could connect over something we both had in common: our love of history and the military.

Watching him intently study General Eisenhower's war plans, I nervously fiddled with nothing in the kitchen for about ten minutes before calling out, "Can I talk to you for just a few minutes? Your Uncle Will and I have been talking over some things, and I would like to discuss them with you."

"Sure." He answered like a polite robot. Always polite. Always robotic. *Would you take out the trash? Yes, ma'am. Would you feed the dogs? Okay. Do you want chocolate-covered roaches for dinner? Yes, please.* He had never expressed an opinion for himself. He never advocated for himself. He answered by rote. Always positively, with zero emotion or inflection. Monotone. Deadpan. Or maybe just dead.

I wrote these rules down as my nephew watched:

The Golden Rules:

1. *Bobby stays clean, i.e., he doesn't drink and he doesn't use. Period.*

2. *Bobby doesn't lie. Not to me, to Will, to Jeff, to his parents, to himself. Period. If he never lies and always strives to tell the truth, he will never have to look over his shoulder, never have to think about what he has said or will say.*

3. *Bobby doesn't steal. Not pennies, not silver, not my last Diet Coke. Period.*

Taking a deep breath, I drilled it home. "There is a no-strike policy. If you break one of these rules, I will sadly ask you to pack your bags and leave."

Pregnant pause.

"Bobby, look at me."

Shoulders hunched and face down, he swept his too-long bangs out of the way with the palm of his hand as he slowly lifted his eyes to meet mine.

"Do you understand this?"

"Yes, ma'am."

"Do you have anywhere else to go?"

"No, ma'am." He was defeated. He made no movement except to shift his eyes downward.

"Bobby, please look at me." I placed my hand on top of his as he rested them in his lap.

"Would you promise me this? Would you promise me that if you get the urge, if you are even thinking about using, that you will come to me first and tell me? You may still end up using, but coming to me will at least give us a fighting chance. We'll take a walk. You'll call Jeff or your sponsor. We'll go get ice cream. Anything until the urge passes. You are kidding yourself if you think you won't have urges. It's been almost twenty years since I smoked my last cigarette and I still get an urge sometimes. But, I know, I know"—I said this with much emphasis—"I will never pick up a cigarette again. I will never put it to my lips nor inhale again. Because I know"—said with same emphasis—"that if I were to do so, one minute of pleasure would lead to months of addiction and withdrawal and I would go straight back to square one. One minute's pleasure for you is the difference between life—and death." I was on a roll, my anxiety showing in my voice as it raised an octave, and I started to speak faster and faster.

"Do you know where you will end up if you give in to just one urge? You will end up in jail, or worse, dead. Dead like Thomas Howard. You will be dead in a back alleyway with only a few of your junkie friends around to care. Please, and I am pleading with you, please tell me when it crosses your mind. Please."

I have this terrible, annoying habit of speaking before thinking, and I was a little mad at myself for coming on so heavy, so I tried to soften it up a bit. Like pizza dough before you cook it in the hot oven.

"In this household, your home and your family right now, I want you to understand that anything I say, anything I suggest is never a command and always up for debate. If I tell you to do something, I am more than willing to discuss it with you, to hear your side of the argument. Always. Except these Golden Rules leave no argument or room for debate. There is NO excuse. Tell me you understand this." I squeezed his hand and he mumbled, "Okay."

I didn't know it at the time, but this conversation was one of the most important conversations we had in the first few months of Bobby arriving. I also didn't know how it would come back to haunt me.

———

HEROIN

I got in bed that night with my computer, determined to understand more about the monster that had embedded in Bobby's soul: heroin.

What I found was fascinating and terrifying. It was late in the night before I turned off the light and rolled over, but my brain would not turn off.

To most people just hearing the word "heroin" conjures images of a back alley junkie, rubber tubing around the bicep, needle stuck in the crook of the arm. Even when someone says the word, her-o-in, they say it in an almost whispered voice, not wanting to be overheard. Say it; say it out loud. Her-o-in. Most say it with judgment in their voices and obvious thankfulness that they do not have *that* problem.

The undisputed truth is that heroin is no longer a dirty, deadbeat, homeless person's drug. It is mainstream, it is readily available, and your children probably already know how to get it. Heroin is now considered a shameful drug only to the most ignorant or uninformed.

————

WEIGHT

When Bobby came to Durham, he was very depressed about his weight. He had been put on yet another new drug three months prior. A side effect of this drug combined with years of unhealthy habits was weight gain—massive weight gain, over forty pounds of it.

I remembered Bobby as always being a slender guy and a snappy dresser, but because of this rapid and recent weight gain, he no longer fit into any of his clothes. As a woman, I totally get that arrow through the heart of the ole self-esteem. Since arriving, he would throw on a camo T-shirt as fast as you could say Duck Dynasty and pair it with oversized, LSU purple-and-gold gym shorts.

I understood his feelings, as I have also struggled with my weight for most of my adult life. It's not so much a health issue, but enough that I skip the bikini department and head directly to the big girl cover-ups.

Although I am athletic and I love to play tennis, I still have to watch the scales. Tennis helps and is not only a great workout but for me it is a wonderful way to meet people.

Over the past years I've suffered from knee problems and have had knee surgery several times, one of which was a knee replacement. At fifty-four years old, I am way too young to have a titanium joint, and recovering from these surgeries has added another fifteen pounds to my frame.

Will and I are both Louisianans originally and we love our food and our drink (especially our drink with our food), but we do try to eat right: veggies and lean meats and chicken. We are not sticklers and "organic" isn't a word we use in our house. We happily splurge when the mood strikes.

The full impact of Bobby's weight gain became clear when I told him to make a list of toiletry items and things he liked to eat and drink so that I could pick them up when I went to the grocery store.

At his request I bought two liters of Diet Coke and put them in the refrigerator. Before lunch the same day, Annie, with finger to her lips to signal silence, motioned me into the kitchen. I looked where she pointed. There, in the recycling bin, were both liters, emptied in a matter of hours. The next time I bought the "buy two get one free" special. I bought four one-liter bottles and received two more free, thinking that should hold him for the week. Six liters. Bobby drank all six in one day. He continued to drink four to six liters a day of assorted soft drinks for several months.

I asked him about his soda intake. He shrugged and said it was a take-home from rehab. I guessed that meant he'd switched one addiction for another. He'd picked up smoking cigarettes as a parting gift as well. I tried not to be judgmental and chewed on this knowledge.

At our next Sunday sit-down before dinner, I gently addressed his eating and drinking habits. I printed out information from the Internet on the effects that drinking large quantities of caffeinated soft drinks had on both the body and the mind. I handed him the paper, and he kept his hands in his lap and eyes to the table.

I wanted to lecture him, but I felt a bit duplicitous. I have to have a Diet Coke when I wake up in the morning—right after my coffee. I also have to have a Diet Coke as a little pick-me-up in the late afternoon. And I mean I have to have it. I'll rip you a new one if you get in my way. I confessed this to Bobby, relieving me of my guilt.

We talked about his horrible headaches, and then I had an epiphany. I suggested his migraines might be due to withdrawal from caffeine and sugar, especially when he didn't have the money to buy the massive quantities he consumed daily.

We eventually made a deal. I promised that I would cut down on my intake of Diet Coke, and he agreed he would cut back on how many liters he drank daily. I suggested we both do this slowly. I certainly didn't want any withdrawal symptoms for either of us.

I hoped that cutting down on soft drinks would help Bobby in other ways too. He complained of a queasy stomach when he woke up in the mornings, and he frequently vomited. Each day he would wait until his stomach settled before he could eat anything, and this might take until well after lunch.

I worried that because of this cycle he wasn't getting the nutrients he needed. I asked him if he had confessed his massive soda intake to the nutritionist Dr. Pate had recommended, although it doesn't take a nutritionist to diagnose that six liters of Diet Coke a day and a couple of bowls of cereal might be contributing to some of his health issues.

A few days later on the tennis courts, I randomly heard about a woman who would cook meals in your home for a very reasonable price. I would do the grocery shopping, and Deborah, the cook, would come for an hour or two once a week and put it all together for me. I thought it over for about two seconds and said, "Dang. That sounds like a great idea."

I can grill a bit and I make about five recipes really, really well. However, I just don't have the patience, knowledge, experience, or creativity it takes to be proficient in the kitchen. I loved the idea of hiring a professional to help me help Bobby. But she did more than that; Deborah was amazing and her healthy, delicious meals were a godsend. I decided after our first week to put Bobby, Will, and myself on a high-protein, no-sugar diet. Deborah would be the solution to all our thorny weight issues.

Hiring Deborah was also masterful because it freed me up to give Will my undivided attention after work, and it lessened my stress immensely, as cooking is highly stressful to me. The three of us started losing weight, especially Bobby.

Meanwhile Bobby's doctor was continuing to reassess all of his prescribed medications, and between the change in meds, cutting back on the soft drinks, beginning a workout routine, and our meal helper, the pounds began melting away. Every five pounds he lost was a cause for celebration. He would even post his progress on Facebook.

Will and I both lost weight too, but Bobby's transformation over a five-month period was remarkable. As he lost more weight, it was like a ship tossing over cargo, slowly rising in the water, buoyant and light. I could see it in the way he moved; gone was the burdensome weight of self-disgust. Out came his snappy clothes and easy stride. It was a process and it was not done overnight. But, in the end, both he and I kicked our Diet Coke addictions, and he slimmed down to the point that I became worried he was too skinny. One day I quipped, "Bobby, you look more like a drug addict now than you did when you were heavy."

I think he took that as a compliment.

———

BACK PAIN

Bobby had too much time on his hands, and Will and I realized that he was not going to be able to get a "real" job or attend school in the near future, due to severe, nonspecific, chronic back pain and his slow recovery from near suicide. His brain still wasn't back to normal after his deadly party in Atlanta, and Jeff said that it might be several more months before he could think clearly.

For a few days I gnawed on the hurdle of what was next for him. I came to the conclusion that he needed a goal, something to work toward, something that might give him a little self-esteem.

But it wasn't easy. Will would ask him to mow the yard,

which is more of a big field, with our riding mower, but, because of his back pain, Bobby found it difficult to sit in the same position for any great length of time. A neighbor asked him to help her plant her garden, but he had to take it very slowly with many breaks because bending over for too long was painful. Another neighbor asked him to help clear tree limbs in his backyard, but he could only cut and drag the smallest of branches. He even complained of pain if he sat for too long at the dinner table. The pain would come and go, and sometimes it would be so severe he took to his bed for the rest of the afternoon. I made a mental note to ask him if his wellness plan, physical therapist, and trainer were helping his back. It had only been a few weeks, but if his pain continued, we would need another strategy.

PLAN: NC DRIVER'S LICENSE

A plan to keep Bobby busy came together after discovering he needed a checking account in North Carolina. Will sent him to several banks and credit unions to gather checking account information so he could make an informed and personal choice on where he wanted to keep his money. He was told the same thing over and over: he needed to be a resident and prove this by showing a North Carolina driver's license or a proof of residency such as a utility bill in his name to open an account. Bingo. He could get his driver's license.

Bobby was gung ho from the beginning, but I could tell he was apprehensive as well. I had warned him that the NC driver's test was not easy. Two of my three kids, names not to be mentioned, failed the written exam and had to take it again. I told him not to be upset if he didn't pass the first time.

I was worried about him failing the test and going into a tailspin. I didn't want to make him more nervous, but I did want to prepare him for failure while hoping for the best.

He listened, but I wasn't sure if it was sinking in or if he even cared. He went about studying as he did most things: robotically, expressing little emotion. But I was pleasantly surprised that he seemed to be taking this driver's test seriously. For the next four weeks he spent most mornings studying practice tests with his computer in his lap and the television turned to a channel that showed an auction of fancy racecars.

From: Renée Hodges
Subject: Monday update
Date: Monday, March 18, 2013, at 11:36 p.m.
To: Mary Costello

My mind is so tired that I can't remember all we covered today because it was a lot. Lots of talk about how to deal best with Will, set structure for Bobby, and to know some boundaries and limitations for myself—ha.

I spent some time talking with Will this afternoon, and I think we came to some understanding although he is down with a major cold and really just needed me to be quiet and let him rest.

I also sat Bobby down to discuss with him things you and I talked about this morning. I told him I had gone to see you for advice (ATTF, Always The Therapist's Fault) and we talked again at length about the things that are "one-strike rules" and those things I expect from him and that I am hoping he will develop into good habits. We talked about "cooperation and compliance." Bobby confessed he was fearful. He said he had never been out in the adult world, responsible for keeping his own schedule and structure. That was a big realization for me. He's a youngster in a twenty-nine-year-old body. I told him we would do it together for the time being and that structure will be the one thing that keeps him from being overwhelmed, and the one thing that will make him feel like an adult.

Anne invited us all for dinner. She and Bobby have bonded deeply. Yep, she tells him she is his third mom. She is loving on him and it seems to do them both good. So happy for the two of them.

Will and Bobby left after dinner. I stayed through Wynonna on Dancing with the Stars; *she gets tens for bravery in my book.*

All is well tonight. For the first time in a long time my mind can go to sleep at a reasonable time. GN

From: Renée Hodges
Subject: Tuesday Update
Date: Tuesday, March 19, 2013, at 6:56 p.m.
To: Mary Costello

Briefly: a fantastic day. Bobby went to lunch with the main minister of the Church of the Good Shepherd, Reverend David Bowen, and has been invited to go to a UNC baseball game with the reverend. I know the real purpose for going to a Carolina baseball game is to turn Bobby away from my beloved Blue Devils and make him into one of those light-blue-tarheel-lovin' people. But I digress.

Bobby kept to his schedule, working out at the Duke Wellness Center and going to see Jeff Georgi this afternoon. My brief time with him came when I told him the litany of courses available to him at Durham Tech Community College. His eyes got so wide that I asked him if he was overwhelmed. "No, I'm excited." Mary, HE SAID HE'S EXCITED, and he said it out loud! He didn't say, "I think I am excited," he said, "I'M EXCITED." After several weeks, just a few little words of emotion. I am so excited too. Wow!

Update to self:

From: Renée Hodges
Subject: update to self
Date: Monday, March 25, 2013, at 11:40 p.m.
To: self

Bobby ended last week on a high, but the weekend brought some new lows. As much as I try to make up things for him to do to keep busy, it seems that he is always at a loss for activities. Reverend David Bowen is trying to help him by introducing him to the Bible, but Bobby is not buying in. I think it is depressing him more than helping him.

He seems to have fallen into a deeper depression. He says his back is hurting again, something that he hasn't mentioned in days, though he did go work out and lifted weights this morning, something he is not cleared to do. In fact, he hasn't been following his physical training regimen at all, but doing his own routine. Jeff Georgi seems to think he shouldn't be out doing any part-time work, but I can't help but feel that he needs some self-esteem. I have sent Jeff a text asking him to guide me.

I went to see Mary this morning. I walk in thinking I am all under control, but she always seems to find that crack in my eggshell armor. We talked about how I have to understand that I cannot "fix" him, no matter how much I do for him. Mary went to a spiritual conference in Austin this past weekend. Lots of things she passed on were very helpful in calming the inner me. I love thinking that everything happens for a reason and there are no coincidences. If I could just hold on to that and not try all the time to make something happen. Have I said it before? I am humbled by my circumstances right now. I am ill-equipped to help my nephew, just as I was ill-equipped to help Thomas Howard. But I am too stubborn to ever give up. And if I won't give up, I want to make damn sure Bobby doesn't either. I think I would bear the guilt forever if he should ever, ever give up.

He met with his new wellness-trainer and liked him. He also met with Jeff Georgi, and I was surprised to get a call from Jeff this afternoon. Bobby has told him he is in a lot of pain and that he is really struggling with the urge to use. Jeff said he wants to put Bobby on a drug that will help him[3]. I can't remember the name of it, but I will find out tomorrow.

Bobby went to a meeting tonight, and when I called up to him, he sounded pretty good. Aside: Anne had a nightmare last night that woke her up. She dreamed that she saw Thomas's face, purple with vomit, and she awoke with a fright. I told her to get counseling, but I know she won't. I also told Bobby about Anne's nightmare. He had asked me how Ms. Anne was doing, so I told him. I am hoping it might make him think.

I hope I can sleep tonight . . .

---

[3] See page 114 for additional information.

NIH: National Institute on Drug Abuse on Heroin

A range of treatments including behavioral therapies and medications are effective at helping patients stop using heroin and return to stable and productive lives. Medications include buprenorphine and methadone, both of which work by binding to the same cell receptors as heroin but more weakly, helping a person wean off the drug and reduce craving; and naltrexone, which blocks opioid receptors and prevents the drug from having an effect.[4]

For more information, see NIDA's handbook, Principles of Drug Addiction Treatment.

EASTER REUNION

Friday, March 29 to Sunday, March 31
Point Clear, Alabama

The tennis tournament trophy is the most coveted bragging right of the Hodges family reunion, held biannually over Easter weekend. Since the first reunion, back in the 1970s, the Hodges family has paired off with each other and squared off on the court, borrowing racquets and outfits, spending a full day at the tennis courts in a bracketed, handicapped mini-Wimbledon, all to claim the engraved two-foot-tall statue.

I have had my name on the trophy two times and am considered by some to be one of the ringers. I have played

[4] NIDA (2014). Heroin. Retrieved November 16, 2016, from
https://www.drugabuse.gov/publications/drug facts/heroin

tennis for twenty-five years, seriously picking up the sport when I was pregnant with my first daughter, Rachel. Tennis has been my workout, my hobby, my sanity. Like everyone else, I take the tournament very seriously.

So I was more than surprised when Bobby said he would participate in this year's tourney. Given his troubles with his back and near constant pain, I had only asked him as a courtesy. We did play tennis earlier in the month when my daughter Katherine came home to visit. Bobby is a nice player, if a little inconsistent, and he'd experienced only minimal pain afterward.

So, he was in. I emailed Julia, Will's cousin, who makes the tennis pairings. Partners are announced the first night upon arrival and they are highly anticipated.

Julia decided to pair Bobby with Nancy. Upon reflection, Nancy was an Easter present from God. One of my closest cousins-in-law, she has known my family as long as she has known me, since we were fourteen years old. She was in our wedding and I introduced her to her husband, Brian, who was my close friend in college. She is athletic and competitive, reliable, responsible, and I know I can count on her for anything. She is a non-bullshitter, having little time for those who do. Ask her a question and be prepared for the honest truth. Driven to succeed, she masters anything she touches, whether it is learning to fly an airplane, traveling around the world, running her self-made health-care business, or playing tennis. That year she was working on her tennis, eyeing the trophy and letting me know it.

Although Nancy knew my brother, she had never laid eyes on Bobby. Nor did she know his history. I decided to call her and tell her Bobby's story, the reason he was staying with me, and that I was hoping that including him in the family reunion would show Bobby what love and acceptance and faith and fun are all about. Just as I anticipated, she crowed, "Renée, I'm happy to play with Bobby. We are going to win the trophy this year together." Did I mention she is a crack smack-talker also?

Will, Bobby, and I drove the ten hours to the Marriott Grand Hotel in Point Clear, Alabama. I was hoping Bobby would offer to drive a few hours to relieve us, but he slept most of the way and generally complained about his back the rest.

A glorious old hotel, the Marriott Grand has been cradled on Mobile Bay since 1847. The whole Hodges family, upward of two hundred strong, have held reunions since the 1980s and booked here every other Easter vacation for ten years now to celebrate the resurrection of Christ, stay connected as the family grows, and win the tennis tournament.

Tennis is held first thing on Good Friday and play continues all day. The hotel's ten courts fill with multigenerational players paired together for optimum mixing of families and balancing of abilities.

Bobby showed up in his idea of tennis attire—camo collarless T-shirt; long, long gym shorts; ball cap turned backward; and mirrored sunglasses. I didn't blink an eye but wrapped an arm around him and started introducing him to the family. They hugged him and welcomed him into the fold.

Nancy zeroed in on Bobby. "Come on. We have to warm up." And off they went. I was surprised and delighted when Nancy and Bobby kept winning their matches and reached the semifinals. I looked at the brackets. Oh no. Their opponents would be my son, William, and his first cousin Hank Davies, both strong contenders.

The excitement was high and most of the family came to watch the semifinal matches.

It wasn't difficult to find the match I wanted to watch. There on center court, right in front of the clubhouse was Bobby, still in full camo like he was headed to war and intently strategizing with Nancy on how to whup up on William and Hank. Maybe this was war?

It was a great match, but the youngsters William and Hank eventually won the tiebreak and went on to play in the finals. I watched as Bobby waved a good game to William and Hank and hugged Nancy's neck stiffly. He packed his borrowed racquet and headed up the stairs.

Everyone called congratulations on a good match, patting him on the back, encouraging him, and supporting him even in his loss. Nancy called out that Bobby was a ringer and gave him much credit for their success in the tournament, even though I knew that probably wasn't true.

He met me at the top of the steps and asked me if he could go back to his room. His back was hurting and he wanted to lie down. Of course, I told him. I gave him a big embrace and congratulated him for getting so far in the tournament. Another prodigy! And I was proud. He was in the midst of a tight-knit group; one that was welcoming him with open arms, but still a group that could be very intimidating at first meeting because we are so large and so loud and loving. As for Bobby, it was the third L that was most intimidating.

The rest of the weekend Bobby was elusive. I tried very hard to keep tabs on him, and for the most part he made it easy, as he stayed in his room for long periods. At night, when it was party-DJ-dance time, and alcohol was free flowing, he would ask if he could leave after dinner to retire for the evening. As much as I wanted him to soak up the faith, fun, and family, I knew it was too early and too much for him.

I retired a little earlier than normal too Saturday night.

After all, the Easter Bunny has to make an appearance every year, no matter how old the kids are. I love a good holiday like Easter where I can go to the dollar store and fill a cheap, pastel-colored, faux-wood basket with plastic grass and jelly beans and have the Easter Bunny visit while the children are sleeping. When the kids were little, I would fill their baskets with Peeps and a chocolate bunny and add a toy like a wind-up chick that would hop all the way across the table. Now I fill their baskets with Burt's Bees lip balm, Kleenex, and mostly useful, inexpensive items. Sometimes, I throw in a Starbucks gift card or a Duke Final Four Championship hat. I always add a small box of their favorite candy and some jelly beans. I ditched the pink and yellow Peeps a long time ago.

I love being a bit cheesy, in only the best way, of course! I can be sappy too. Not too much, but just enough—although my kids might not agree. I thrive on getting a response from them.

This year, with Bobby, I had four baskets to make. The morning before leaving for our Easter reunion, I'd stopped at Target for some sunscreen. Striding quickly, I was focused on the task at hand until I jerked my body like a squirrel in the middle of the road as my attention was drawn to the dollar bins. What is this? I stopped and picked up a one-inch square cardboard box with the smallest terra-cotta planter I'd ever seen inside. Peering closer and pulling out my readers, I realized it was a miniature tomato seed planter. I picked up four of the wee boxes and thought how much fun it would be for the kids to have a miniature plant in their apartments or on the kitchen window. I know. Cheesy. The only child that even planted the seed was Bobby, several weeks later.

On Easter Sunday, Father Hampton, one of Will's fiftyish first cousins, always celebrates a Mass for everyone in an upstairs convention room in the lodge. Anyone from the hotel is welcome, as praying together and openly is important to us.

I kept looking for Bobby to arrive, but when Father Hampton said, "Let us pray" and we stood, he was nowhere to be seen.

I glanced over my shoulder every fifteen seconds until finally I saw him in the back of the room. I had saved him a seat on our row next to our kids, but he zeroed in on an old high school buddy, Jake, the son of Will's cousin, and sat next to Jake and his family. I don't know why this made me sad. I shouldn't have taken Bobby's seating choice personally, but I did, as if sitting next to his friend was a slight to me.

I was being irrational and self-serving, but I wanted Bobby to feel a part of us so badly that sitting elsewhere confirmed to me that I had a long way to go. I prayed hard that morning and I held Will's hand throughout the service.

ONE MONTH ONE DAY

From: Renée Hodges
Subject: Update
Date: Thursday, April 4, 2013, at 5:59 p.m.
To: Mary Costello

A nice Easter break from writing! Hope you had a great and relaxing holiday.

Bobby seems to be really trying, but has lots of weird mood swings and physical ailments at odd times. I sometimes think that he has such high anxiety that he tenses up and that creates backaches and headaches. But when he is feeling well, he is laughing and smiling and the world lights up. He is very loving and very gentle when he is happy.

However, I do see a rougher side of him when he is not feeling well. He will push the dogs off him with a harshness I don't often see and is not intrinsic to his personality. Or he will close down and barely look me or anyone in the eyes. This is not often, but I can see a lot of hurt inside him at these times and I bet he could be scary if he started raging, if he allowed himself to show anger. But, then, couldn't anyone? He keeps it all locked up inside.

I am a bit miffed at and almost disappointed in John and Jill. Jill keeps in contact with a smattering of text messages to him. They did not call him on Easter. I hesitate to judge them as I can see how emotionally twisted all the relationships are. I realize there is a lot I don't know about what they've been through. I do know that he needs to feel their love though.

———

FAVOR

Thursday, April 4

Even though Bobby rarely talked about his immediate family, I knew his addiction has caused great despair and anger between him and his parents and sister. I hurt for Bobby, as I knew exactly how it feels to be estranged.

He didn't or couldn't vocalize how much it hurts, but I understood the pain, the self-doubt, the "what can I do to fix it?" feelings. I was estranged off and on for close to fourteen years from my family because I have refused to turn a blind eye to the disease in our family. One of the deeper regrets I have is that by taking a stand, I wasn't a part of any of my niece's and nephew's younger lives and they were not a part of my kids' lives. Without intervention or understanding, addiction ultimately divides and separates families.

Bobby's immediate family, John, Jill, and Elizabeth, had waged war on alcoholism and opioid addiction for several decades, first with John and now with Bobby. His family was angry and they were tired and I didn't blame them one bit. Addiction is exhausting and relentless. Hidden inside of every loved one dealing with addiction in their family are bloody wounds, ripped raw—over and over again. If you care, if you love, if you hope, addiction crushes you. Even if you personally never take a drink—or pop a pill or use a needle—it is still a tragic family affair.

When Bobby came to live with us in Durham, I sensed from his family a feeling of relief, of giving up or maybe giving over. I could hear the release of air from deep in their guts, slowly exhaled, affirming deliverance. He was someone else's mission now. Yes, it was exhausting.

John had already said enough: enough money spent, enough time spent, enough hurt. John loved his son but realized Bobby had to make his own recovery and no one could do it for him. He wanted to protect Jill and his daughter, Elizabeth, and he had to protect his own recovery.

The most powerful thing John told me recently was that he sat his adult children down several years ago and told them he was sorry: sorry for his disease, for the pain and suffering he inflicted on them individually and as a family. He had apologized a million times before. This time, John also told them it was the last time he would apologize to them, that he had to move on and he couldn't move on if he continued to feel guilty. Powerful, painful, and daunting.

I admire John for moving on. As a member of a family molded through addiction, accepting where you are now and pushing ahead instead of regretting the past is something I have labored over for many years. Although he doesn't know, this declaration to his children helped me to move forward as much as it did John.

However, unless your family is dead, moving forward is hard when there is no communication from them, positive or negative. It creates a feeling of abandonment and neglect, a hole in your heart, and this elephant is always in your room.

Bobby was lonely in North Carolina. I knew this because he told me. He had no friends, no job, no money, no girlfriend except some girls he talked to online, not even someone to have lunch or go to a movie with. He missed Louisiana: the food, the fun, the family. He missed his highs.

So I understood how he felt: isolated, forsaken. I wanted to bridge healthy contact between Bobby and his mother, father, and sister. In my heart, I believed they must want that too.

I once considered Bobby's mother one of my closest friends. But since my father died in 1991, Jill and I had both changed unimaginably as a result of our dealings with our addictive family. We both fought the battle, I by running away to the security of another state while Jill stayed fighting in the trenches. War is hell.

Jill is tall, with the longest legs, so long that they appear to start at her waist. She wears her light brown hair long and straight, bangs covering her tall forehead. She is super fit and should be as she is a compulsive exerciser. She is very bright, a special education teacher turned mother. She is sharp, and her wit is quick. She is also a brilliant piano player, but I don't think I have heard her play in almost twenty years.

Patient and kind, Jill has a heart of pure gold. When you get to know her well, you realize that she is also terribly unreliable and indecisive, possibly because of her anxiety, but because it's her, this trait is almost endearing.

She almost never answers her phone, and even when asked to call me, she will send a text instead. It is hard to imagine the silent damage she has sustained in her lifetime. Growing up with a stepfather who was an alcoholic, she learned enabling and codependence at an early age. Then, after escaping her childhood, she repeated the cycle by marrying my brother, John.

I admire her immensely for staying by John's side throughout his drunken years, rehabilitation years, and now, thankfully, his recovery years. She is an angel; there is no other way to put it. And I love her!

Elizabeth, my niece, severed contact with Bobby several years ago. They were very close as children until he became too sick with addiction and anger and started acting out. Weird postings and pictures on social media, embarrassing antics out in public, and the accumulated bad habits of a drug addict (lying, secrecy, isolation, and moodiness) were all too much for her. Elizabeth and her fiancé, Charlie, who was once one of Bobby's closest childhood friends, stayed as far away from Bobby as possible.

I sent an email update to John, Jill, and Elizabeth with Bobby's progress over the last four weeks in hopes that I could move mountains in their broken relationship.

From: Renée Hodges
Date: Thursday, April 4, 2013, at 4:00 p.m.
Subject: Favor
To: Jill Redford, John Redford, Elizabeth Redford

Dear Jill, John, and Elizabeth,

Bobby is doing well. He is studying to take the NC driver's test. Most fail on the first go-around so we'll see. He is now working out daily, by himself and several days with a trainer, and he is using the Duke Wellness Center pool.

He has been asked to join a darts team, and he is interested in Civil War reenactments, which are very big around this area. He is doing odd jobs, is keeping an accounting of everything he spends, and we are budgeting week to week. The response and willingness of others in the neighborhood to help him has been tremendous.

He is very interested in going to automotive school and his eyes light up when he talks about it. We are pursuing this. He has also been offered the opportunity to become a Driver's Ed classroom instructor. If you have any reservations about this job or anything else, let me know now, please.

He and his partner, Nancy Wallace, came in third at the family tennis tournament over Easter at the Hodges reunion in Alabama. They were knocked out by William and his cousin. He had a good Easter and seemed content.

Lastly, I can't tell you how important it is for you three to send him a card every once in a while. Jill, he has your Easter card on his bureau, wide open so he can see your "Love, Mom" from his bed. He needs to know you all love him. You don't have to write anything else in the card or get into anything serious. You can just sign it. Just send "thinking of you" cards, funny cards especially, so that he feels your love.

Elizabeth, do you think you can do this? Go buy ten funny cards and sign them, address them, stamp them, and send one out each week. Jill, please call him at least once a week and just shoot the bull. Nothing heavy, just light stuff. Maybe ask him if he wants you to come visit? He loves you so much and misses you something fierce.

John, send a nice card or two and I'll let you know how he responds. He also loves you so much and doesn't want to let you down.

I won't ask you all again because you have to want to do this. But he is on his way to a new start and he is inching his way out of a black hole. Every little bit you can do to help encourage him is so important, especially right now.

Love, Renée

I received this email from his dad in response:

From: John Redford
Subject: Favor
Date: Thursday, April 4, 2013, at 11:29 p.m.
To: Renée Hodges

Hey there, thanks for the news! I'm thrilled Bobby is doing okay for now. Automotive school is a start but not sure if it will sustain his wannabe lifestyle? Just saying he needs to think it through. But it does sound low stress though, just what the doctor ordered!

As far as writing him, well, there has been a lot of anger about his last usage the night he left for Durham, and how it happened . . . not to mention the money and years of his "I'm through," all the hurt and lying and manipulating . . . well, you get the picture. Every time we come into his life, we feel like we're the ones responsible for him going back out there and using again. I can't begin to tell you the fear we have been subjected to over his usage. The disease is so selfish.

I don't want to be Debbie Downer here, but it seems the best way for him to grow up is with us, for the most part, out of his life until he gets some clean time under his belt and can show a commitment to sobriety we haven't seen before. That looks like at least a year of sobriety.

Elizabeth tried to understand for a while, but with Bobby's constant Facebook posts she has been embarrassed for the last time. His sightings of aliens and continuous suggestive pics online only fuel her embarrassment . . . she is in the happiest time of her life and I need to keep it that way . . . these days are for her, because the last four to five years have been for Bobby.

Jill's love reminds us of the love Anne Howard had for her son . . .

Renée, we feel guilty he has chosen your place and not a sober living community to possibly start a new life. We wrestle with what we could have done to achieve a more positive outcome. Our guilt is driven by our values and, naturally, we don't want to get hurt again. We are worried for you as well . . .

This is not anybody's fault, but we're trying to heal while he is healing and unfortunately, we are not close to thinking he's through . . . I know we're not there and can't see what you see . . .

Bobby knows our love for him, but I want to make sure it is not an unhealthy love for him . . . he has never experienced healthy love due to the euphoric nature of the drugs and alcohol and therefore he can't recognize it.

Don't want to drag this out, but I've gone from doing everything I can for his recovery and comfort to now wanting to protect the family, this means you and yours too . . . But when he wants to write, I'll listen . . .

Love you more than you know and Bobby,

John

———

SEEING RED

I was irate when I first read that email from my brother. How could John not even want to send his son a funny card every now and then? How could he preach to me about all he's done and then tell me he was through, done, kaput, now that Bobby was living with us? John talked a lot about what he had been through but had barely mentioned helping Bobby. And Bobby was doing so well.

For twenty-four hours I was consumed with all sorts of conflicting feelings: first anger and rejection, then disbelief and a bitterness that finally turned into a smolder.

I had to step away from the email because it stressed me to the point of obsession. It took awhile to calm down, but I finally decided I couldn't change what was said. So the best thing for me to do was to walk a mile in John's boots. I placed myself on the other side of his email to try to experience how he might feel, and what logic he might use to protect himself and others he cared about.

I attempted to feel the up and down emotion of having a child you love so much, your only son, addicted to a drug that makes him unrecognizable to his own father. And what about the amount of money John's family had spent for treatment, living expenses, and short- and long-term rehabilitation centers for Bobby? Insurance should cover more. (The maximum twenty-eight days covered by insurance are not sufficient for the majority of patients to detox, face their demons, and then change their patterns. The insurance companies should give each patient a readmission form as they leave the treatment center premises: Here, sign this and we'll see you in a couple of months. We'll even keep the light on.) Addiction is an expensive disease and John and Jill would go broke if they continued to support their grown son. When is enough, enough?

And, of course, engaged and planning a wedding, this was Elizabeth's time in the spotlight. I know from my own personal history how the unaddicted child lives in the shadows, silent and obscure. We are not loved less: we are just healthy and not requiring the life-and-death attention a sick child needs. I can see this clearly now but, as a young adult, I did not.

John was right about Bobby's ideal lifestyle. I generalize here, but it takes a lot of hard work and a lot of money to sustain the lifestyle to which Bobby was accustomed. Unless he was willing to change the way he lived and spent his money, automotive school would not finance his extravagant shoes, designer clothes, and expensive hobbies. Bobby did need to think through his priorities, because from John's email, it looked like the gravy train had stopped with a screech.

I could understand all of that. But I still couldn't comprehend John not wanting to send cards to Bobby or be in his life for the next year.

But my attitude changed after thinking about all the hurt and mistrust and wounds John and Jill had endured for this disease. Bobby needed some good old-fashioned tough love instead of being rescued again. John—who understood the struggle to overcome addiction firsthand—felt that his past actions had not helped his son and he must release himself of that strongest emotion: parental guilt.

His decision was to stand firm with love while protecting Jill, Elizabeth, and himself from further harm. Now this I understood. This was my first experience of helping Bobby and we were having some positive results, but there had been many prior recovery attempts—none of which had been successful.

My initial anger at his email had all but evaporated. I realized I was taking the noncontact too personally, feeling once again that I had been abandoned. But really, tough love was exactly what Bobby needed from his family. Not money, not acquiescence or complicity, and not contact with his father. John was indeed displaying a healthy, non-enabling kind of love. And this is the greatest love of all for an addict.

The fact that John was acting from a place of love was

most evident in the fact that John did not shut the door. He clearly stated that if Bobby wrote, he would listen.

As I digested John's email, I learned a lot about myself and the process of recovery. I was grateful to John for standing firm—with Bobby and with me.

From: Elizabeth Redford
Subject: Favor
Date: Friday, April 5, 2013, at 8:13 a.m.
To: Renée Hodges

Thanks for checking in, Aunt Née! It's nice to hear about what's going on over there. Sounds like Bobby is starting to come into his own again! I'm very grateful that he is in such great hands and beginning to experience real life by taking on day-to-day responsibilities and becoming more open to extracurricular activities!

I know, I know . . . a day at a time :). I guess one thing hasn't changed though . . . Still the ladies' man! Give him a hug and a punch on the shoulder from me! I'll send him some stuff. Thanks for the guidance. Call me if ya need me!

Love you, Elizabeth

———

From: Renée Hodges
Subject: Favor
Date: Friday, April 5, 2013, at 9:46 a.m.
To: Elizabeth Redford

Thanks for your email, Elizabeth. I know this is very hard for you, so please know that I don't want you to do anything that makes you feel uncomfortable. But if you feel you are able and willing, you will not believe what just a funny card with a "Love, Elizabeth" will do for Bobby and his self-esteem.

Since I have been dealing with addiction most of my life, I know what a toll it can take on a person. But I also know that there is much hope, especially when you look at your father and what a great man he has turned into, and the battles he had to win in order to get to where he is today. But any contact you have with Bobby should be something you want, and not something you are doing for me.

I love you and your parents and am looking forward to getting to know Charlie better in the future. I know I will love him as well!

Love, Aunt Née

———

JOHN AND RENÉE EARLY YEARS

My family—Bobby's family—is complicated, as are most. My brother John and I are closer now than we have ever been. It has taken decades of slow, painful growth, but each new bloom in our friendship is a blessing to me. We have finally realized that we are not enemies or rivals. We moved past competing for a place in the family and decided that we are family, which trumps all.

We can now accept each other's warts (and there are many) and that is nice because we haven't always been so generous. Sometimes we still don't like each other, as I have some grumpy control issues and am quite adept at stirring the pot and John can be holier-than-thou, preaching and teaching from past experiences. John is also the most defensive human being in the world—next to me. He puts up a defensive line that the New Orleans Saints would envy. We are both working on our defensiveness and that is a very good thing for any relationship.

The best part is that John and I have learned we can agree to disagree on most subjects and still respect each other when for most of our lives we simply turned away. It is freeing that we can stay securely planted and listen to each other openly and hear what is said. We are more accepting of our differences and revel more in our similarities. I know that we love each other and that is a solid foundation for our relationship.

I am in awe of John. All signs pointed to us burying him before he was forty years of age, so I have only the utmost respect for my brother and what he has accomplished.

John is a recovering alcoholic, who turned his life around nearly thirteen years ago. In 1971, when John and I were thirteen and twelve, my dad retired from the Air Force and moved us back to his Southern roots, a small town in Louisiana. John is only fifteen months older than me, but back then it might as well have been a fifteen-year gap for all we had in common. First, I was awkward in middle school. I was gangly with straight, oily hair. I had an oversized nose and was top heavy; it was a battle for your eyes to determine which part of my body you looked at first. In seventh and eighth grades we were all at that terrible pimply stage, that strange growth and hair spurt stage, that wild and raging hormone stage, but I didn't recognize that commonality—I could only see myself in the mirror and it wasn't a pretty sight.

Another endearing quality I had as a preteen was my compulsion for following the rules. As an Air Force brat I was raised to say "yes, sir," and "no, sir."

Following rules, or orders, was drilled into us military brats from infancy. Even the height of the grass on our front lawn was regulated. Let it grow a quarter of an inch too long and the family would receive a citation. Being a rule follower was simple. There was no thinking involved, only compliance. It never even crossed my mind to not comply. In middle school none of my attributes served me well, least of all the rule following.

Conversely, John was not a rule follower. He had so much excess energy that I'm not sure he could sit still long enough to even comprehend a rule. If I could have harnessed even a little bit of his energy, I probably could have run the local power plant for a year. He had ADHD before we knew what that was.

In middle school he grew tall and lanky and had a perpetual tan. He loved the outdoors, particularly waterskiing. He would wear his thick wavy mass of dark hair long over his ears and to his shoulders if he could get away with it. He loved hard rock and would close himself off in his room, oblivious to the outside world, with his record player on full blast, listening to runs of electric guitar from the likes of Deep Purple, Led Zeppelin, and ZZ Top. He was a beautiful, sensitive young man, and has remained very handsome.

John and I tried to assimilate into our new community and school, which was easier for John because he had a wonderful, exciting charisma about him, radiating energy and charm. I was shy and insecure, not sure of my new surroundings, and although we had visited and even lived in Louisiana when I was younger, it was as foreign to me as if we'd moved to Outer Mongolia.

Our new town was mostly agricultural, and many of my classmates were expected to start full-time on the farm the day they received their high school diploma. My young memories of my new hometown were of a small, close-knit community, with a downtrodden, gloomy, and crumbling downtown, identical to hundreds of small Southern towns in the 1970s. Even though I loved growing up there, and still love the Southern way of life and the people, I couldn't wait to graduate high school and move to the big city of New Orleans.

I was late to alcohol by Louisiana standards, starting as a middle schooler who looked down on them—the rule breakers, the other thirteen- and fourteen-year-olds who were sneaking beer and vodka and climbing out of their bedroom windows in the middle of the night, my brother included.

John was invited to every party in middle school, every dance, and was never without an entourage at lunchtime. I was virtually invisible, keeping my head down and my nose in the books, trying to do the right thing, whatever that might be.

When it was time for high school, popular John followed the path of most students and entered the local public high school. I, however, needed a new start—a school with the structure and discipline I had become accustomed to growing up. My path was the local Catholic high school where uniforms were mandatory and nuns and priests made up the majority of the teacher population. I was thrilled to apply and be accepted, and wear that cute, shamrock-green plaid and pleated skirt that hung to my shins. I felt a part of something from the very first day.

In the ninth grade I decided I was tired of being the rule follower, the one never invited to the bonfire or the school dance. This was a turning point in my life; I took control and directed my destiny. It was also in the ninth grade that those professional Catholic drinkers tutored me in the fine art of mixing Seagram's 7 and Coke Icees, watching the whiskey melt the ice until it became my very own intoxicating Slurpee. It was then that I realized how drinking made you a part of the crowd, how much fun it was to drink, and, go figure, how good at it I was.

I learned quickly that street cruising and boozing were the favored entertainment of all the cool teenagers. We received our driver's licenses the day we turned fifteen, and if you were needed to work the farm, you could get it earlier. There wasn't much entertainment, so we entertained ourselves.

John only lasted one year at the public high school due to some academic troubles and a few fights he had before he too was enrolled at the local Catholic high school for the tenth grade, therefore making us both new students at a new school again in 1973. John did not find his new Catholic school as wonderful as I did. He had a hard time fitting in and making new friends. I loved the discipline and uniforms. John chafed at the rigidness. But we both found out early that the more we partied, the easier it was to be included. Lord, it is a wonder we were not killed.

My first car was a standard, gorgeous chocolate, two-door 1974 Monza I received when I passed my driver's test. I could drive, smoke a cigarette, and talk on the CB radio all while swigging straight from the bottle of that mother of all upchucker wines, Boone's Farm Strawberry Hill. A high school favorite for about a year, it was a wine so sweet and seductive that it tasted like dessert. At fifteen, I could consume a whole bottle by myself only to taste it a second time as I left it on the side of the road.

My friends and I were masters of cranking the car window down in record time, rolling it round and round as fast as we could go—*hurry, hurry . . . bleh.* You see, even my puking was a connection. I felt connected to my new friends as I bent double, heaving while my high school friends held my hair back out of my face and looked the other way. If you have never had a friend stick their finger down your throat or hold your hair back while vomiting—well, I won't go so far as to say you are missing something, but there is a delicious feeling of comfort, of tenderness, and, in my young heart, a feeling of true friendship. John's drinking wasn't so different. We both did it to fit in, to feel a part of the group.

My friends and I constantly pushed the envelope, young and carefree, always looking for just a little bit of trouble. So many nights we cruised the thoroughfare or the back roads, our imaginations bigger than our little town; we loved life and we wanted to have fun. My imagination has always been fertile for just skirting trouble, like walking the beach and getting as close to the waves as possible without them touching your bare feet. Most times, I was fast enough to get out of the way, but the odds were there. Do it enough and one of those times your feet will get wet. With wet feet, sand sticks.

John happened to be the unlucky one. At the time no one knew it, but he had won the family gene-pool lottery, inheriting the family's addiction gene and with it an insatiable craving for alcohol, following directly in our maternal grandfather's and uncle's footsteps.

In 1976, John graduated and went off to college, frat life, and 24/7 partying. He had a few DUIs through high school and college, which were mostly, if not completely, paid off by my dad—an easy and common thing to do in the seventies and eighties.

I do remember my parents arguing behind closed doors over what to do about some of John's exploits, but it wasn't until well after I graduated from college that the realization struck me that he was truly addicted. I was too self-absorbed in my own teenage world to recognize the signs of alcoholism in John back then, and I was living in a glass house, abusing alcohol too.

The signs were clearly there. Alcohol fueled John the way jet fuel sends a rocket to the moon. He would lose all his inhibitions. Stories would trickle down to me that would take my breath away. Like when the college boys headed down to New Orleans in a party van and the driver, going eighty miles per hour on the interstate, was shocked to see an upside-down face with a silly, drunken grin, suddenly plastered (no pun intended!) to his windshield. John had gone out the back door of the van and climbed on top of the roof, holding on to the top rails like a Hollywood stuntman, inching his way to the front. Holding on somehow, he'd flopped himself on the glass and began a wild-man wiper motion with his arms. It was a wonder the driver didn't slam on the brakes. John was out there; he was a drunken daredevil, pushing every boundary, and it is astounding he is still alive today.

Alcohol could also send me to the moon. My college days were alcohol fueled as well, and going to school in New Orleans is a permission slip for partying and drunkenness. It was common and accepted, and mostly expected. There is no doubt in my mind that many of us had alcohol problems, drinking far more than I think is humanly possible, and some of us became alcoholics or addicts. But I loved my college years, the feeling of immortality that youth and alcohol gave me. I have great memories and greater friends. Still, I am regretful in so many ways that with alcohol and lack of accountability, I squandered much of a wonderful education, not taking advantage of every class, every learning opportunity.

With maturity I can confess this, but as with regrets— recognition is one thing and moving forward is another.

Throughout our teenage years my father worked hard to create a new business, as starting over after retiring from the Air Force at the age of forty-one is not easy and the stress is enormous. My father was a workaholic, receiving his high from wheeling and dealing, always looking to expand and make more money, and it paid off in a big way. Dad was not a harsh man or a mean father; in fact, he was loving and generous to a fault, except with his time during our high school years, when he was focused on growing and expanding his business. Because he never had a father figure except for Uncle Sam, Dad demanded respect and allegiance. He wanted his kids to be like him: a disciplined and brilliant financial shark, a business visionary, a resounding success not only in one career, but two. The expectation for all of us was that we would go to college, graduate, and return to the family business someday.

The only problem was that John was not cut out to be a shark. John was more of a beautiful dolphin: friendly, playful, and trusting, dancing through the water in the middle of the pod, just happy to be alive, busting at the seams with pent-up energy. He was good with people, and his thoughtful and generous sides were his best assets. Sometimes I feel that pigeonholing my brother into someone he was not, somebody that he could never be, drove him to find solace and acceptance in a brown bourbon bottle. And, of course, John was genetically predisposed to alcoholism.

I can now see that my brother needed help with his alcohol problem as early as high school. Heck, back then we both probably needed help. The difference between the two of us is that I am not an alcoholic. I have never craved a drink or felt I had to have a glass of wine. Even now there are times that I really look forward to and want a drink, but I never had to have one. I used to love the feeling of being drunk, of how spontaneous I felt, how imaginative and happy. How deep I could think. How deep I could love. But it was all an illusion. For the last two decades I have watched it destroy my family, and being drunk no longer holds the same appeal for me.

John and Bobby are similar in their personalities; I think that is why both these men found themselves deep in addiction. Neither had a role model to help them understand that their sensitive sides were normal and beautiful. Bobby is very much like his dad, a bright and loving boy, with huge magnetism, full of kindness and creativity. Like his father, Bobby was trampled by his dad's own insecurities, a generational cycle of misunderstanding, lack of acceptance, and low self-esteem. And add in alcohol and John and Bobby's relationship was destined to be rocky.

As a young adult it was tough having an alcoholic brother. The family took sides. While my father was alive, there was enabling, avoidance, and denial, but my dad's strong bond held us all together. It wasn't until Dad died that my family started to splinter. Without Dad to hold us together, our bonds unraveled. I was the first one to face the fact that addiction was a solid member of our family. For the rest of them there was still enabling, avoidance, and denial many years after the last handful of dirt was thrown on my dad's coffin.

Looking back, I let my righteous feelings morph into defensive feelings, then morph again into judgmental feelings. I was affected by John's addiction every bit as much as if it were my own and I were the one who must bring the bottle to my lips every day. I wish I had sought help from Al Anon or an addiction counselor specializing in alcohol many years ago, so that I could have understood that I was not alone, that there are so many people out there who have felt my anguish.

I sometimes imagine what would have been different if my parents had openly sought help to understand the alcoholism in our family, had openly talked about the disease, treatments, anger, and frustration together, maybe over Sunday's fried chicken dinner. I imagine how it would have been to express our fears and hurts, to be able to bond as a strong unit, to take the shame and secrecy and power away from the disease. We would not have been alone, addict or family: we would have openly faced addiction, together. This dream of mine is so strong and poignant that when I think about it, I have to wipe my tears away to be able to continue.

When I look back over the years my brother cannot remember and scrutinize every little aspect of my behavior, I am forced to admit it is ugly. I was angry and helpless, and I had no control nor ability to change these circumstances, ignorant of the facts of addiction. I lived with a feeling of self-disgust, a debilitating cross between self-righteousness and terrible, obliterating shame and hopelessness.

Addiction is equal opportunity in this way. Spouses, children, extended families, and even close friends can own that painful feeling of humiliation and disgrace. Shame is stealth. It creeps and niggles and then parasitically embeds in one's soul, and one doesn't even know it is happening. How can a feeling be this powerful, hurtful, and destructive? Believe me. It can.

But, together, shame can be overcome. And only by owning the monster together, can the healing begin.

Today John is an amazing success in his own right. He is sober, physically healthy and fit; he has found God and faced his demons and is now giving back. He and Jill, seeing a great need in their Louisiana community, have started a fledgling drug and alcohol rehabilitation center (too late and too close for Bobby) and are looking to give others another chance at life, too.

Most of all, John is a shining symbol of hope to all he encounters: addicts, alcoholics, and family members alike, because he knows we are all in this together. Truly, John has walked the walk. And his strength and success gives me hope for his son.

ONE MONTH SIX DAYS

Tuesday, April 9

REPORT CARD

After several days of Bobby not feeling well and staying in bed, I texted Jeff to ask for a consult. Will and I had become more and more uncomfortable, not just with Bobby, but with our roles as supporters and facilitators. We desperately needed some guidance.

We were now struggling on all levels. Bobby was still up all night, sleeping until eleven or twelve every morning. He was non-communicative, answering questions with one word replies, if at all. He would leave the house without a word, come back and go straight to his room. He wasn't eating breakfast and was—after cutting back for several weeks—consuming massive quantities of caffeinated soda, five or six liters a day. He would finish a bowl of Honey Nut Cheerios when he did eat, and the only way we'd know was because of the dirty bowl he left in the sink with round remnants stuck to its sides. Since he had no money, he couldn't afford fast food, but when he had even a dime, he would go to Chick-fil-A.

Since returning from Easter in Alabama, Bobby had regressed, complaining daily of nausea, headaches, and general feelings of illness. During the day, like a phantom guest, unseen and unheard, we were unable to keep him under our thumb. And since he wouldn't come down for dinner and didn't speak when he came down to smoke, I was at a loss as to how to connect with him.

Will and I met with Jeff and I rattled off questions, some

of which I'd acquired in my Monday session with Mary. She had been helping me form strategies and also letting me know when it was time to contact Jeff. She didn't have to tell me this time.

I was happy that Will joined me at Jeff's and that he too was able to vocalize all his questions, fears, and feelings of discomfort.

Will and I were unprepared for what Jeff shared with us; his insight totally blew our minds and I realized I was such an innocent—no, scratch that, an ignorant. Jeff felt Bobby had PTSD (posttraumatic stress disorder), something affecting many children of alcoholics. Children of adult alcoholics experience higher abuse rates and PTSD than those without alcoholic parents, whether from verbal or physical abuse or just from plain old neglect.

Once my shock wore off, I was so saddened by this revelation. It made sense, but Jeff stressed that Will and I must realize that there was no way for us to know for sure what happened in Bobby's childhood or even if anything traumatic did happen. But nevertheless, we must start from here, from how Bobby was feeling today.

I didn't quite understand. If Bobby had PTSD, something caused it, right? The wind was knocked out of me, and I felt I should say something in my brother's defense, in my family's defense. I was embarrassed by this revelation from a stranger, and my embarrassment turned to defensiveness. Like a dog that had been kicked and didn't see it coming, I wanted to turn on Jeff and snarl or run or howl. Instead I went deep inside myself, to a place of paralysis, numbness.

Old thoughts and memories ran through my head in a matter of seconds. John and me, growing up. John pushing my father's limits with insubordination: lying, sneaking out, drunken stupors. Yes, John was a rebellious teen but he wasn't alone.

I never questioned my dad's love for John, for all of us. He showed it in many ways. I miss his laughter and love so badly sometimes I can't breathe. But something was there. I dug even deeper into my thoughts.

My dad was raised through twenty-five years of military service and four tours of war.

Why did my dad ride John so hard? Who knows? It could be that John was wired differently from my father and needed something Dad couldn't give him: room to be different. John needed acceptance and encouragement as well as safety to find his own unique place. He was a lot like our father in that he was a gregarious people person, but he was not a hotshot fighter pilot or cut out to be a wheeling-dealing businessman. He is incredibly sensitive. I have a memory of him taking all of our old blankets on a cold night and giving them to the homeless people who were huddled shivering and dirty on the street corner.

Old memories flashed through my brain like the Times Square ticker tape, moving so fast, I had no way to stop them. I sat trembling on the leather cushioned chair in Jeff's office, vaguely aware of Jeff and Will discussing something, but not hearing anything except what was going on in my head.

I thought of how secretive my family is with each other, compartmentalized, especially about troubling or financial matters. They were still like this today, years after my dad's death. Only selective conversations were had with me when I still lived at home, and they never included mention of John. But a few times I knew that all was not well. Several re-pressed memories popped up of Dad and John interacting, arguing with voices raised, a few physical tussles. One time ended with John becoming so frustrated he put his fist through the wall.

Of course, I didn't see any of this as I always locked myself in my room and listened to "Bridge over Troubled Water" or other soul-soothing music, but I imagined what was happening through the thin ceilings and walls where reverberations could be felt to the core of the earth.

We didn't talk about things like that, but continued as if everything was fine. We were masters of secrets and avoidance. And it has taken me many years to realize that these are two characteristics of an addict and an enabling family. I was struck once again by how different everything would have been if all the bad times could have been dealt with openly—without shame, blame, or secrecy.

There were many loving times too, but as a lonely and vulnerable teenager, I seemed to be affected most by the emotional ones, the scariest, and the events with the most upheaval. The ones that were never spoken about, shrouded in secrecy, and where I was left to my own imagination. I liken it to making an F on a report card. The scary emotional incidents were the F. It takes a million happy A memories to bring one F grade up. And, even then, the memory of the F is the one that never goes away, that haunts. Could this be Bobby? Did he have an F he couldn't let go?

John's behavior in our teens was a cry for help, and, looking back, so was mine, in entirely opposite ways. We were both seeking attention—John, the negative, and Renée, the positive. I craved my Dad's recognition, and I successfully gained it in high school with academics and extracurricular activities. I was drinking too much, yes, but I also excelled at school; I knew when to put the bottle down. To have my dad boast to a friend that his daughter was senior class president and made all As on her report card was better than a year's supply of Strawberry Hill wine. I thrived on it and kept my focus.

The more accolades I received, the more John found trouble. His behavior only made me look better; his out-of-control drinking only made mine seem normal. We were headed in polar opposite directions, and we shared nothing much in common except our last name and our ability to down a Miller Pony in ten seconds flat.

Sitting in Jeff's office, I thought, *no way, no how could John hurt Bobby. He loves him.* But, as I sat there, I realized there might be some truth to it. A behavior pattern passed down from father to son, unconsciously reenacted generation after generation. My dad unwittingly and inadvertently bullied (by modern day definitions) my brother, trying to make John conform to his idea of what a successful man should be; he also unintentionally shamed him. And John, in his alcoholic haze, passed on the things he learned at my dad's knee. Of course, the decades have changed the way we discipline our children, from leather belts, paddling, and switches to time-outs and communication. Physical discipline is no longer acceptable.

Bobby had some work to do because I knew he would never succeed if he continued to be held by the umbilical cord of generational shame. Leaving Jeff's office, I felt great sadness. It looked like in order to help, I would have to look deeper into my own childhood and relations between Bobby, John, and my dad—between all of us. Even sitting with Will in the car, I felt very alone, old haunts and anguish seeping to the surface like blood through a bandage. Damn, love hurts. It hurts so badly.

———

SANTA: REFLECTIONS FROM 1996
LOUISIANA

I was estranged from my family off and on for many of Bobby's formative years, so I don't have many memories of him as a child. One holiday we did spend together stands out in my mind. It was Christmas 1996, and he was just twelve years old.

My father had been dead five years, and I was nervous about this reunion with my mother, brother, sister, and their kids, if you could even call it a reunion. It was more that we were all in the same town, at the same time, and it was Christmas Eve.

The truth was, for a while I had no idea what had gone wrong with our family. Before my father died, I was so close with my much younger sister that we talked every day, sometimes twice, losing touch after the funeral. I was also very close to Jill, and I adored having another sister in the circle. Jill was my confidant—the older sister I did not have. John was John, my big brother, and we had not been close since grade school.

Today, because of the passage of time and the knowledge I have gleaned about addiction, I can look back and see so clearly where the break in our family began. I can trace it back to when my mother was growing up, the oldest of six in a household with a loud, alcoholic father. Sometimes, the children would hide under the bed when he came home from work, quaking in fear of his drunken rants and verbal abuse. I think the breakup of my immediate family began when my father died and my mother went back to her safe place, hiding from the pain of having to deal with an alcoholic son and the grief of losing her spouse too early. Instead of tough love and professional help for John's inherited addictive gene, my mother thought that if she gave him a job and free rein over my dad's amazing company, he would find self-esteem and settle down—no more three-day binges, no more car accidents, no more gambling debts. Unfortunately, it doesn't work that way. Giving money to an addict never helps. You cannot continue to hide under the bed.

My mom and I were not especially close during my childhood. In fact, our relationship was pretty superficial now that I am able to compare it to my relationship with my own girls. In fairness, I suspect that she had a similar relationship with her own mother and that was all she knew. I also think my mother was groomed to always conceal her feelings, anything that was emotionally heavy. She learned this from her family of origin, being the ACOA (short for adult child of an alcoholic), and from being the wife of a fighter pilot whose job left her by herself with young children in strange locales for long periods of time. She excelled in the military mottos: "Don't let 'em see you cry" and "Distraction could be death."

I have struggled to understand this side of my mother my whole adult life, as I freely and happily show my emotions. I'm not afraid to cry, to laugh out loud, to touch, to love, or even to let my anger and fear show through. I sometimes am too much for someone not used to my effusiveness. I tell my children every time I talk to them on the phone that I love them. I tell my friends the same. I tell my husband every morning and night, and if we are romantic, I tell him again. And if I don't tell someone, I show it by being loyal and giving—to a fault, as Will would say.

When Bobby came into my life, he made me look in the mirror, come out of my own safe place, and rethink, with maturity and grace, many of the prejudices and judgments I harbored about my family. I realized I had been hiding under my own bed.

Back in 1996, my family was invited to Will's mother's home to spend the Christmas holiday with her. Will and I share the same hometown, and upon arrival I was taken by surprise when I heard that my mom and siblings were in town also. Ever since my father had died in 1991, my mother never stayed home for the holidays, preferring a cruise or an exotic adventure to being home with her memories of my father. My mother-in-law, Hope, was adamant we split the holiday: Christmas Eve with my half and Christmas Day with Will's family. Hope knew I was crushed by the unraveling of my family bonds, and she was hopeful I might have a holiday reconciliation.

So I called my mother on Christmas Eve morning and announced, "Surprise! We're just across town." Could we join them for that night's gumbo dinner, a Louisiana tradition? Haha. What could she say, really? No, you can't come?

We hadn't spent a Christmas all together since my dad passed away. Heck, I don't think my mother had seen my kids but fleetingly for over several years. Will and I had attended my sister's wedding and the christening of their first child, but beyond that, there was little, if any contact. I became wistful and saddened by the gulf between us and desperately wanted to see them all again and to be together this Christmas Eve.

I was so hopeful and a bit nervous as we loaded our children, dressed in their Christmas best, and headed to my mom's house. They were already gathered when we arrived: my sister and her new husband and their beautiful two-year-old daughter, who'd traveled all the way from Brazil; John and Jill, and Bobby, twelve, and Elizabeth, eight.

John hadn't changed one bit since I last saw him; a good-looking man, cocky and boisterous. Jill was quiet and evasive. She never sat still, always busy, silently looking for some task that didn't need to be done. I winced as she dodged me most of the night, and I sensed the connection between us was broken, as with the rest of my family.

It should have been apparent that this night was not going to go well when the five of us traipsed into Mom's house through the kitchen door and my sister was handing everyone Santa hats smartly monogrammed with everyone's name in white block letters. Everyone except our family.

As my mom put on her bright plush red hat, fixing her hair in the mirror, I quietly inquired if they would be willing to wait to wear the hats until the next day when we would not be there. Mom gave me a surprised look; she hadn't even considered that these monogrammed hats separated the family like the Atlantic Ocean. But my kids were old enough to understand that they didn't get a hat. And I was old enough too.

I could see indecision on her face. For the first hour or two she refrained, but in the end, she wore the hat. I realize now that I shouldn't have taken the hats so personally; I could have called sooner and let her know we were coming. That night only made me feel more left out, bringing my loneliness to the surface. I think it was the knowledge that they had been planning to be together at Christmas long enough to put their names on hats. Ouch.

When Bobby and Elizabeth, the first grandchildren, were born, my dad began playing Santa Claus, much to their delight. Sadly, my father passed away before he could play Santa for my kids. When I heard John planned on playing the jolly old fella for the children who still believed in Saint Nick, I was thrilled.

The memory of John playing Santa Claus twenty years ago is still as vivid to me as if it were yesterday.

After Christmas Eve dinner John had looked at Bobby and signaled. "Son, come upstairs and help me put on the Santa costume." Bobby slowly followed his dad up the back stairs.

Fifteen minutes later Bobby was back downstairs pulling on my arm, wide eyed and whispering, "Aunt Née, my dad needs help."

I quickly followed Bobby back up the stairs to the cedar closet, a small storage for seasonal items, where Santa was housed for 364 days a year.

John was plopped on the bench that lined one side of the room, red polyester plush pants jumbled around his feet. He had attempted to put on the soft felt-like jacket with an attached jet-black plastic belt. He had one arm in, and hanging inside out behind him was the other jacket arm. He was futilely trying to grab the stray sleeve.

He let out his best "ho ho ho!" and I suddenly realized John was so dead drunk he could not put on the Santa costume without help.

"Bobby, why don't you go downstairs and I'll help your father," I softly told him.

"He's not going anywhere. Son, you are going to help your father."

I saw it: a look of fear crossed my nephew's face and he answered too quickly, "Yes, sir."

It took the two of us to pull John up. How in the hell did he get the pants on backward? John struggled for balance while putting one foot in the pants and then the other. Bobby was trying to use his shoulder to keep his huge father from falling backward.

John is a big guy, six foot two, broad shouldered, a fitness freak even when he was drinking. His muscular, hard body makes him weigh as much as an eighteen-wheeler. This night he was an eighteen-wheeler on ice skates.

During the cedar closet struggle, John would emit another "ho ho ho!" every few seconds and lock his thumbs in behind the two black suspenders and tug. He had brought a small chair cushion to use as his belly, a square double-corded pillow that had little give in it. Putting the cushion in the pants and covering it with his jacket and suspenders took creativity and patience, but I jammed it in there, buttoning him up, lacing the black jump boots, while he fooled with his beard and Santa hat.

John was happy, but even in his upbeat mood, he was hard on Bobby, riding him constantly, finding nothing that Bobby did was right. "Son, pick it up," John said after he had dropped the hat for the second time.

Bobby scurried to pick it up and give it to John. Then he drew his hand back to his pocket quickly.

John was finally dressed. I was told to leave to announce Santa's arrival. As I turned, I took Bobby's hand and said, "Come down and help me get everyone together, Bobby."

John reached out his right hand and placed it on Bobby's shoulder, a silent warning. "Go on, Renée. We'll come in a few minutes."

The children were beside themselves with the delicious anticipation of a visit from Santa. "Santa's coming, Santa's coming!" The little ones ran around announcing it to everyone over and over, assuring us of his imminent arrival.

Santa made a Crown Royal appearance. Loudly ho-ho-hoing, John swayed into the living room, a grand entrance, chair cushion slowly sinking lower in his pants until one corner was pointed straight down to the floor, with the other double corner at his armpits, making him walk like he had just gotten off a long trail ride.

John took a seat in a nice wide chair and waved his hands for all the Santa believers to come to his side. It was at that moment that I noticed something was not quite right. John's Santa hat was riding low on his brow, almost covering his eyes. The elastic on his white, fuzzy beard-mustache had slid up, pulling the holes where his mouth and nose were supposed to be to just under his eyes.

When John would "ho ho ho!" all we could see was a white mass of wavy Santa hair wiggling on his face, a Santa that unfortunately had no facial characteristics other than two jolly red eyes filled with mirth, barely peeking out from under his hat.

I was completely caught off guard. Although it shouldn't have been funny, I burst out in laughter and could not stop; I snorted whenever I saw his face. I couldn't control it and my eyes were tearing up. I had to wipe away the wetness to see.

It seemed John's antics had the same effect on every grown-up in the room as the adults were all loudly laughing by now, tragically contagious. John could have been a Saturday Night Live skit.

The little ones, including my three children and my two-year-old niece, were all completely quiet, several backing away from Santa very slowly, not understanding what was happening around them.

"Come here, little girl. Come sit on Santa's lap. Ho HO HO!" he bellowed, oblivious to our merriment at his expense.

John pointed to my daughter Rachel, the oldest of my children, who at six was still a believer, and crooked a finger, bringing her to him with an invisible pull. With more than a little encouragement from the crowd, Rachel braved a visit to Santa's lap.

"What is your name and what can Santa bring you tomorrow, little girl?" Rachel stared at the mass of moving hair on John's face, a close relative of Cousin It from the *Addams Family*, and she proceeded to tell him the gift she really, really wanted: a three-story, three-foot-tall and three-foot-wide Barbie dollhouse.

"Have you been a good little girl? 'Cause if you have been a good little girl, I'll bring you a Barbie dollhouse." Rachel squealed with delight, vigorously shaking her head, yes, she had been a good little girl.

Suddenly it wasn't so funny anymore. What idiotic Santa stand-in promised a child that he would bring her anything she asked for the night before Christmas?

I slid my finger across my neck in a stop-it-before-I-slit-your-throat motion. Did I get her the dollhouse? Nooooo. Now her biggest surprise on Christmas morning would be that Santa did not believe she was a good little girl. I was doomed.

Rachel scooted off Santa's lap and Santa looked around for another victim. Seeing two-year-old Katherine gripping my leg so firmly she would leave ten little blue marks where her fingertips had dug in, John zeroed in. "Ho HO HO!" he barked. "Come see Santa, little girly."

I could hear him speak, but without lips it was a most unusual and confusing sound.

The corner of the cushion in his pants kept him from standing up, so John leaned over and stretched his hand out as far as he possibly could, reaching and reaching until he almost touched Katherine. "Katherine, have you been a good girl?"

Katherine's face was buried in my leg. She turned around to peek at Santa and, seeing his hand inches from her face, she let out a bloodcurdling scream, stamped her feet, and ran away. Setting off a chain reaction, her cousin also began screaming and William started yelling and all the innocent little children who should have had sugar plums dancing in their heads were instead going to be having nightmares about a hairy, faceless Santa Claus.

In hindsight, I was uncomfortable throughout the evening. There was no cohesive family atmosphere, no warmth, no worship. It was painful to look at Bobby and Elizabeth because they too were laughing with the adults at their father, the drunk Santa-It.

I was so happy and so sad when I told everyone goodbye. Light embraces, barely touching, with empty promises to stay in touch swallowed by the air, like our kisses, before I even crossed the threshold.

ONE MONTH ONE WEEK

Wednesday, April 10

EXPECTATIONS

I made a list of expectations and house rules for Bobby to give him some direction. I liked this idea as it would cut down on my nagging and give him expectations in a kind way. I printed out a copy for him since he still wasn't checking emails.

Dear Bobby,

Jeff suggested, and I agree, that now that you are physically feeling better, we should relay things that will make the house run smoothly. There are always extenuating circumstances, but for the most part, these are what we expected or would expect from any of our kids.

1.   *Sunday is a day to sit down and plan for the next week.*

2.   *Out of bed by at least eight thirty on weekdays. Eleven on weekends unless we go to church. This is to help with sleep patterns. It is hard to sleep all day and then get to sleep that night.*

3.   *Please make your bed every morning.*

4.   *Please put your towels and dirty clothes in the laundry chute on Monday morning so that Annie will be able to start her week. She is happy to help you out whenever you need it. Also, if you are out of toilet paper or soap, please let me know.*

5. *Please don't put wet towels on the floor or bed, hang them up.*

6. *Please be extra vigilant and keep no food or trash in your bedroom. This will help with our ant problem.*

7. *Bring all dirty glasses, plates, etc., to the kitchen and put them in the dishwasher.*

8. *My expectation is that you will have three meals a day. You must eat well to feel well and that is our goal! Also, you can't lose weight if you don't eat, a proven fact.*

9. *If you can subsist on a protein drink at breakfast, that is okay by me, but I would talk to your nutritionist to see if it is sufficient to give you nutrients you need for working out.*

10. *Every day you are to do your stretches, whether at the house or the gym.*

11. *You are responsible for scheduling your workouts, meetings, and counseling, and you have done a great job with this!*

12. *Please let us know when you leave the house, where you are going, and when you return. Please use the alarm. I am somewhat paranoid living so secluded on this hill and this will do much to help me with my anxiety.*

13. *Our expectation is for you to have dinner with us when we are sitting down to dinner. If you plan to be away for dinner, please let me know so we can plan. Dinner is a good time to catch up with each other. As a courtesy we all stay at the table until everyone is finished. Sometimes this is the only time we get to see each other during the day!*

Also I expect everyone to help set the table and clear the table.

14. Please keep your ashtrays clean and take care that there are no lit cigarettes in the trash can.

15. TV is okay but you should limit how much you watch.

16. You should be actively keeping your schedule, investigating things that will help you in the future, looking for pick-up work.

And, as always, things can change. If you have any questions or feel uncomfortable about anything, please let me know as this is your home too, and we all need to work to make it comfortable and "homey" for each of us.

Love, Aunt Née

———

MAIL!

Update to self:

From: Renée Hodges
Subject: 4/11
Date: Thursday, April 11, 2013
To: self

Elizabeth has sent Bobby his first card! YAY! He was so excited to get it and it is prominently displayed next to his mom's card. And guess what? He went straight out and bought the funniest card ever for Elizabeth. It was perfectly suited for her, and it showed he put some time and much effort into finding just the right card. I love it!

ONE MONTH THIRTEEN DAYS

April 16

DRIVER'S LICENSE TEST

On the morning Bobby decided to take the driver's test, I waited for him in the kitchen with Mr. Pig, a housewarming gift from some of my close girlfriends eighteen years ago that has been residing on our kitchen counter ever since. A three-foot-high pinkish ceramic work of art wannabe, he stands upright and holds a black chalkboard in his pig knuckles, like he is holding a tray he's about to serve. He is dressed in a ceramic chef's hat and coat, and his pig ears are stuck out to the sides as if a wind has just blown through the room.

He is a beloved part of our family, helping communications amongst us. Over the years, his chalkboard has held many inspirational messages.

The first message I wrote for Bobby was "Welcome Home," written the day of his arrival to Durham. It stayed on the chalkboard for several weeks until one day it was erased. In its place was a message from Bobby: "Believe."

A silent game had begun, and throughout Bobby's stay, the chalkboard would publicize many things, including "Happy Birthday," "Merry Christmas," and "Happy Mother's Day." It would also cry out things we did not want to voice aloud: "Trust in God with all your heart," "One day at a time," "You'll never succeed if you don't try," and "Reach for the stars." Annie Walters would often surprise Bobby with her own words of encouragement or a Bible verse.

This communication helped Bobby in many ways. It assured him that we were thinking about him, whether it was his birthday or a milestone or when he was struggling. It also helped me to show him encouragement and love in another very concrete way.

I have come to cherish Mr. Pig and thank him kindly for being a reliable and dependable messenger for the household. I like to think he's helped us all become better communicators. The day Bobby was to take his driver's license test, Mr. Pig said, "Do your best; that is all you can ask of yourself." This is exactly what Will and I have always told our children before an exam, internship interview, or a big lacrosse game. I waved as his truck headed down the driveway. Then I paced and ditzed around the house like an expectant father waiting for a baby.

Finally, I heard Bobby coming through the back door. His face was solemn and I could read failure across it. I rushed over to console him, but the little rascal couldn't hold this sad expression for too long. He broke into the most beautiful grin, ear to ear and all teeth, and sheepishly boasted, "I made a hundred."

He whipped out his wallet and handed me a newly laminated North Carolina driver's license. I looked at the picture and stopped dead still. Our celebratory moment was over.

Bobby had taken the picture with his hair deliberately messed, sticking up and out and hanging in his face, and making the ugliest scowl he could muster. It did not look anything like the good-looking, boyish young man who stood in front of me.

"Bobby, why did you do this?" I gently questioned.

"I don't know," Bobby answered. "I just don't know why I do things like this."

Much later Jeff would tell me that it was because of Bobby's shame, that he didn't feel he was worthy of anything good in his life. Even passing a driver's test with a 100 percent.

Update to self:

From: Renée Hodges
Subject: 4/16
Date: Tuesday, April 16, 2013, at 9:52 a.m.
To: self

I am still trying to balance Bobby and Will, and I think it is working better, but I am so tired sometimes I feel I can't make it through the day without a nap.

———

TRANSFORMING

Bobby was transforming in micro ways, but I could see the changes. As we were waiting for him to become brain and body healthy, we were gingerly looking to the future and with his input had tentatively come up with two options for him to pursue. The first thought was for him to go to automotive school and become a car mechanic. The second was for him to become a classroom teacher of a Driver's Ed course.

Gail Brooks, a Driver's Education instructor, is one of my friends who went the extra mile to try and find Bobby work. Gail is both real and insightful. She has a darkly playful side, loves to shock, and is not afraid of anything taboo. I'd like to say I love her despite this side, but really I love her because of it. She needs to know that you will get to know her insides and will love her no matter what she says or does.

Gail is the consummate caregiver, needy not in the derogatory way, but in only the most giving way—needing to
give as much of herself as she possibly can with no thought
for return on her investment.

I understand this. We are very much alike in this regard.
I would trust her with my life, as I know she would save me
from the fire before she saved herself. Heck, she would save
you from the fire first, as well. I would have to think about it.

Gail has had to fend for herself since the breakup of her
second marriage while she was still young. She teaches
Driver's Education. It gives her some flexibility and she is
awesome with young people. When she heard that Bobby
was in need of a job, she went to bat with her boss to give
him a look-see. She quickly arranged for him to watch a
Driver's Education class that she was teaching. She didn't
hesitate to tell me that she really liked Bobby but that he was
"unprofessional in appearance and dress" and in her opinion
would not be offered a job until he did something about it.

I couldn't have agreed more, but with all the battles to be
fought, that was one I'd thought could wait. Until that moment. The first battle would be the hair. Hair is such a personal
choice. Bobby wanted to wear his light brown hair long. I
suspected he would have preferred really long, but he knew I
would disapprove, so he kept it shorter than he would have
wanted. It was as straight as a Tiger Woods tee shot and
hung limply, unshaped, sideburns and all.

When I asked him to comb his hair, he would style it like
Justin Bieber, fanned sideburns slicked at a slant toward his
pale cheekbones with the rest straight and hanging low over
his brow. He still hung his head, not able to meet anyone's
eyes, so this style made him look like he was in high school.

Some of the worst fights my father and brother had were

over, not John's grades or alcohol consumption, but his hair. My father was raised from age sixteen by the military. Yes, Dad lied. He dropped out of high school and ran off and joined the Air Force. It was pre-Korea, peaceful, but my dad couldn't sit still in class and he felt the call and excitement of duty. He also felt he needed to support his mother, my grandmother. When John began letting his hair grow in the seventies, I never understood why my dad took it so personally. Every rock star or screen star was wearing it over the ears.

"Cut your hair or I'll cut it for you," my father would say. Or "No son of mine will be a longhair-hippie-freak," a meaningful phrase from a man who had recently returned from two tours in Vietnam. And then the skirmishes would begin. Every six weeks or so I could predict the conflict over the haircut even as the Vietnam War was coming to an end. And I'll never forget the time my brother dropped the bomb, "If you want me to cut it, you'll have to catch me." The chase around our block was one of the lighter moments in my childhood. My dad, scissors in hand, flying down the sidewalk after John, his locks swaying with the wind, bouncing. Of course, my dad won the clash over the hair length every time. Interesting that the hair battle raged on with another generation. Like father, like son, I suppose, but this time it was Bobby who was rebelling.

Remembering the constant push-pull of my father and brother, I had been hesitant to say anything, but I finally decided to sit Bobby down and be frank.

"Gail Brooks thinks you need to clean up your appearance and look more professional."

He hung his head, shuffled his feet, hands clenched in front of him as the extra-long gym shorts he wore had no pockets.

"What do you mean?"

"I mean, you need to do something with your hair. You are wearing the hairstyle of the kids you would be driving around. You need to look the part of the teacher."

"I like my hair long."

A sigh from me.

"I'm not going to chase you around the block with a pair of scissors. You will have to cut your hair on your own. What I am going to do is promise you that when you are a full-time grad student, have a full-time job where you are the boss, are a self-made millionaire and don't have to answer to anyone else, I will stop nagging you about your hair. Until then, you must take care of it. There is nothing wrong with wearing it long if that is what you prefer. But if you are to keep it long, you need to keep it styled. Styled in a grown man's hairstyle, out of your eyes, sideburns trimmed, combed and neat."

"I do have it styled."

Sigh again.

"Yes, but it is not the style of a twenty-nine-year-old." I wanted to let him down gently, but there was no getting around it. "You are too old to wear it like this. Especially if you plan on teaching Driver's Ed. You will look like your students."

Silence. I couldn't tell what he was thinking, as his eyes were covered with his mop of hair and pointed downward.

Okay, I thought. *Just spit it out. Honesty. Painful honesty.* "And you have to make more of an effort when you dress for an interview. Gym shorts are out. Wrinkled shirt and pants too. A potential employer will look at your appearance before looking at your resume. In the first fifteen seconds he will have made his assessment. I read this somewhere." I think.

"Aunt Née, I can't fit into any of my clothes. They are all too big now."

God, I'm a dunce. I hadn't thought of that.

"If you can't fit into your clothes, you must tell me. Please tell me these things. And let's celebrate that you can't fit into those clothes!" *Can we burn those gym shorts as part of the celebration, pretty please?*

Bobby went out the next morning and came home with a new haircut. It was short on the sides but still long in the front—maybe a bit passive-aggressive or maybe just a first step to a more conservative haircut. Still when he used gel and slicked it back, I swear he resembled a GQ cover model. I decided to consider it progress.

LATE APRIL

WATERING THE PLANTS

Bobby's routine began to stabilize; he was going to bed at a reasonable time, and I didn't hear him wrestling with insomnia as much. His screaming nightmares woke me from time to time, but he was now able to wake from them since he was not as heavily medicated. I could feel an ever so slight change in his demeanor. Spring was in full bloom; the days were lighter and longer and birds and flowers were in abundant supply.

I had asked—no, I had told—him to set his alarm clock in the mornings, but he still had difficulty getting out of bed.

Nine thirty, then ten thirty, eleven passed. I watched the clock, tick tock. By eleven I went to the stairs and called up, "Bobby, it is time to get out of bed." I admit that I had a little posttraumatic stress because of Thomas. I held my breath every morning until I heard him groggily yell back, "Yes, ma'am. I overslept."

Forcing him to get up and out of bed in the morning before noon was not a punishment but rather a tool. A good sleep cycle is next to cleanliness and godliness. Setting an alarm for a designated time each morning would help to regulate his sleep patterns and keep him on a schedule. I used Jeff Georgi's tools. If he could spin taking a drug test each week into something positive, I could take this situation—which could be construed as a negative—and make it into a good thing too. Lemons into lemonade. Aside from this positive technique, I believe that without sleep, life can look bleak and hopeless. Just ask me after I have had a poor night's sleep.

When Bobby began getting up before 10:00 a.m., I could hear him dragging down the stairs, slowly and begrudgingly.

I would stop anything I was doing and make a beeline for the kitchen, wanting to arrive first so it didn't look like I was waiting for him, which of course I was.

Mornings do not show my best side either, so I had to work at putting on my brightest smile and saying, "Good morning, Bobby."

In the early days he would grunt or mumble a nearly in-distinguishable "Good morning," and go straight for the re-frigerator to grab the liter of Diet Coke, and pour a tall glass to take outside with him for a first smoke.

I usually sat in the kitchen fiddling with my cold coffee or rechecking emails on my phone for the tenth time, patiently waiting until he returned. Like in the movie *Groundhog Day*, I would offer to fix him breakfast each morning, and he would always reply, "I can't eat right now. I'll get some cereal later." For the first seven to eight weeks this was our routine. If Sonny and Cher had been singing "I Got You Babe" in the background, I would have sworn we were part of that movie.

But one day in April Bobby arrived in the kitchen and instead of going for the Diet Coke, he went straight to the windowsill. There, sitting all alone in a blaze of sunlight, was a miniature terra-cotta pot, so small it had to be made for the Lilliputians.

I'd seen it somewhere before . . . ah, I remembered. That sweet and lovely Easter Bunny had left it in the kids' Easter baskets this year at the family reunion, a single tomato plant seed and baby pot in which to plant it. Bobby had done just that and I watched that first morning as he carefully filled a glass with a baby amount of water and poured it into the container.

He slowly developed a routine as he acclimated to waking

up earlier and earlier. Wake up, come downstairs, go straight to the plant and water it, get a Diet Coke, and walk outside to smoke.

Pretty soon there was a small sprout peeking out of the soil, and the tomato plant continued to flourish as spring turned into summer, summer into fall. I watched this ritual most mornings out of the corner of my eye as I pretended to read the newspaper or look at my cell phone. Sometimes I saw him lovingly move it to different areas of the kitchen sill, perhaps to gain sun or shade or just to break the monotony.

I do not have the gift of gardening. I love flowering plants, fragrant and colorful, exotic or simple, but I simply cannot keep them alive. Over the years I have given it the good ole college try, but I hate feeling guilty about the wasted money and time, not to mention the ugly death of so many plants. Silk plants are my friends now.

But I do own a few living plants. A small bamboo, braided intricately, is my longest surviving plant, as it is not needy. It lives despite me. I have another ivy-looking plant that is very prolific, and I don't think I could kill it if I tried. These plants also sat on my kitchen windowsill, perkily coexisting with Bobby's tiny tomato plant.

Several months after Bobby's routine commenced, I began to notice that my two plants were not looking so well; the bamboo was jaundiced yellow and the ivy wilted like cooked spinach. I scrutinized the patients but I had no diagnosis. These plants had lived and suffered for many years in my household, yet now they were on life support.

I decided to take a closer look at Bobby's routine and, upon investigation, discovered that Bobby was also taking care of my plants each day, watering them at the same time he watered his tomato plant. I didn't have the heart to tell him that each plant needed a different amount of water, and he was killing my plants with his nurturing and good intentions.

To stop the slow death of the plants without hurting Bobby's feelings, Annie Walters and I made a production of rearranging knickknacks in the family room and pulled Mr. Bamboo, limping and on his last leg, and Ms. Ivy, bloated and sickly, and placed them well away from the kitchen. It took a few weeks of good old familiar neglect to revive them, but they are both still alive and well today.

He groomed his tomato seed, soon to be a thriving plant, for the next fourteen months, replanting it several times as it continued to grow tall and taller still. Two lone wolves, depending on each other for survival.

About six months after Bobby first watered the tomato seed, Will and I were out to dinner with a young doctor and his wife who had recently moved in down the street. Linsey and Duncan Hughes, outgoing and energetic, are magnets for anyone looking for a fun time. Both Linsey and Duncan were tennis players, familiar with Bobby's struggles and very supportive of him—and us. Linsey and Duncan were younger than Will and me; I was hoping we could keep up with them. Over cocktails at a small plates establishment, the conversation turned to gardening and my black thumb. I related the story about how Annie Walters and I had to hide my only two plants to keep them alive because Bobby was so conscientious about watering them. "And he is obsessed with this single tomato seed plant I gave him for Easter. It is the heartiest plant in the house!"

Linsey's expression was not of amusement but of wonder. Setting her glass of wine down, she placed her hand on my arm and said, "Renée, you know that is one of the tenets of Alcoholics Anonymous."

Huh? My blank look urged her to continue, and she picked up steam. "In your first year of sobriety, if you can take care of a plant, and it lives until the end of the year, it means you have nurtured and taken care of something other than yourself. This prepares you for having a relationship. The lessons you learn in caring for something else prepare you for the time and effort that a relationship takes."

Of course. Duh.

"How do you know this?" I asked.

Linsey picked up her glass of wine and sat back, a reflective smile on her face, then told us: Duncan's great-great-granduncle William Duncan Silkworth, or Doc Silkworth, was the cofounder and original doctor of Alcoholics Anonymous. Duncan was named after Doc Silkworth.

I was mesmerized to be sitting with greatness. Once again, sharing Bobby's story openly and honestly had connected us with support and encouragement.

Linsey continued with her story:

Bill W. was an alcoholic from New York who had a vision of the way to sobriety and was introduced to a like-minded doctor from Akron, Ohio, Doc Silkworth. Their first meeting led to the creation of a twelve-step recovery program and a book that would change the lives of millions. Doc Silkworth is known for writing the chapter "The Doctor's Opinion" in the AA handbook. While Doc Silkworth was treating Bill W. for alcoholism, he gave Bill W. a plant and told him if he could take care of this plant for a year he would be able to take care of himself.

Yes, it was exactly what Bobby was doing. It all made sense. As I sat back on the comfy couch and ironically ordered another glass of prosecco, I smiled openly, unable to contain my inner happiness.

The following day, I researched Doc Silkworth and Bill W. I love the following story about the foundation of AA for many reasons. I think it shows courage and resolve, fellowship and compassion. It is a pay-it-forward action and, for the alcoholic, a 911 distress call.

If you ever go on a cruise, it is likely that the morning agenda slipped under your door while you sleep will announce daily: *Friends of Bill W. meet in Salon Room C.* Or if you are in an airport awaiting the departure of your plane and the loudspeaker blares, *Would a friend of Bill W.'s please meet Becky at Gate 12?* it is not because Bill W. is a habitual traveler with a lot of friends. This is a method and code for anyone who is in recovery and in distress, needing support from another recovered alcoholic or friend.

The Alcoholics Anonymous website tells the following condensed story. It states that the seeds of this tradition began in 1935 when the newly sober cofounder of Alcoholics Anonymous, Bill W., away on a business trip, found himself craving a drink. (Bill W.'s last name is initialed to help with anonymity, which was particularly important in the 1930s, when overt drunkenness was likely to land you in a lockdown facility for the mentally insane. To this day, only his first name and last initial are used.)

On this business trip Bill W. was put in touch with a struggling alcoholic surgeon who also needed help staying sober. Bill W. and Dr. Bob's meeting lasted for hours. Afterward, Bill thanked Bob for his fellowship, saying, "I know now that I'm not going to take another drink and I'm grateful to you."

But the relationship did not end there. Bill stayed with Dr. Bob for the next three weeks, and through their friendship, Dr. Bob also gained sobriety.

171

Over decades this first connection has morphed into a worldwide help network. Any recovering alcoholic who needs help can ask for and receive immediate support with this method.

"Friendship" with Bill W. has become a stand-in for sobriety—a useful secret bond between addicts navigating an often judgmental world.

Because Bobby was having such a hard time with his incessant cravings, his ties to Alcoholics Anonymous were ever more important and I urged him to regularly do just what Bill W. did a hundred years ago: call on a friend.

ONE MONTH NINETEEN DAYS

Monday, April 22

THE LITTLE THINGS

I make it a point to do little things for my kids and anyone else I love. My family was never much about the small things and, as I get older, I realize that those details are important and what I partly think love is all about.

For example, getting picked up from the airport and not having to take a cab is wonderful, but our family takes it a step further. How nice is it when you have been gone for a long period of time and you are met at security, big hugs and kisses are exchanged, your rolling suitcase is taken from you immediately, arms link together, and you are kept company while you wait for your luggage to arrive?

No, we didn't do it every little trip. Sometimes, knowing I would probably be met at the airport, I would text, *Don't get out of the car, it is too late in the evening*, giving dispensation. It is perfectly acceptable to be picked up on the curb after baggage claim.

But if someone makes the effort to come to town, we make a special gesture by parking and greeting them at security, instead of simply pulling up to the curb and scooping them into our car. If our kids went off to camp or a community service trip, we would always meet them at security with open arms and bear hugs. Posters and flowers were displayed for a junior year abroad.

After almost seven weeks in Durham, Jeff still did not believe that Bobby was well enough to stay alone when we went out of town. His mother volunteered to come spend a long weekend with Bobby while Will and I traveled to New Orleans for a reunion with my college girlfriends. Jill overlapped with us by coming a day early, so that we could visit and strategize about Bobby's continued recovery.

It felt important for Bobby's mom to have those first moments privately with him, so I asked him to pick her up from the airport alone.

I did give some thought to the little things, and the day before Jill arrived, I explained our airport pickup tradition to Bobby, hoping he might take the hint. As usual, there was no comment and no expression of comprehension.

When I heard Bobby and Jill returning from the airport, I went to greet them at the back door. I was so excited to see Jill.

Jill's eyes danced as she jumped out of the cab of Bobby's white truck. She carried an array of multicolored carnations and a "Welcome Home" balloon. Bobby had stopped at the local grocery store and paid for these gifts out of his own hard-earned money, then he'd parked and met her at security.

Jill choked up as she showed me the flowers and balloon. Dang, I choked up too. Sometimes I had no idea whether or not he was listening. I was glad he'd listened this time. I couldn't imagine the feelings of apprehension Jill must have had seeing Bobby for the first time since he'd stormed out of her home on a suicide mission. She'd probably turned the corner at the Raleigh-Durham Airport and BAM! There, front and center, was Bobby grinning madly, carrying balloons and a bouquet, maybe swaying back and forth with anticipation and his own anxiety at seeing his mom. And I could picture the embrace. The first touch between mother and son, both desperate for assurance that everything was going to be all right.

From: Jill Redford
Subject: Update on Bobby while you are out of town
Date: Sunday, April 28, 2013, at 5:59 p.m.
To: Renée Hodges

Hi Renée.

I hope you are having fun at your reunion. All is well here. Bobby just went upstairs so I can write. He has been good.

We talked over the two options for tech schools. One requires some training prior to enrollment and the other could conflict with Gail Brooks's Driver's Ed training. He told me he would have a better understanding of Driver's Ed this week.

He completed the garden work but did not get a chance to walk the neighbor's dog. She will contact him this week.

Jeff was not available for another session, but I am working on watching his DVDs on addiction. The Reverend Bowen and his wife dropped off brownies and texted Bobby as well. He completed the CD shelf and has been consistent with the dogs, Saint and Roux. I have found just a little reminder or update keeps him on track. I am hoping soon all projects become more manageable for him.

Renée, you've done what no one else could do. You gave him a chance to get back on his feet again. The support that Will and you have given him is nothing short of a miracle. It is a miracle. Thank you.

That being said, I am available twenty-four seven to help in any way. Please let me know if you need me to follow up or stay over. I am ready to visit when you take your thirtieth anniversary trip to England this June. Send the dates and I will make arrangements.

Much love, Jill

PS. Bobby also completed meetings for the week!

Will and I arrived home from my New Orleans college re-union exhausted and very late on a Sunday night. Coming down the escalator to baggage claim, I began texting Bobby that we had arrived and we were headed to get our luggage. I glanced up to make sure I wouldn't miss the last escalator step and do a face-plant, and there I met his blue eyes.

He was waiting for us at the bottom of the escalator, holding the "Welcome Home" balloon he had reused from when his mom arrived a few days earlier. I was most proud that he did not spend money on us. After all, it was the gesture that counted.

I wasn't expecting this airport welcome and I was caught off guard. My eyes welled with tears as I began to comprehend. Bobby had that contagious grin on his face, and he looked so young and innocent and proud of himself. I felt his strong embrace. I felt the warmth and emotion behind it. It was a two-armed, spread-open, squeeze-the-stuffing-out-of-ya bear hug.

Yes, I truly believe it is the little things.

ROUX, SAINT, AND BOBBY

It's important at this juncture to introduce my two dogs: Roux, a chocolate lab, and Saint, a golden retriever. When the realization struck me that I would have a home devoid of children as the last child headed off to college, I impulsively added two more family members to the household to soften the blow. They were one-year-old rascally puppies when Bobby came to live with us.

He spent more time with the dogs than anyone else in the

house because he is a smoker and the smoking section is anywhere that is not in the house. At the beginning of his journey to recovery, Roux and Saint were Bobby's only friends, but they are loyal ones.

Since his arrival in Durham, I noticed Bobby had a difficult time connecting with people, not just Will and me, but everyone. He was not just guarded, but walled off, reminding me of the Great Wall of China, taking many years to build and almost impenetrable.

Still, as he paced around the backyard smoking, those two tongue-hanging, tail-wagging bundles of energy and fur followed closely on his heels, vying for any attention he might give. He was strong but firm with these young pups. He fed them routinely and bathed them several times a week in his bathtub. I never said anything about this odd ritual of bathing because it seemed to give both the dogs and Bobby a lot of pleasure and the dogs had never smelled so good. We did have to make sure he wasn't using the good guest towels to dry them.

He taught Saint to retrieve tennis balls, tossing the yellow ball as far as he could and watching as Saint would bound happily after it, picking it up in his soft mouth and bringing it back. Now if only Saint would learn to drop it instead of us having to pry his jaws open to retrieve the tennis balls.

I began to think of Roux and Saint as therapy dogs, as the more they interacted with Bobby the more his mood would lighten and sometimes, just for an instant, I could see a normal kid on a normal afternoon playing throw and fetch. As he became healthier, his interactions with our sweet dogs became more loving, and their puppy enthusiasm seemed to permeate his sad exterior.

One afternoon, I went looking for Roux because he had been missing for a while. I called and called for him, inside and outside the house, but he didn't come. After searching for him for over an hour, I started to get worried.

Finally, roused by my calls, Bobby came out of his room on the second floor, and his exclamation was filled with delight. He yelled down proudly that Roux had been sleeping outside his door the whole time.

Roux sat or slept outside of Bobby's room many more times in the next months, protecting him from all seen and unseen enemies. I believed this chocolate Labrador understood that Bobby was vulnerable and in need of his protection and love.

The unconditional love that my puppies had for Bobby began chipping away at his defenses, allowing him his first connections in many years.

Woof.

From: Renée Hodges
Subject: update to self
Date: Friday, May 3, 2013, at 12:17 a.m.
To: self

Jill Redford came here for a long weekend] to stay with Bobby while Will and I went to New Orleans for my reunion. Jill is smart and very loving and she was so excited to see Bobby, and to see him doing so well. I did set out an agenda for them to keep Bobby on schedule. I really wanted Jill to help him nail down a career path, but that didn't happen because there was so much to do. What did happen though was she made sure he had a good trainer and is getting proper care for his back. She took him to get shoes and toiletries and spent lots of quality time with him, and he felt both loved and wanted. All in all, a very successful trip!

Here is the cumulative update on Bobby's progress in order of when my brain thinks about it:

He has lost twenty-five pounds and is so happy about that. He says it is because he has cut out fast food. And because he has cut out fast food, he also has money in his pocket. He is sleeping better at night so he is better able to get up in the mornings. He has worked for several of my friends and because they are trusting him with their dogs, gardens, and errands, he seems to be gaining some self-esteem. This is so important to his recovery. Thank you friends!

He has decided not to pursue the Driver's Ed route but to go back to school or to apprentice somewhere and become an auto mechanic.

He went to Durham Tech and picked up applications and is taking a welding course this summer and looking at what other classes he can take. I have set him up to meet the owner of a European sports car shop. He has called the owner and they will meet next week. I have found two other sources for him to follow up on—but that is for next week.

Jeff has been out of town, but he did have one session with Jill and Bobby before he left. Jill said that it was very emotional as Bobby asked her why she had stayed with John during his alcoholic days. I let her speak and I didn't go into it deeply with her because I really don't need to know, and I probably know it all anyway.

I did get on Jill for buying Bobby that remote control he has been wanting for his race cars. I think I nicely called her an enabler, saying that a lot of his problems were that he had never been accountable for any money. But I guess if she were to buy him something extravagant, I am glad it was the remote. It gives him something to do and something to tinker with, both great things for him. And he loves those cars.

I was supposed to go to the beach for an overnight with some of my girlfriends. Will was disgruntled about my going, so I canceled it. My friends understood and Will is right. He isn't comfortable staying with Bobby and he said this to me. But I think he would have been disgruntled if I went whether Bobby were here or not. I am just too fragile to push it. Maybe next time . . . Good night.

TWO MONTHS NINE DAYS
CURRENT EVENTS

Since college, Bobby had been in and out of rehab centers. The facilities have strict rules for the patients' welfare, rules about what they can read, what they can watch on television, and what they can receive in the mail. I learned this when I tried to send him a *Sports Illustrated* magazine in a box with some chocolate and a Duke Blue Devils championship ball cap. First, what I considered innocuous was anything but to a recovering patient. What a birdbrain I was to not understand this before dropping the box off at the post office. In fact, it never even crossed my mind.

It only took one instance of my present being sent back to me to learn my lesson. Nothing can be sent with pictures of party scenes, alcohol or drug use, or implied sexual content. Pick up a Sports Illustrated magazine—or any magazine for that matter—and thumb through it. Every other page is an ad for alcohol or a prescription drug. Most have scantily clad women in suggestive poses selling it. Many ads deliver messages like "Just Do It," or "The Most Interesting Man in the World." Think about Red Bull and its message. Even Dove's soap ad campaign has a slew of young women in their undies promoting "real beauty." The patients' television viewing is strictly monitored and social media is nonexistent.

Most patients are working so hard to overcome their addictions that they could care less about what is happening out in the world beyond the doors of their recovery center. The war is within themselves and stock market quotes, Super Bowl football games, or skirmishes in the Middle East are far from their thoughts.

When Bobby moved in with us, I forgot these facts. I'm a current events and history junkie. Both Will and I usually know what is happening in the world, in our state and city, in the stock market, in the NFL, in Hollywood—well, you get the drift. We subscribe to three newspapers, although I must confess I rarely get through but one or two papers every day. Will devours all three.

I DVR the world news every night and can't help falling in love with each consecutive ABC anchorman and anchorwoman as they bring current events into our home. I love the human interest and people-of-the-week segments at the end of each broadcast as they make me feel uplifted even as murder, war, famine, and terrorism reign supreme.

Will and I are well-traveled, a privilege of having money, but also because we are interested in other countries, cultures, peoples, and their histories. Even when struggling financially in our early days, we would save our pocket change in a big glass jar to use for trips and travel.

Debate, discussion, and heated conversations over just about any topic are a mainstay in the Hodges household. We are all experts on everything; just ask us. I love that all my children are open to the world, learning from the past and keeping up with the present, which will be the past tomorrow.

In the early months of 2013, the world was in an upheaval, but no place more than in the Middle East. Even though the wars in Iraq and Afghanistan were winding down, the unrest in Libya, Egypt, Syria, and Turkey led to the Arab Spring uprisings. The Arab Spring was a revolutionary wave of demonstrations and protests (both nonviolent and violent), riots, and civil wars in the Arab world that began on December 17, 2010, with the Tunisian Revolution, and spread throughout the countries of the Arab League and its surroundings. While the wave of initial revolutions and protests faded by mid-2012, some started to refer to the succeeding and still ongoing large-scale discourse conflicts in the Middle East and North Africa as the Arab Winter.

When my children came home for Mother's Day in 2013, it was difficult to go anywhere without seeing a headline about the upheaval in the Arab world. It was a topic of conversation at parties or the pool, and of course at our dinner table.

Katherine, a student and lover of Middle Eastern history and politics, was to embark on an academically accredited summer-at-sea program that would sail the Mediterranean, with ports of call in many Middle Eastern countries. Because of the uprisings sprouting like mushrooms, her itinerary was tentative and subject to change with the shifting tensions. Will and I were concerned for her safe travel but trusted the program to keep her away from any trouble. Sitting around the kitchen table, I listened as my kids conversed about the current state of affairs in the Middle East. Bobby sat quietly as everyone injected their differing opinions. He finally piped up, asking, "What's the Arab Spring?" Katherine proceeded to summarize the political unrest and violence in each country.

Bobby soaked it in, listening intently but asking questions, like a visitor who just arrived from Pluto. He had no knowledge of world events. Heck, he had no knowledge of what was happening outside of our house.

Late the next afternoon, after the last of my children had headed back to college after Mother's Day weekend, I sat down with Bobby for our weekly planning meeting. I was gentle as I pushed the *Wall Street Journal* across the table to him.

"What's this?"

"The *Wall Street Journal*. I want you to read it every

morning when you get up. Take it to the porch and have your Coke and cigarette while you read. Take it to your bedroom. Put it next to your chair in the family room. I want you to read it cover to cover. Please do this as a favor to me." He looked confused.

I continued, "Part of getting healthy is getting your brain healthy too. Healthy enough that you may rejoin the world at large. And to do this, you must be able to converse intelligently about current events. No one can live in a bubble and be healthy, and during the last few years you've been living in one. It's time to rejoin the world. By reading the newspaper, you will be able to go anywhere and talk to anyone intelligently about current events. We, together, are going to work your brain, just like we are working your body."

I tapped the headline: "Historic Pakistani Election." "Go and read." And he did. Every day thereafter I would find him reading the newspaper. He became a CNN fan and would turn on 24/7 news programs and listen while he worked on his computer. He eventually started to read the news online.

Weeks later, Bobby was having dinner with me, Will, and a group of friends at a restaurant down the street. I can't recall the exact topic of conversation, but it was of global importance. "Has anyone heard the latest?" someone at the table asked. Bobby was the one to bring the rest of us up to date. I barely listened to the conversation, which is why I can't recall it, because I was so intently watching him converse knowledgeably, intelligently, and with confidence, an adult speaking to other adults. He was asked questions and he had the answers. I just sat there dumbly with my mouth agape.

Welcome to the world, Bobby.

From: Renée Hodges
Subject: update
Date: Tuesday, May 14, 2013, at 10:53 p.m.
To: Mary Costello

Mother's Day weekend all the kids came home. Bobby at first was distant and didn't say much until I cornered him and told him he must engage in the family. I told him he is a part of our family now and that was my expectation. Staying in his room was not an option. After that, he opened up more and he even played darts in a heated game where he showed he is quite a good player!

I asked Anne to spend Mother's Day with us as she would have been alone. Her daughter had to be out of town for this first holiday without Thomas.

When I told Bobby this, he replied with "I'll go get her a Mother's Day card." Special.

On Mother's Day, he had a card for me and a present, too! A book about Catherine the Great that I have been talking about reading. I was very touched as he had put some thought behind it.

He drove to Charlotte to interview at an automotive school that touts links to NASCAR. An impressive facility but at an astronomical cost for eleven months. He was so excited, but I have pulled him back to reality by making him compare pros and cons of tech schools vs. for-profit schools and he is now doing his due diligence.

I contacted Jill and asked her, if Bobby were to go to this school or another one, would they give the money to him? If they did, I suggested it should be a loan. After he graduates and he gets a job, and proves he did his best, then and only then could they decide whether to forgive the debt or not. I just don't think this should come easy for him.

My deal with him is that if he goes to an auto tech school I will buy his tools, which could be as much as seven thousand dollars worth—and jeez, are not included in the astronomical tuitions. I would own them, and, again, if he graduated and got a job, I would forgive the debt. But if he dropped out or regressed, I would sell the tools. We would sign a contract on this so he would not be able to pawn the tools. At least, I hoped this contract would make him think twice.

Will and I are doing our dance and keep stepping on each other's toes. We are fine at the moment—for now. Just some tender tootsies.

TWO MONTHS TWO WEEKS TWO DAYS

SOS

From: Renée Hodges
Subject: SOS
Date: Sunday, May 19, 2013, 4:36 p.m.
To: Jeff Georgi

Dear Jeff,

I am very worried about Bobby. These past few days he has become withdrawn and unengaged. We sat down today for our weekly look-ahead meeting, and I asked him what he was feeling. He said a whole lot.

1. He is obsessed with taking a drink and is very close to doing so. I asked him what I could do to help him. He gave me several suggestions and I am following them. I asked if we should take all alcohol out of the house and he said no, he could get it anywhere, but I have moved it all to one place and locked it away, nevertheless. I think I need some advice on this subject, especially since Will and I love our cocktail hour.

2. He says he doesn't know how to be happy. I gave him a lot of examples of times this past week when I thought he was happy. He agreed with my examples. Then he said he is having a lot of nightmares. I said he must be processing something (that's what Mary tells me :)). He says he has some dark secrets that he can't tell anyone. He has written them in a journal that he has at his mom and dad's home. I told him he needs to learn to trust Jeff or me and that there isn't anything that would change the way we felt about him. I told him everyone has things that they wouldn't want to share but that if it was something that was affecting him so much, he needed to try to find the courage to face it.

3. He only feels safe in his room, so I suggested he read his book in the library tonight. It is a very warm and comfy room where he can close himself in with the books. It will get him to spend time in another place, and I do so hope he likes it.

4. I suggested he change AA meeting groups and see if he can find a girl in the group that would be his friend. Someone that he can trust and who would know what he is going through. He said he thinks that is a good idea.

5. He said he appreciates that Will has tried to talk to him. He said he liked having Will as another father figure. That is nice that he could vocalize it.

Until the last few days he has been doing great. Engaging, smiling, keeping a schedule, being thoughtful and helpful, etc. I don't know what precipitated this turnaround, or if anything did. I just know it is going on now.

Thanks, Renée

RED, WHITE, AND ROSÉ

I searched the honeycomb wine rack in the locked closet for just the right color and blend and found it, pulling the dusty bottle from its resting place. I am not a connoisseur, but I am particular about my wine. I have tasted enough vintages, blends, and colors to know just what I don't like, and, as the saying goes, life is too short not to drink fine wine.

When Bobby came to live with us, I was conflicted. I

knew I had to change our lifestyle to keep him safe. Will and I had partially built our world around wine, which included discovering, searching, crafting, and of course, drinking. It is as hard for those who have an addiction to alcohol to understand how and why the other side can drink without consequences as it is for those like me to understand why there are those who cannot partake.

I was being a hypocrite, and I knew it. Every day I worried and obsessed over the alcohol locked up in my home, knowing that Bobby could never take another drink in his lifetime. Still, I love to drink. If it is wine, I am an equal opportunity drinker; no preference for white, red, or rosé. I do love a good bubbly and relish the tingle in my toes I get from French champagne, though my frugal nature often keeps me in the cava and prosecco families.

Will and I love to find just the right house wine, one which tastes like a Robert Parker score of ninety-nine but costs more like a Two Buck Chuck on special.

Will is the connoisseur in our family. Almost fifteen years ago he decided he wanted to make wine in our detached garage. Today he orders cases of grapes from Napa Valley, overages from a name vineyard, and has them refrigerated and trucked across the country during the harvest in September or October.

He then spends nearly three days crushing, de-stemming, fermenting, and whatever else he does in his man cave, producing his most recent vintage.

Our children grew up knowing the chemistry of wine, learning the ins and outs of beakers and sulfur, yeasts and sugar points. One of my children used their wine-crafting experience as a college application essay. Will and I were proud of that essay, which described the science behind the hobby, the precision behind the process, and the craft of producing a fine wine.

I remember passing by the bar on my way to the kitchen to fix breakfast one morning before school. Eleven-year-old William was bellied up to the bar, back to me, with three wineglasses sitting in front of him, each a third full of red wine. I stopped and remained silent, watching to see what he was going to do next. He carefully picked up a glass, swirled it, peered closer to see the opacity, swirled it again, dipped his nose into the glass, inhaled deeply, and then set it down. He repeated this process with each glass of wine. Suddenly he popped his head up and shouted to his father in the next room, "Dad, there's too much sulfur. We need to put a penny in it."

Even though I am a bit biased, I have to admit Will's wine is damn good these days. His early batches usually produced sangria or went down the drain, and his joke was, "If it is a good batch, I'll give you a bottle. If it is a bad batch, I'll give you a case." But his recent vintages rate right up there with the famous winemaker Helen Turley, and I tell him this often. Today's vintage, you'll be lucky to get a glass.

When the kids were born, Will researched their birth year and we bought a case of wine for each child, which we have held in the cellar for many years. We open a bottle on special occasions, such as graduations or engagements.

Alcoholics and addicts are so misunderstood. They do not want to crave a substance so much that they will ultimately give up their lives if they do not get help. *Just say no*, we think. *Why can't they just say no? Are they weak? Are they crazy? Don't they care about themselves, their job, their wife or kids?* Our addicted loved ones tell us over and over they are going to just say no and we want desperately to believe them. The humbling truth is that without intervention, it is almost impossible to quit drinking, quit using. And, even with help, it takes many months to years for the addict to understand the underlying emotional issues. After the physical symptoms of withdrawal are in the rearview mirror, it is the core issues that need to be addressed: the shame, the insecurities, the whys.

Why is it that my little family of Will and our three children can be so enriched by the craft of wine, but for my brother and his son and the multitudes of alcoholics in the world, a single glass of cabernet sauvignon might lead them to death? It is so unbelievably unfair.

I must try to be more empathetic; we all must try to understand that addicts do not choose to drink. They are not weak or malicious, irresponsible or crazy. It is the disease of alcoholism or drug addiction that forces them to make the poor decision to drink or use, a decision that for them will most assuredly have negative ramifications.

During the first few weeks after Bobby's arrival, we didn't know he had an alcohol problem—until the session with Jeff. Our bar stayed open and stocked and wine was poured freely at dinner. A few months later Jeff told us Bobby struggled with abstaining from alcohol and that to assure his full recovery from drug addiction, he should never drink again.

It was earth-shattering to hear Jeff say this. Seriously, I wondered if Will and I might have a problem with alcohol when I considered the strong resistance I had to Jeff's suggestion of an alcohol-free home.

No more wine with dinner?! No more cocktail hour or late afternoon mojito?! My hands started to shake at this notion. Could I do it? Could we do it? Houston, do we have a problem?

We knew we had to change and we did. We put away the alcohol, quit drinking anywhere around the house and around Bobby for what seemed like an interminable time.

At a much later session with Jeff, Bobby confessed that he felt very guilty that we had changed our lifestyle for him and asked if we would please not do this, to drink freely as we should choose.

Did I feel a flood of relief when he said this? Did I miss alcohol so much that Bobby's well-being was secondary? Did I have a problem?

No, no, and no. Sure I missed the feel of an aged bordeaux as it tantalized my taste buds, the slight heat in my cheeks after a few glasses. I missed the way my muscles relaxed and how I could sink into the furniture on the terrace and pretend I didn't have a care in the world. I missed the easy laughter that comes with a few glasses of vino or a vodka and soda, and the sharing of these feelings with close friends.

But I did not hesitate to tell Bobby that we would not be putting the bar back and that if we drank at all, we would not flaunt it. The occasional drink, whether it was a glass of champagne or a Heineken, went into a red plastic cup and was kept far away from him.

It took awhile for Will to get the swing of the red plastic cup, but he begrudgingly complied, caring for Bobby as he did. So did all of our friends. It was a compromise we could all live with. Bobby didn't want us to change our lifestyle and we were concerned for his health, so a little bit of discretion worked for us.

Heck, by using plastic cups, I never even had to do the dishes.

From: Renée Hodges
Subject: Please advise
Date: Wednesday, May 22, 2013, at 10:46 p.m.
To: Jeff Georgi

I received this email from my brother in response to an email I sent to Jill last week asking about tuition for automotive school. Please advise on all accounts. Thanks for all you do.

Begin forwarded message:

From: John Redford
Subject: Bobby
Date: Wednesday, May 22, 2013, at 9:41 p.m.
To: Renée

Hey there, I have a call in for Bobby's counselor, Jeff G., about his take on Bobby's wanting to go to school. I am of the opinion that Bobby needs to stick to the original plan of getting a job. If you remember our previous conversations about his wanting to do too much too early, and then not finding that it works for him, he may use failure as an excuse to be unhappy enough to use again. I call it setting himself up for failure. I think Bobby should not be trusted to make prudent decisions for himself until he is deemed able by his doctors and counselors.

You requested a guide for Bobby's working through his first year and suggestions as to what he needs.

Maybe this will help:

*We can and will only be responsible for Bobby's needs if he is doing what he's supposed to be doing to take care of himself, or at least learning how to take care of himself. He and we will now and always work toward his independence financially.

*He should have exhausted all means available to him for financial help before he turns to us. For example, applying for disability, state or federal financial aid, school loans, or the sale of assets. He should have as big or bigger stake in his future than we do.

*He should be close to carrying a full-time job. If he cannot because his support group is against it, he needs to have one lined up for the day they authorize him. At least he'll have that to look forward to.

*We will only give supplement if he is working and has no way to make ends meet and can prove that.

*We will only support him if he is working with his support group in Durham as scheduled and working some sort of spiritual program.

*We will continue to support him only when he completes at least a year's worth of stable work history and he decides he wants to better himself or go to school part-time. We will not gamble money on what he feels he needs, only what is recommended by his support group with that backed up.

*We will always cover Aunt Renée's expenses and anything she or the support group has deemed necessary . . .

God puts people in lives for reasons that are beyond our understanding . . . I feel he works through others . . . All of Bobby's needs, wants, and dreams will come to him as opportunities and must be worked for. When he becomes healthy enough, he will recognize them, and he will begin his recovery and journey with God.

All my love to you, Renée, and my only son.

John

———

From: Will
Date: Thursday, May 23, 2013, at 10:34 a.m.
To: Jeff Georgi
Subject: Bobby R

Jeff:

John's analysis of Bobby's "failure cycle" is compelling and one I have glimpsed in our interaction with Bobby at home. He still has not shown the desire I would expect to get a job or research automobile mechanics careers.

Last night he went to a welding class at Durham Tech. When he returned, he had a "bad stomach." I don't know if his stomach problems are physical or emotional (i.e., anxiety . . .). It is a repeated ailment, and it worries me that he may be "paralyzed or sickened" by some insecurity or anxiety—especially when there is pressure or expectation. That said, can we expect him to do well in a classroom setting learning automobile mechanics? Could we, as John says, be setting him up to fail?

I want desperately for Bobby to transition to living safely and happily on his own and understand you are working on an exit strategy. I am equally concerned with the downside. Through all of John's musing, this rings truest to me.

Should we continue to push Bobby to pursue mechanics school or should we pull back? Are there other issues we should address? I need a clear line between what you and Bobby are doing and what we, as his supporters, should be doing. Both Renée and I are pushy and well intentioned. I just want to make sure our intentions are compatible with your goals and what he can handle.

Thanks, Will

———

From: Renée Hodges
Subject: Slowly unraveling
Date: Thursday, May 23, 2013, at 10:25 a.m.
To: Mary Costello

Hey Mary,

Things are slowly unraveling, thread by thread. Bobby has become withdrawn and unengaged. Will, Bobby, and I met with Jeff Georgi Tuesday. Jeff tried to explain/define shame and how Bobby is viewing the world. I simply have to get a grasp. I am so afraid of doing the wrong thing with Bobby, and I am letting his success/ failure become my own. Damn, damn, I have a jumpiness and on-edge feeling I can't shake.

Renée

———

REACHING OUT AND COMMUNICATING

On May 23, 2013, at 11:19 a.m., Renée Hodges wrote the this text to Bobby:

Hi Bobby,

Did I ever get your birth certificate and important papers back for the safe after you got your driver's license? If not, I would like to know they are safe and sound, so if you could please give them to me today sometime. Thanks and have a great day!!!

Love, Aunt Née

From a text from Bobby to Renée:

I will bring them to you today. I love you too. Sorry I'm being distant. I'm just having a tough week and it's easier for me to not engage so I don't have to worry about saying something I will regret.

From a text from Renée to Bobby:

Bobby, I am trying to understand and I thank you for letting me know. Just communicating like that helps me immensely because I sometimes don't know if it is something I have done. So, I really appreciate the communication.

When you are able, we need to sit down and reevaluate everything based on where you are now.

And, just pointing out, when you were busy and had set goals the first two months, you were happier than you are now!

Love, Aunt Née

PART TWO

Condensed History of Heroin

Approximately a hundred years ago, in 1898, heroin was first marketed as safe and a wonder drug by Bayer Co., Ltd. It was widely prescribed to everyone including children until Bayer stopped making it in 1913. Around the 1920s heroin was pulled from the market because of its highly addictive nature. This is why the majority of people understand the dangers of heroin. Today, OxyContin, Percocet, and others are some of the frequently prescribed opioids used to treat pain. Both are narcotics containing the active ingredient oxycodone. The molecular structures of heroin and oxycodone are almost identical. Prescription opioid narcotics come from the same place heroin does—the opium poppy. This is the primary reason we are seeing an epidemic of death and addiction caused by prescription opioids, far surpassing those of illicit drugs.

—Excerpt from ARPO Advocates for the Reform of Prescription Opioids (Rxreform.org, http://www.rxreform.org/prescription-opioids/similarities-to-heroin/)

TWO MONTHS TWENTY-EIGHT DAYS

Friday, May 31

SHRIMP BOIL

It was a beautiful day, cloudless with a cool breeze to keep away the insects. Perfect for a good ole Louisiana shrimp boil. My husband and I, along with close friends, have held a shrimp boil annually for nearly fifteen years. For the last few years we have honored our high school seniors as they graduated and headed off into the world. In 2013, sadly—or happily?—we were all empty nesters and had no one to celebrate but ourselves.

Everyone who would be invited to this party cared about Will and me, and I believe they now also cared about Bobby. He had been with us for nearly twelve weeks, and most of the friends attending this party had at one time or another offered odd jobs to him, given him leads or advice on schools and work, or had sent me encouraging emails and offered prayers. Several had reached out to Bobby with lunch invitations, introduced him to their adult children, or included him when they invited Will and me to dinner.

For nearly three months Will and I had laid low socially, as we were worried about exposing Bobby to an environment where alcohol would be readily present. For the first time I grappled with the question of whether to cancel this annual, much-loved celebration. I gnawed on how I might have the boil and keep him safe at the same time. In my mind, he had made huge progress, starting to open up emotionally to his counselor, Jeff Georgi, finding a routine, taking a welding class, beginning to structure himself and be accountable with money. The last week though had worried me as he had backslid, once again becoming moody, feeling poorly, and being non-communicative. I would eventually learn that this is normal and there are many ups and downs during recovery, both for the addict and their family.

A week prior to the shrimp boil, we sat down and talked.

"After talking with Jeff, Will and I have decided to have our annual shrimp boil. If you want to come and help Uncle Will, we would love to have you, as you are such a good cook. But you need to know that there will be beer and wine available. If you are uncomfortable at all or feel like it won't be a safe place, I need to know and we can find some fun alternative plans for you."

I could see that the thought of digging into some zippy Louisiana cuisine excited him. I think he even did a little dance move as he told me, "I would like to help Uncle Will cook. I have been missing Louisiana food. I'll be fine."

Done. The tightness in my shoulder blades released. For a second there I was trying to get them to touch. I assured myself that this would be the perfect place for Bobby to begin socializing, safe here at home with people he knew and people who cared about him, eating Cajun cuisine.

I was excited about the party and his enthusiasm for it. I also hoped that having something to look forward to might help pull him out of the depression he had on and off for the last few weeks. When he was down, he seemed to have more physical problems. I confess I ignored my sixth sense that whispered to me that I was taking some chances by inviting him to participate, like he was already healthy and capable of integrating back into society. After all, there had been several weeks of warning signs.

I did take a few precautions. I requested of each friend

that they not drink the alcohol of their choice out of a bottle or clear glass but instead pour it into a red plastic cup and ditch the evidence. Nothing visible that might identify whether Coors or Coke. I told them to be cautious with their cups, to keep track and refrain from setting them down half-full.

I also explained that I had talked with Bobby and Jeff Georgi and they were fine with us drinking, but that I wanted to be courteous by not flaunting it.

I love my friends. No one batted an eye, and I silently patted myself on the back as much for having such good friends as for having the cup idea. Allowing others to support Bobby and us would be truly instrumental in his success—and for keeping my emotional sanity.

Will played a big part in my decision to go ahead with the party. This is the party where Will is a superstar, center of his own little universe of pots brimming with boiling water and pungent Zatarain's Crab Boil, steam so strongly seasoned that whoever wanders too close to the chef finds their eyes watering.

Ice chests of shrimp are on standby, pounds and pounds of headless delicacy waiting to be pitched into the bath at the precise moment. Sweet shucked corn broken in half, new potatoes firmly cut to half-inch pieces, extra-large heads of garlic sliced right through the middle, and, my favorite, bunches of tender, tantalizing green asparagus, all just waiting in line for their time in the boil. This mixture is boiled until it has married with the Cajun spices Will has concocted like a mad chemist in his gurgling vat. At the exact right time, the dinner mosaic is pulled from the pots and drained by supersized strainers. It takes several men to hoist the strainer up and carry it to the eight-foot round table.

The table is laid with heavy-duty black garbage bags taped to the undersides then covered with several weeks' worth of old newspapers to sop up the excess liquid. On three, the entire contents of the strainer are dumped into the center of the table.

"Shrimp!" Will always announces with a wide, energized smile. And our guests are drawn to the round table to stand, peel, and eat, like farm animals to troughs, chowing down until the sun starts to drop below the tree line and appetites are sated, jovial conversation flowing across the piping mound. Every year, it is a magical party. But not this year.

Boom. The first landmine went off after dinner. The women had segregated themselves under the canopy to rest and digest when Bobby walked up, animated and energetic, and began to engage the group in conversation.

Spontaneously and very loudly he began to sing a strip-tease melody, while suggestively turning into a Chippendale on the spot. This should have been my first clue something was off. What little I remember of Bobby as a teenager, I recall he was always this funny, and I was psyched that he was using his comedic gifts tonight. He removed his shirt and suggestively rotated it like a helicopter above his head while his other hand perched on the opposite hip. The ladies howled with laughter, a few surprised snorts mixed in as drinks went up noses. I was laughing as hard as anyone, slapping at my leg as he feigned undoing his front button on his shorts. His eyes shone brightly and he had the hugest grin on his face. I could tell he was having so much fun. Thankfully, he stopped at the top button and zipper, to sighs of disappointment that the moment had passed. He was gone as fast as he arrived, with a wave of the hand.

Okay, yes, I should have recognized that Bobby was not acting in the sullen, depressed way that had been the norm since his arrival, especially the last week, and that a striptease was a little out of the ordinary for anyone attending his aunt and uncle's shrimp boil. But please. Sometimes I need a sledgehammer.

Half an hour later, I saw Peter Herbert and Anne conversing with Bobby. I was relaxed and comfortable as the sun dropped quickly and the coolness of the evening was weighing down my eyelids.

As I watched them talking, I noticed their body language first. Peter's back was straight and he was leaning into Bobby's face, scrutinizing it through the shadows of twilight. Anne was frantically looking around the yard.

It hit me: full on, the Enola Gay, blindsided.

I catapulted out of my chair and covered half the distance to them before my feet hit the ground. Anne saw movement and her eyes locked on mine. Damn it. Damn it. She didn't have to say a thing but she did. "Something's not right, Renée. Something's not right with Bobby."

I gave Anne a half smile, something between a grimace and a failed don't worry look, patting her on the back as I bounded to Peter and Bobby. I couldn't see Bobby's face, but I saw Peter's. I was crestfallen. I was in disbelief. Surely there was some mistake. Peter looked at me and shook his head from side to side as if to say, "Sorry, but it's true."

Bobby was on something.

He must have seen Peter's signal to me because he broke off and started quickly toward the back door, thinking he would find sanctuary if he made it inside before I could reach him.

Hurtling over to him, I placed my hand on his shoulder, and I ever so slowly turned him around, prolonging the moment for as long as I could.

At six foot three Bobby is close to nine inches taller than me. Even with his head hung, I could tell. Bobby was high.

The creep of bad news spread ever so slowly through the party like spilled molasses, sinking into every crack and crevice; no one wanting to spread it, but leaving no one untouched. The raucous noise of our friends laughing and eating together ebbed under the weight of this new development.

Will appeared by my side. He put his arm around me and asked me to tell him what was going on. His face was stern, lips tight.

"Go take care of the party," I instructed him gently. "I'll find out and let you know."

So as not to make a scene, I took Bobby by the elbow and marched him into the house.

"I want to go to my room," he demanded, slow and slurred, his strength propelling him toward the back stairs even as I tried to hold him back.

"You are not going to your room. Sit right here." I motioned to the stairs that were in front of us.

He sat compliantly, but dejectedly.

"What are you using? What have you taken?" He told me nothing, playing with an imaginary piece of lint on his shorts.

"What is in your pockets?"

"Nothing."

"Pull them inside out."

He hesitated.

"Now!" I was emphatic. I was even a little afraid of me.

He was truthful. There was nothing in his pockets.

"Tell me. Tell me what you are using."

"I took some Xanax. The doctor gave me a prescription for Xanax this morning for anxiety and I took a few." He got it out, but his mumbling and slurring and his fear were making it hard for me to understand his words.

"Xanax? Xanax is a benzo. No doctor in his right mind

would give you Xanax. Are you telling me the truth? What else are you on? Tell. Me. Right. Now."

Behind me I could hear friends in the kitchen, clearing dishes and cleaning up from the party. Their sad faces pierced me, eyes darting over to catch glimpses of us. They were all out there feeling sorry for me, sorry for Bobby. Damn it. I began to well up, tears on the brink of an uprising. Bobby was slouched over with his head leaning against the wall under the cherry banister.

"Get up. Show me this bottle of Xanax."

Once in his bedroom Bobby began searching for the prescription bottle, but I could tell it was a superficial search. Thrusting his hand in a sock drawer, looking under the bathroom sink. Shaking out the duvet covers, as if the bottle might be stuck in the feathers.

All the while I was talking, demanding answers.

"I was having some anxiety about the shrimp boil, and Dr. Smith gave me Xanax to help me. I filled it this afternoon."

Okay. That makes sense, you stupid doctor, I thought angrily. *Prescription meds were the beginning of his problems.*

"Bobby, how many did you take? I need to know. Please." It was the pleading "please" that was persuasive.

"Maybe four or six. A handful. And then I drank some old wine I found in the bar."

Shocked. Stunned. I grabbed his chin and turned his face so he had to look me in the eyes and blurted out, "Bobby. Why don't you just put a gun to your head? Wouldn't it be easier and faster?"

I hit Jeff Georgi's number on my speed dial, looking at my watch and praying Jeff would pick up.

When he did, the words tumbled out of my mouth, as I told him everything.

Jeff clarified the situation for me. Xanax and alcohol together can be extremely deadly as they depress the respiratory system. He instructed us to find out the quantities of both pills and alcohol Bobby had consumed and possibly take him to the emergency room. And, comfortingly, he told me to keep in touch, understanding that tonight was a step backward. Hell, it was a quantum leap.

When I told Bobby what Jeff Georgi had said on the phone, he refused to listen.

"Bobby, this is not a game. This is serious and I am scared. Jeff says six or seven Xanax could kill an elephant, especially when taken with too much alcohol. We need to go to the emergency room right now."

"I'm not going." Bobby gave up pretending to look for the prescription bottle and crawled under his covers.

"How much alcohol did you drink? Tell me truthfully."

"Hardly any. I couldn't find any in the bar except an old bottle of wine. It had gone bad." Phew. This was good news.

I headed back down the stairs to find Will alone in the kitchen putting the last of the utensils in drawers. The party was over and cleaned away just like it never happened. It seemed a lifetime ago.

I quickly brought Will up to date. "We need to find that Xanax bottle to see how many pills he took," he said. "Did you try his truck?"

When we did, there wasn't much in his truck other than some fast-food trash and a secret stash of Mountain Dew—that little cheat.

"Renée, we can't take him to the emergency room if he won't cooperate. Let's have him sleep in the daybed where we can watch over him. If he seems in distress, we'll call the paramedics."

Together we went up to his room to roust the elephant out of his slumber.

"No emergency room for you just yet, Bobby, but you have to sleep downstairs where I can keep an eye on you. That is the deal. Take it or leave it."

Will held on to him all the way down the stairs as I ran ahead to pull the sheets down. The daybed is in the master bedroom. It is the bed that every one of my kids has slept in when they were growing up. Fever? Daybed. Tonsillectomy? Daybed. Nightmare? Daybed. Possible overdose? Daybed.

As soon as Bobby was tucked in, I flew up the stairs to his room and began systematically rummaging through it, privacy be damned. I was going to find that pill bottle or I was going to find something else. Unfortunately, I found nothing.

Wearily, I set my alarm clock for every thirty minutes so that I could check on his breathing to be sure he was not in any distress. Long minutes passed before I began to doze and I popped up at the sound of the alarm. It was a pattern throughout the night: doze, alarm, breathe. By six o'clock in the morning I turned the alarm clock off for good, as he was sleeping soundly and breathing regularly. I was asleep before you could say "exhausted."

It was about nine o'clock in the morning when I rolled over and realized last night wasn't just a nightmare. The daybed was empty, cover rumpled. Bobby had woken and left the bedroom.

I put on my robe and headed out to the kitchen, calling his name. No response. I called again. I hesitantly climbed the stairs. My mind was still half-asleep.

I asked myself what had happened last night, trying to sort through the jumble of thoughts. I'd believed Bobby and I were making some progress.

Then the guilty feelings came: What could I have done better? Did socializing at the shrimp boil set him off? Was I going too far and too fast with him when he wasn't ready? His door was ajar and he was standing at his bedside, back to me, dressed in athletic shorts and a T-shirt.

"Bobby." I knocked and slowly pushed the door open. I was struck in the stomach when I saw he had pulled out his gym bag and was stuffing what little he owned into it. The sound of the zipper closing ripped me.

He turned around, looked at me, and declared with a blank face, "I can't stay here anymore."

"What? We need to sit down and discuss this, discuss what happened last night. Put your bag down and let's go get some coffee."

"I can't stay, Aunt Née. I can't stay here anymore. I broke one of the golden rules. I have to leave now."

It slowly dawned on me what he was saying. I pleaded with him to stay so that we could figure out what set him off and how to learn from this situation. My words were left behind in his bedroom; he was already halfway down the stairs, bag thrown over his shoulder.

"Where are you going? Bobby, you have no other place to go. Let's talk. Come on, come to the kitchen," I cajoled him. I said all this very calmly. No way would he leave right now, right at this very moment. But I was getting no response from him, and I was talking to his backside all the way out to the garage.

"Bobby, please. I don't understand. Please don't go. Please don't go. I love you. We all make mistakes. Let's talk about it so I can help you."

He swung his gym bag, this time into the back of his truck. Was it only twelve weeks ago he'd arrived? I didn't want to beg, but I did. I was searching for something that would slow him down enough that I could get a grasp of the situation. He was slipping away from me.

"I'm sorry, Aunt Née. A rule is a rule and I broke it, and I promised I would leave if I ever broke the golden rules. I love you." Eyes downcast. He hugged me. I held him tightly and he gently broke free. "Thank you, Aunt Née, for everything you did for me."

As he pulled out of the driveway, I instinctively grabbed my phone out of my robe pocket and started taking pictures of his truck. He rounded the corner and I zeroed in on his license plate. *Click, click, click,* until his bumper was gone from my view.

Like a patient in shock, I walked back into the house. For someone who always has a game plan and contingencies, in that moment, I was clueless. I walked into the kitchen and there, against the hard cold black of the marble countertop, sat a solo Duke Blue Devil key. I did not plan for this.

————

LOST

I was fatigued to my pinky toes. Getting ready for a party is tiring to begin with, but the emotional swings and waking every half hour for Bobby's respiratory checks had taken their toll. I was weepy, wiping tears I didn't even realize I was shedding. Will was wonderful and he didn't push me to talk, instinctively realizing I couldn't put two words together without a meltdown.

The house and yard were immaculate, since my close friends stayed late to make sure I had no extra work on my hands this morning. I almost wished I had some dishes to wash.

I looked to Jeff for some miracle solution, and I was crushed when he told me that Bobby had always been high risk and that the longer he stayed away, the lesser the odds he would make it. He called Bobby's cell phone and left a message, hoping to talk him down from the ledge.

It was a beautiful day and I was bewildered by the gloriousness of the first day of June. I paced outside on the terrace, sunshine on my face. It was a cloudless day with a slight breeze and the multicolored flowers that were planted in the garden seemed to be fragrantly taunting me. I was gripping my cell, checking over and over to be sure the ringer was up and on.

I called Bobby's mom and condensed the situation, not wanting to alarm her until, if and when, I needed to alarm her. There wasn't much for her to do from Louisiana, but I did ask her to call him and urge him to come back.

Since it was Saturday and not a workday, I texted my therapist, Mary Costello.

Text from Renée to Mary Costello:

Mary, Just thought you'd want to know that Bobby ran away this morning. He took some Xanax and drank some alcohol last night. He left his key.

My phone rang instantly, making me jump. "Hey, Renée," Mary said, and, damn it, the unspoken sadness in her voice put me over the edge.

I broke down, a good wailing, snorting, nose-running cry, weeks of tension released in a few minutes. I knew Mary was talking to me the whole time, but I couldn't register anything except my own heartache.

"Mary, I told him to just put a gun to his head and pull the trigger. I told him it would be easier for him, for all of us." There it was, my confessional. I felt I might have put the bullet in his gun, and I was wracked with grief and guilt. "I'll never be able to live with myself if he takes his life, Mary. What have I done?"

Mary said the most remarkable thing. She told me that sometimes putting our deepest fears into words actually had the opposite effect and that Bobby would be thinking about this and hopefully see the effect of his actions. Was this psychobabble or did she really believe it? I didn't know, but after discussing with Mary, I dried my tears to a sniffle and turned my thoughts toward doing something productive to find Bobby. I began by sending an email.

From: Renée Hodges
Subject: update on Bobby from last night
Date: Saturday, June 1, 2013, at 3:43 p.m.
To: Close Friends

Dear Close Friends,

Something set Bobby off last night (we have some ideas), and he took four to six Xanax and drank some alcohol on top of his regular meds, enough minimally to possibly take down an elephant and, maximally, to cause respiratory failure. I assure you that before last night Bobby has been clean and in my estimation, on a wonderful, upward trajectory.

Sadly, this morning Bobby packed and left in his truck, leaving behind anything positive, i.e., his school notebook, his computer, and his Duke notebook. He's had no contact at all for the morning hours even with repeated texts, calls, and emails from me, his counselor Jeff, and Reverend David Bowen.

I sent him a text around 1:30 p.m. pleading with him to come home and not to throw out the progress he has made. We have had no communication.

I have always known Bobby is "high risk." I am hoping for the best and not thinking about the worst. I will let you know when I know something. I am not giving up on him just yet!

And, lastly, I was so glad that it was YOU here last night because I felt like I could do what I needed to do and not worry about you nor worry about what you would think. That is a wonderful feeling, my friends!

Love, Renée

———

From: Renée Hodges
Subject: update on Bobby
Date: Saturday, June 1, 2013, at 7:23 p.m.
To: Close Friends

Dear Friends,

I wanted you all to know that Bobby has made contact by text. He wrote that he is "fine and not to worry." We still don't know where he is or what he is going to do. He said he was not coming back here, but I am trying hard to keep a dialogue open. I will let you know if things should change.

And thanks for calls, emails, prayers. Needed and appreciated.

Love, Renée

———

From: Libby Reaves
Subject: update
Date: Saturday, June 1, 2013, at 10:05 p.m.
To: Renée Hodges

Bobby is so fortunate to have family like you in his life & that is exactly what I was thinking last night. I would have not wanted to be anywhere else but at the shrimp boil. I will pray that he realizes this. I know you will do whatever you can for him if he will let you. In the meantime, remember to take care of yourselves. Your friends are here for you through thick and thin!

oo & xx, L

———

From: Renée Hodges
Subject: Struggling
Date: Sunday, June 2, 2013, at 6:12 p.m.
To: Mary Costello

Mary,

I feel like I am suffocating. My mind is playing tricks on me. I will stop and cover my face and moan loudly and not even know I am doing it. I don't know what comes over me.

I tried to play some tennis . . . ha . . . the next thing I knew I was hanging on the back fence like I had completed a triathlon, bent over with one hand on the fence, the other arm over my eye and hyperventilating. I thought my tennis people were going to call an ambulance.

Sometimes I am talking to someone but don't know what I'm saying and I have no idea what they have said. Totally disconnected. Is this what a breakdown looks like? Get out the straitjacket, Renée has gone looney?

I haven't had any communication with Bobby since he texted yesterday. I have begged him to let me know if he is okay. I texted Jeff Georgi, his counselor, earlier and asked if he has had contact and haven't heard back from him—so my paranoid brain thinks that Bobby may have pulled our privacy agreement. I told someone today that I feel like I'm on a suicide watch but not able to intervene to stop it. I can't take his shoelaces or belt. I'm not sleeping, can't let my mind relax. I can't think about it. I can't. I just can't. I can't let myself go there.

THE SEARCH

I made a list of anyone who might be geographically close enough to provide a bed or couch for Bobby if he passed through, anyone at all. Did he have a cousin on his mother's side? Did he have a Match.com friend he might still keep in contact with? After twelve weeks, I could only come up with two substantial relationships in our vicinity, the Reverend Bowen and an AA sponsor who was very sick.

I called Reverend Bowen, the minister Bobby had developed a relationship with over the past three months. Upon hearing about him, Reverend Bowen asked me to pray with him. I closed my eyes and listened to our mutual plea to Jesus to keep Bobby safe and bring him back. I'm such a terrible out-loud pray-er that this was very welcome. Reverend Bowen called Bobby's cell and left another message urging him to make contact. He left multiple messages in the next four days, sharing his Jesus-like love and tenacity.

Not for the first time I was overwhelmed with gratitude that, as horrible as Bobby's absence was, I didn't have to face it alone. Will was hovering even more than usual, gently rubbing my back or kissing my cheek each time he passed by me in the kitchen, where I stood at the window blankly gazing out at nothingness. My friends emailed, called, searched, texted. Reverend Bowen and Jeff Georgi kept Bobby's message box filled with kind words and support. Dinner was delivered for the first few nights, and I maudlinly thought about the similarities between this situation and a funeral.

I texted Bobby, thinking that he could ignore voicemail but he would have to see the texts. I reinforced how much I love him, how we all make mistakes and he wasn't the only one to err on Friday. The golden rule had been a mistake of mine; it was wrong to hold him to those absolute standards so soon after he came to stay. I explained that there are always extenuating circumstances, and even though it seemed black and white, this event definitely was not. I asked him to please come home for at least an hour so that I could explain myself. To come home for me, not for him. To give me a chance. I was begging. I knew it. I didn't care. I was afraid.

I was distraught by his absence, furious at myself for the no-strike policy. Everything had been going so well, for the most part. I'd convinced myself that he would truly make it. But now that he was gone and there was only silence, I realized for the first time how much his parents must have suffered over the years. I did not know if he was using or not. I did not know if I would ever see him again. I had to keep reminding myself to breathe.

Will and I asked Jeff if we should call the police to help find Bobby's truck, since I had his license plate number and a picture. Jeff discouraged us from doing this until we had more evidence that Bobby might hurt himself, reminding us that he was a grown man and not considered a runaway. Time stretched on interminably.

Katherine, my youngest child, had heard about what happened. Because it was a Saturday, she'd hopped in her car, drove the three and a half hours from her college, and arrived after lunch. Katherine is not an overly sentimental or empathetic child, so this concrete action of hers meant so much to me.

For the next two days Katherine secretly left the house and would drive all over town searching for Bobby's truck, traveling from parks to rescue missions, low-budget hotels and parking lots. I was overwhelmed with love when she told me about her jaunts to find her cousin. She had searched high and low and exhausted almost all the options we could think of where he might have gone. But she still had one more idea: she knew Bobby liked to race his cars at parks, and asked me if he had a particular favorite.

We dashed to the car and rushed to a park on the other side of town, unfamiliar to me. It was dusk and eerily lonely. We checked the multiple parking lots; we spoke with the few people we came in contact with, but we found no sign of Bobby or the truck. We got home frustrated and out of time; Katherine had to get back to school.

There is a country-western song I like whose chorus talks about how you "find out who your friends are." When you were most in need, when your circumstances just stunk, that is when your friends would come running.

These lyrics were never so true for me as when Bobby ran away. I was stuck in a ditch in the middle of nowhere, and every last one of my friends cranked up their car to be there for me. Most sent a beautiful email or text, or made a phone call to offer support, and to let me know that they too were saddened by Bobby's choices. They offered us help in any way we might need.

Our friends' emails were uplifting and loving, but it was their love and concern for Bobby that struck me so powerfully. These weren't polite thank-you emails so we could gloss over an unpleasant incident at the next cocktail party. These were deeply caring messages of support, heavy with genuine concern for what might now happen to Bobby, sadness about the fact that he might have given up; we were all so sure Bobby was going to make it. The knowledge that so many in my neighborhood cared kept me positive.

It is hard to put into words just how a little text now and then kept me safe from my own imagination. Each one was a small assurance that things would be all right. Promises that my people would not abandon me. An affirmation that each of them would hit the gas, get there fast, and never stop to think.

For the days that Bobby was AWOL, I was a walking zombie. I tried to go about business as usual, but I was wound up tighter than a Red Sox pitcher one moment, in the fetal position in bed the next.

Several of my tennis friends suggested we play tennis on Monday to take my mind off my problems, and I jumped at the chance. I zoomed to the tennis courts, played several hours of horrible tennis, and dejectedly walked up the hill to my car.

Holy shit! I couldn't believe it. There, sitting in the parking lot, was my minivan, engine purring like a contented kitten. I had forgotten to turn off the ignition.

And that was just how I went about those few days, with my engine running and no one at the wheel.

From: Renée Hodges
Subject: update to self
Date: Monday, June 3, 2013, at 5:02 p.m.
To: self

Dear me,

Look at what has kept me going all these years, my confidence that I was so right and had all the answers. But there are no answers with addiction. Yes, there are paths, but we are really quite helpless when it comes down to truly helping the diseased. Right now I can't even help myself. I am wallowing in something and can't put a name to it. It's like I'm diseased also. I can't help myself. I can't stop my brain from the thought that I can't help Bobby, that I couldn't help Thomas, that I couldn't help others in the family.

Save me! Give me some peace please.

———

FOUND

Tuesday, June 4

After four of the longest days of my life, wrought with angst, worry, and so much guilt, he called. When the phone rang and his name flashed on the display, I jumped and fumbled to push the answer button.

"Bobby?" A rush of blood to my head made me feel faint, a swoon so strong I had to put my hand on the wall to steady myself.

"Hi, Aunt Née." Curt. "Can I come by and talk to you for a minute?"

That was it. Short, sweet, and to the point.

"Yes, please. Come on. I'll be here waiting. Come home." I nearly fell to my knees with relief.

Time stood still while I paced, scenario after scenario going through my head. I had no idea in what state I would find him, where he had been for the last four days, and, most importantly, what he had been doing. After four days on the run, would he have given up all the progress he had achieved? Was he using again? Would he come back to us? Would we take him back? I was afraid, afraid of the unknown. I knew in my heart that he was running out of options, chances, money, and sympathy. Could I muster the energy to begin again? I was exhausted, barely able to think.

Will was not home when Bobby's truck rumbled up the driveway. And I couldn't reach him on his cell phone, so I was flying solo.

I raced outside to the garage, arriving as Bobby was opening his door. It was awkward. My impulse was to throw my arms around him and . . . and . . . wring his neck. I hesitated and the hug/kill moment passed.

I observed that he did not get his duffel bag from the truck; it was plainly sitting on the rear seat. He purposefully headed into the house, stopping only to ask me where we should go to talk.

We settled in the library, a serene wood-paneled room, the scent of ink and paper bringing a calm atmosphere—diametrically opposed to the way I was feeling. I sat on the brown leather love seat, and Bobby took a seat across from me in an upholstered side chair. He fidgeted and procrastinated. I began, understanding that this was going to be a difficult talk.

"I am so glad you called. I have been sick with worry about you."

Emotions crossed his face that were inscrutable to me. He tried to begin but changed tacks until finally he apologized. A deep, heart-wrenching sincere apology. He didn't want to hurt us. He didn't want to worry us.

I told him that I knew he didn't mean to worry us but that we would always worry about him because that is part of loving someone. I know he must have worried about how we were coping too. I thanked him for the text he sent early on telling me he was fine, the only text he sent. Even though I was in the dark, that single text kept me from falling apart.

"Aunt Née, I needed time to think." He paused, unsure how to proceed.

"I needed time to think as well. I want you to know that I made a huge mistake, and I want to talk about it before you say anything else. In the beginning, I made some rules that had a no-strike policy. One of them said if you used, you were out. I was wrong." My voice started cracking here, popcorn kernels stuck in the throat. "I was wrong when I drew a line in the sand. Listen to what I am saying. I made a mistake. You had extenuating circumstances, and I should have known that nothing is ever black and white. Nothing."

By the look on Bobby's face I knew he was confused, but I cut him off before he started to speak. "No, let me finish. For four days now I have had time to reflect. First of all, you were given a prescription for Xanax by a respected doctor, albeit a nitwit, but respected. You will have to figure out why your anxiety was so high that you felt you could take more than the prescribed amount. That is where you went wrong. What you did after taking the Xanax is something I want to believe you did because you were out of your mind."

I had a flashback to the first week Bobby arrived. His eyes were downcast, shoulders slumped forward, body language heavy with turmoil. I heard his emotional struggle when he said, "Aunt Née, I am so tired of being a failure. I don't want to be a failure anymore."

I winced at his admission, then and even now as I replay it in my mind's eye. If he had looked up, he would have seen that I was held together by a thread. He would also have seen someone who loves him, warts and all, who understands that life is so damned difficult, so full of pain and yes, so full of choices. God, give me strength and put the words in my mouth that will help this gentle young man.

"You are not a failure. You are twelve weeks of hard-fought, bloody, nail-ripping success. Yes, you made a mistake, but it is only a problem if you don't learn from it. If you can't look back on this experience and say to yourself 'I will never abuse drugs again, prescription or illegal, and I will not drink either,' you will not have learned anything and that would be the mistake. And I think you need to go a step further . . . I think you must find out why you did so in the first place. Why you felt you needed to take more than the prescribed amount of Xanax. Once you do this, then this experience is no longer a mistake. It will be a valuable lesson. For heaven's sake, the best way to learn a lesson is when you make a mistake. We are human. And I'm sorry to break this to you, but this will not be your last mistake either. You will make many, but learn to turn them into something positive. Evaluate each and every one and learn from them." I got down off my soapbox.

He sat quietly for a second and then softly confessed that the worst part of messing up was that he'd embarrassed Will and me in front of our friends.

I adamantly dissuaded him of this false belief. I told him that was untrue. He had not embarrassed us. Our friends had been the ones most worried about him because they loved him as they loved us. I promised him that I would share my friends until he had some friends his own age, assuring him that my friends would be there for him the rest of his life.

These were strong statements and I couldn't predict the future, but I deeply believed in the innate goodness and kindness of my close friends. Throughout this journey, they did not prove me wrong.

"Aunt Née, I promise you I did not use while I was gone. I wanted so badly to buy some beer and sit and drink it in my truck the morning I left, but I didn't."

"What did you do? Where have you been?"

"The Salvation Army. And I have been thinking this whole time."

We had searched the city for him, going from park to park, motels and hotels, rescue missions, and homeless shelters. How did we miss the Salvation Army?

Damn.

Then I asked him what made him return to us.

He described reading his text messages and listening to voicemails when he turned on his phone. He thought they would be critical, judging him as harshly as he judged himself. But instead they were loving. Caring. Urging him to come home, proclaiming their love and hope over and over. Even his father called and urged him not to give up. Bobby knew that coming back was his only chance to stay sober. He did not want to give up; he did not want to fail.

From: Renée Hodges
Subject: update to self
Date: Tuesday, June 4, 2013, at 9:05 p.m.
To: self

Dear me,

Bobby returned today. I feel like I barely crawled across the finish line of the Boston Marathon . . . but I am so ecstatic that I made it. I am also so very humbled.

THREE MONTHS

June

SUMMER BEGINS

The week after Bobby returned, I was fragile and weary but determined not to give up. The knowledge that he had not used alcohol or drugs while he was away was the fuel that kept me going.

I reasoned that it must have been difficult for him to inhabit that emotional state when he realized that by leaving his house key on the kitchen table he no longer had a warm bed, three meals, or a place of love and safety. By walking out, he had given up his home.

With one decision to misuse his Xanax prescription, he became a drifter, a lone star forever traveling through space until it finally and ingloriously burned out. I shook my head in wonder at the courage he drew upon to refuse the urge to use, and I realized we both had come too far to throw in the towel.

Carved in my psyche was the memory of Jeff Georgi gently telling me that Bobby was a high-risk patient and that his shame-based diagnosis was one of the most difficult for an addict to overcome. When we connected during Bobby's absence, Jeff's voice was firm but caring and tinged with something else. Sadness? Resignation? "There is a high probability that he is not going to come back. Statistically, after several days an addict will turn to what he or she knows best for comfort. You must open up to the idea that he might not make it."

He meant that Bobby would not be coming back to me,

to sobriety, to a future. But I couldn't hear him. His words were too heavy to penetrate my brain. I couldn't let them in; I chose not to let them in. It was my way of survival, the ultimate stage of denial.

But Bobby proved us all wrong. During the four days he spent at the Salvation Army, he punished himself—angry at yet another failure—embarrassed by his actions, saddened that he may have embarrassed us in front of our friends. He was sick that he stumbled and broke my golden rule and ignited my no-strike policy. He told me he passed four days in self-pity and recrimination and several times he was ready to give up and call it quits, to start using again. This time would definitely be the last time he would use, he said to himself, planning his death by overdose.

Instead, miraculously and against all medical data, he decided that he wanted to get well. He wanted to recover, to stop being a drug addict once and for all. As I stared deep into his tortured face, blue eyes glinting with tears of shame, I believed him when he looked at me and said once again, "Aunt Née, I am so tired of being a failure."

Could this be the turning point? Was he ready to commit to recovery with his whole being, instead of just going through the motions? Commit and dedicate the rest of his life to sobriety and health, love and life?

I couldn't be sure, but I wanted so badly to trust him, to believe in him. This need to trust and believe is the plight of those of us who love an addict. It is a vicious cycle of love, caring, and hope that gets shattered time and again by relapses, lies, and manipulation. There are those who enable, who cannot bear to go through the cycle and choose to believe the addict over statistical data and past history. It is easier to believe that your loved one will never drink again . . . this time. Will never have a one-night stand with another man or woman . . . this time. Won't forge your check or pawn your watch . . . this time. My experience is that all addicts are liars. But so too are all enablers. They just lie to themselves.

Over and over I had been told that Bobby's recovery was Bobby's recovery. I could not be an enabler. I could and would give him a safe place to live. I could and would give him love and compassion. And I would not lie to myself—or anyone else.

On a deep level I understood some of what he felt. I have always felt like I haven't lived up to my potential, specifically to what my father expected from me. I call it my "failure to launch" syndrome. This syndrome can be paralyzing at times, and it is something I thought only I could understand. When Bobby returned, I explained to him that I had these feelings of failure, of incompleteness, and that maybe we both should look at what was driving these emotions.

New beginnings, fresh starts for both of us. *Let's do it together*, I told him.

For Bobby, a fresh start entailed several things. He must open up to his counselor in order for Jeff to be able to help him. He needed to find a job, full- or part-time, to make some money, or go to summer school, or both. And he needed to make long-term goals and plans.

I needed to figure out what drove me too, and what was causing these feelings of inadequacy and insecurity. For someone so confident on the surface, I am a big pile of mush on the inside.

It was too late for Bobby to apply to summer programs, so I encouraged him to make decisions soon if he wanted to apply for the fall. Since he still hadn't sorted out what he would do with the rest of his life, career-wise, it was overwhelming for him to make the decision to go back to school for another degree. To my surprise and delight, I learned he had an okay GPA at his undergraduate institution, even though, due to drug and alcohol abuse, it took him six years to graduate.

He had taken the first of eight welding classes at our local community college before he ran away. He was very animated when he returned from that first class. Will and I thought welding would be a great profession for Bobby as he loves working with his hands, loves cars, and it is something he could do in any city in any state. It also pays very well.

In late June, Will and I would be celebrating our thirtieth wedding anniversary and had long planned a two-week trip. Jeff was not comfortable leaving Bobby by himself yet, especially when he had just come back from running away, and, frankly, I was downright scared to leave him alone. But Jill had already agreed to stay with him and he would attend welding classes while we were out of the country, so I felt better about our anniversary trip.

From: Renée Hodges
Subject: trip
Date: Saturday, June 8, 2013, at 10:33 a.m.
To: Jill Redford

Hi Jill,

Would you send me your Durham arrival and departure schedule, please? I will print it out and make sure you are picked up. You have full use of our cars here since we will all be away. Do not rent one, please.

I have put out a little feeler to my girlfriends letting them know you are going to be here for two weeks. I gave them your cell number and the home number. They are going to be calling to check in on you and see if you have questions or want to play tennis or have lunch, to invite you and Bobby over for dinner, to include you in a museum tour (Bobby has already seen it with me!), and to generally make sure you have things on your calendar while he keeps to his schedule. I think you know all but two of the girls, having met them over Mardi Gras, and they are all excited to know you are coming.

Every one of them knows about Bobby's struggles, and most were here the night he ran away. Ninety percent of them have either a substance abuser in their close or extended family, or a family member dealing with another deadly addiction (anorexia/bulimia). Most of them have walked or are now walking in your shoes.

It is amazing to find that so many of my friends understand completely about Bobby and about struggling family members or friends. I am blessed beyond measure to have them as a support system. I know you will find them easy to be around and a comfort if you need a friend. They are excited to be able to get to know you too!

Love, Renée

The week before Jill arrived and we left for our anniversary trip, it poured so much and so fast that the creek enclosing the front side of our yard swelled and began to overflow, drowning a small bridge that crosses over the road. This creek bed is usually dry or a trickle, but when there is a deluge, its banks are too narrow to contain the runoff water. When the creek and bridge succumb to the rushing water, so too do our lawn and driveway, engulfing the whole yard in front of our house. Fortunately, our house sits high on a hill overlooking this flash flood, so the family and home are safe.

As the rain slowed to a slight drizzle, Bobby announced he was going to walk down our overrun driveway in an effort to assess the damage. He roamed the flooded driveway in his hunting boots, staying clear of areas where water was over a foot deep. Reaching the main road at the end of our driveway, he turned to the right, where a hundred yards up the street the creek bridge was inundated with a fast roiling current, making it dangerous for vehicles to traverse from one side of the bridge to the other. There were cars on either side of the bridge, indecisive drivers contemplating the risks of continuing over the bridge and down the road or turning around to find alternative passage. Several people got out of their cars to take a closer look at the force and depth of the water.

Holly Barton, a neighborhood resident, was considering her options. She exited her car with her teenage daughter, Erin, and walked to the edge of the flooded bridge. She greeted Bobby, as she does everyone, with a friendly handshake and welcoming smile. Holly and Erin struck up a conversation and they listened as Bobby told them how he had moved to North Carolina to start over, living with his aunt and uncle while looking to change jobs and make Durham his home.

This short visit was enough for Holly to log Bobby's contact information into her phone. She promised to pass it on to her husband, Kennon, a successful commercial real estate broker, in the hopes that Bobby might find an interest in real estate and Kennon might have a job for him.

The wheels were in motion even before the water receded. This small interaction was the beginning of Bobby's journey toward his professional purpose. The small kindness of a complete stranger lit a spark in him that I hadn't yet seen. I think it was hope. Someone wanted to take a chance on him, give him a leg up.

He had hope of a job, maybe even a career, in an established business and respected field. This chance encounter could not have come at a better time, just days after he had returned from the Salvation Army, at a time when he was questioning himself, still raw from his latest mistake.

I was thrilled that he would have something to think about while we were out of town. In the days leading up to our departure, we came up with tasks for him. He must gather information from several of my friends about the pros and cons of the commercial real estate business, research how much time and money it would take to complete the test, and spend a day shadowing Mr. Barton.

He was also supposed to discuss other future job possibilities—in case he didn't like real estate—with his mother. They were in the process of finding an apartment for him. He would need to secure a job that could cover his living expenses. I knew he was not ready to move out, but he had to make informed decisions rather than simply jumping into the first thing that crossed his path. Knowing how much he needed to make each month to live was a great start.

From: Renée Hodges
Subject: Somewhere over the Atlantic
Date: Tuesday, June 11, 2013, at 6:53 p.m.
To: self

Dear me,

I know I need to get away for a while. I am mentally exhausted and I didn't really know how badly until I felt the airplane wheels retracting into the undercarriage.

I am trying to keep control of the situation even though I am passing the baton for the two weeks we will be away. I am still stinging from Bobby running away and the only way for me to relax is if I feel I have done everything I could do before we left for the airport.

Feeling slightly guilty for all the orders I left, I also suggested they take a little time off and go to the beach or the mountains, both within several hours of our house. See? I'm not so bad.

I am so excited for our anniversary vacation, and as I clicked my seatbelt and rested my head on Will's shoulder, I felt the anxiety dissipate from my body—like an early morning fog, slow and melodious, lifting until the world came back into focus. I realize the fog will be back . . . but for today, I am not thinking about it.

———

From: Lily Mayer
Subject: Bobby lunch
Date: Sunday, June 23, 2013, at 12:34 a.m.
To: Renée Hodges

Hi Renée,

Hope your trip is going well, can't wait to hear all about it!

I had lunch with Bobby and Jill on Thursday, very good time, talked all about real estate. Don't know if I helped, but he seems to want to move forward and understands what he's getting in to! Great kid.

G'night for me means almost good morning for you!

Enjoy, TTYSOON

XXO L

From: Bobby Redford
Subject: Hi!
Date: Monday, June 24, 2013, at 10:04 a.m.
To: Renée Hodges

Hi, Aunt Née! Everything is great! The dogs are great! Happy as pigs in slop! Hope y'all are taking great pictures! Love, Bobby

---

FINDING A PATH

June 26

When Will and I returned from our trip near the end of June, rested and refreshed, we got caught up on the real estate excitement we'd missed while out of town.

Bobby's meeting with Kennon Barton went fabulously. Kennon promised him a job if he passed the commercial real estate license examination and even offered him the use of his office for studying and test preparation.

Although we were happy that Bobby was so excited about this opportunity, Will and I were of the opinion that welding was still a much better fit for him than real estate, especially commercial real estate. Having a successful real estate career means self-starting, keeping one's own hours, and organizing one's time—tasks which were new to Bobby. Welding just fit with his personality as I was getting to know him.

I tried to explain the thoughts that had been going through my head, and there were a lot of them. I threw out well-worn bits of advice like dice at the craps table.

There *is* a difference between a job and a career. No matter what he ended up doing, digging ditches or brain surgery, I wanted him to be passionate about it. I wanted him to "sing behind the plow." If he could do that, he would be happy and successful.

He had been given a second chance to find a career. He should use it wisely.

I wanted him to think long term, to wake up every day with a smile on his face and say, "damn, I'm lucky I get to go to work." How many people even have this choice?

FOUR MONTHS

July

BACK PROBLEMS

One of my main goals when Bobby arrived was to assess and identify his back problems, fix the issues medically or surgically, and further strengthen his body. My reasoning was that if his back pain lessened, he wouldn't feel the need for addictive pills.

During March and April of 2013, Dr. Pate thoroughly examined Bobby, including an MRI, CAT scan, and X-rays of his back and neck.

We already knew that Bobby had a slight curvature of the spine and he was initially put on OxyContin for back pain at a spine clinic in Texas when he was twenty-one years old, thus triggering his addictive tendencies.

At twenty-nine years old, he learned that the curvature of his spine was not as severe as previously indicated. No other physical reasons could be found for the crippling pain he experienced.

He was working out with a trainer at the Duke Wellness Clinic two to three times a week, all in the hope of building up his muscles and subsequently lessening the hurt. The workouts were great and some of the discomfort in his back was alleviated. However, he still had to lie in bed at times, and it was hard for him to do manual labor or heavy lifting.

When Will and I returned from our anniversary trip reinvigorated, the first item on my to-do list was to figure out Bobby's back issues. Through my children's school I had become acquainted with Dr. Hay, a top-notch neuro-spine surgeon. I felt that if anyone could diagnose Bobby's physical problem, it would be him.

Dr. Pate didn't think that Dr. Hay was the correct specialist for Bobby, though. He wanted to enroll Bobby in a pain management clinic. I felt this would be an option only when everything else was ruled out completely. As I saw it, the only thing that helped Bobby during the six months he spent at the last pain management clinic in 2009 had been the prescription pain medication. And look where that got him.

Eventually, with Bobby badgering him because I was badgering Bobby, Dr. Pate referred Bobby to Dr. Hay. The appointment was made, and all of his many years of previous test results were sent to Dr. Hay's office for review.

When the day came for Bobby to go see Dr. Hay, he called for directions on his way to the Raleigh office. What he was told on the phone was a game changer.

Dr. Hay would not see him. After studying his tests and charts, and after all of his previous medical appointments, X-rays, CAT scans, and MRIs through the years, Dr. Hay could find nothing structurally wrong and felt he could do nothing for him.

Bobby called to let me know he had turned around and was coming back home. He was confused by the diagnosis, but I can't say I was really surprised at Dr. Hay's assessment. The pain in Bobby's back had never been medically evaluated to the degree Dr. Hay investigated, with the cumulative gathering of records and tests. As I waited for Bobby to return, I began to think about the connection between the body and the mind.

"Sit down," I instructed when he walked into the kitchen, clearly fatigued and defeated. "And listen well. I believe you have severe back pain. I know it is there. I believe you. Just because you have nothing structurally wrong with your back doesn't mean you are making things up. You. Have. Back. Pain. Period. It is real and you feel it."

I could tell he wanted to believe that I believed him. But he was so dejected that I was afraid he wouldn't be able to comprehend what I was about to tell him.

"This appointment with Dr. Hay is it. No more. You have had test after test to find a physical reason for why you hurt, and the overwhelming consensus is that there is no physical reason. Zip. Zero. You are healthy . . . physically."

Pause.

"We must start looking at other reasons you are in pain. And the most logical is that you are having physical reactions to emotional problems."

I could tell he was scoffing at me, and I didn't really blame the poor kid. He'd been through so much, I almost wished there was some physical defect we could fix with a knife. It would definitely be easier.

But I had been there myself. In 2003, Will and I lost some close friends in a small plane crash. We had had dinner with them just a week before they left for the trip from which they would not return.

When I heard the awful news of the crash, I immediately felt a shooting pain in my lower back. This stinging wouldn't go away, and I had no idea how or why it came on so suddenly. One day while I was shopping in the grocery store, the shooting pains were so bad that I had to lie down on the floor until they subsided.

Structurally, nothing was wrong; multiple doctors confirmed it. Yet the hurt was real. What I eventually learned was that I was carrying many things in my back muscles: grief, hurt, anger, worry—all the emotional struggles I couldn't process.

My muscles became the receptacle for what my brain couldn't hold. It was only after I was able to release, understand, and accept the tragedy that I became well again. It did not happen overnight.

I had an intuitive feeling that Bobby's back pain might be the same, brought on by emotional trauma. He needed to find out.

He and Jeff discussed my theory. Chronic pain is a common symptom in people with anxiety. Bobby could indeed have anxiety-driven pain that had begun many years ago when he was a young adult. Plus, taking painkillers over a long period of time may in fact increase a patient's sensitivity to pain, a syndrome called hyperalgesia.

Although Bobby still suffers during times of high anxiety or stress, he now understands that it is his back which holds his mental pain and that he does not have a physical problem. And he can deal with that without prescription pills.

————

LAUGHTER RETURNS

I remember this day so well. It was the first time I saw a bit of the "old" Bobby I remembered.

I strolled into the kitchen, dripping sweat from a tennis match while looking through the mail. I was multitasking, not something I do well or often. And I wanted that apple I'd been thinking about all day. A beautiful, rose-colored Pink Lady, crisp and shiny, hidden in a triangular stack of oranges, apples, and grapefruit on the blue ceramic platter one of the kids had made in kindergarten. I had paid a bloody fortune for that platter in the school auction, and I was damn sure going to get my money's worth out of it.

I reached my hand for the apple and I felt it before I saw it. Slick, hard, thin with stiff tendrils and appendages. Yuck! I instinctively whipped my hand back as fast as I could, letting out an involuntary shriek for good measure.

Ribbed and winged, a two-inch coffee-colored roach was resting just where my fingertips grazed it.

It took a second but scrutinizing closer . . . ah, I was right. That little stinker. Sitting smack dab on top of the apple was the most lifelike imitation of a Louisiana cockroach I'd ever seen. Except, haha, I *had* seen it before. That gross plastic spectacle had been making the rounds in our home since being caught at a satirical Mardi Gras parade several years ago by my son, William—a packet of hard, molded roaches falling into the happiest boy in the world's outstretched hands.

I had secretly thrown all but this one lowly creature into the garbage, hiding them as deep as I could for fear of reappearance. This last roach had become our family prank for the last few years, a nasty-looking creature hidden where you least expect it, eliciting a shriek or scream or titter when you stick your hand in the dryer looking for a sock, in the soap dish as you take a shower, in my makeup drawer cold cream, and surprise! Your hand makes contact. Gross.

It has made more appearances in the kitchen than Emeril and has been found in all of the major food groups. I must say, I don't miss the little bugger when my kids are not home.

I grabbed up the roach, wrapping it tightly in the palm of my hand, fingers clenched in a fist. *Yes.* Then out loud. "Yes, yes, yes." I flicked it up in the air and caught it high, almost punching. Pulling a fast one on old Aunt Née is fun! I recognized signs of life, of laughter, for the very first time since my nephew came to stay and I smiled broadly to myself even as I called out as loudly as I could, "BOOOBBBYYYYY!!!!!!!"

———

TAKING THE REAL ESTATE TEST

In late June, when Bobby was already signed up for the Real Estate License course, he met with a close friend of mine who is a residential real estate broker to discuss just what it took to have a career in real estate.

Although she stressed how difficult commercial real estate would be, that Bobby would need to be a self-starter and hours were irregular, he was a hard-charging bull, only seeing the red of the cape. The first testament to his motivation was the fact that his evening classes were in Raleigh, a good thirty-five minutes away if the traffic favored you.

He never missed a real estate class and he spent hours in his room studying. The legalese sections were a breeze for him. He enjoyed learning and memorizing terms and definitions. It was the math that gave him fits.

There was much enthusiasm in the house as we all dreamed of his new career and the job offer extended from Kennon Barton, but there was also an underlying apprehension.

For Bobby, passing this test, receiving his license, and starting a career—not just a job—was everything to him. He felt he could restore his life with one successful exam, show all the naysayers and judgers out there that he was not a failure, and make something of himself.

I received this email confession the night before Bobby took his test:

From: John Redford
Subject: Bobby test
Date: Thursday, July 25, 2013, at 10:31 p.m.
To: Renée Hodges

... don't tell Bobby unless necessary but I flunked the real estate test first time ... just made me mad!

On test day Mr. Pig was sporting a new message for Bobby: "Believe you can!"

As Bobby rolled his eyes, I went through a checklist: "Pens? Pencils? Water bottle? Peppermints?" An old wives' tale maybe, but our family believes popping a peppermint will give the brain an extra burst during a test.

For two days after taking the exam, he checked and double-checked email, hoping scores would be posted. He said he felt fine about the test, that it had been difficult but that only the math problems gave him any concern.

Like the dropped anchor on a frigate, we felt weighed down, chained to our anxiety until his grades were published.

On the third day, when Bobby did not come down the stairs in the morning, I became anxious. The real estate test is known for being a difficult exam, and many an intelligent person has failed it, including, I had just learned, my brother.

But Bobby wasn't just any person. This exam meant so much more to him. It meant not being a failure.

Around noon, Bobby came down the back steps dressed for the day and veered right toward the back door, steering clear of the kitchen. I figured he was heading out for his first smoke, but the sound of his truck startled me.

I texted him, *Good morning. What's on your agenda today?*

He texted back, *Going to a meeting.* I concluded this meant an AA meeting and that was the end of it.

Later that afternoon Bobby returned and went straight to his room, electing to bypass the kitchen and conversation once again.

I heard his bedroom door softly close. Why I sent him a text and didn't just go to his bedroom is beyond me. Modern communication, I suppose.

Have you heard anything about your test?

There was a long pause, more than just an uncomfortable length of time, and I knew without him having to tell me. But he texted anyway.

Failed.

Damn. I sat down at the island in the kitchen and placed my cell phone on the hard countertop in front of me so I could lay my head in both hands, hunch over, and dejectedly stare at my screen until the full weight of comprehension hit me. Failed. Bobby had failed the test.

Okay. I didn't plan for this, the eternal optimist that I can be, or maybe just eternal avoider. *Think. Think. Now what do we do?* I slowly climbed Mt. Everest to the top of the stairs. So disheartened and spent, I didn't know how I made it up to his room.

Knocking lightly, I asked if I could come in.

Bobby's back was to me as he lay curled in his bed, knees almost to his chin. He did not turn over.

I sat on the side and gently rubbed his back with the palm of my hand, for his assurance and mine that things were going to be all right.

"Bobby, I'm sorry. What a bummer." *God, that is an eighties word*, I chastised myself. *Can't you think of something better to say?*

"Listen. It is going to be fine." I moved my hand in a wax-on, wax-off pattern. "Many people do not pass the test on the first go-around. It is supposed to be difficult. I don't know if you know this or not, but your dad also failed the real estate exam on his first go-around. Yes, that's right. I understand your disappointment. I am disappointed for you. But you have gone through much worse. This is not the end of the world. I am going to give you the rest of the day to feel sorry for yourself because I know you are sad and need some time. Get it all out and I will do the same. Because starting tomorrow morning, we are going to wake up, put this behind us, and move on."

And that was just what we did. Bobby called his teacher to see if he could find out which problems he missed on the test, but to no avail. So we did the next best thing: he signed up to take the whole course again, beginning the next week.

FIVE MONTHS

August

STAYING BY HIMSELF

July just flew by. Why is it that the summer months go twice as fast as the winter ones?

I have marked the end of summer for almost forty years by our annual trip to upstate Wisconsin. We spend one week on a beautiful lake enjoying a rustic family resort. We love our yearly trip there. Each family has a separate sparse cabin, with no AC or TV. Cell service is a brand-new concept in the region. With feet dangling off the pier, toes touching icy water and setting off concentric circles, yes, this is definitely a place that can bring peace to those who have difficulty finding it.

We have always gone the first week in August, and this year we were to leave Saturday, August 3, meeting up with Will's sisters and brother and our children, whoever could make it.

I asked Bobby to join us, but he declined the invitation. He was attending his real estate prep course again and did not want to miss a class. As much as I wanted him to join us, I was proud of him for making the right decision, albeit a hard one. Class or lake? Studying or fun?

I was thrilled when Jeff Georgi gave him permission to stay by himself in our house for the first time. I knew Bobby was nervous; hell, I was too. I knew I had to go by what Jeff said but I felt so . . . so . . . accountable for Bobby. If I were here in the house with him, I felt safer, or I should say I felt that Bobby was safer. I knew this was all in my head, that he could be in his room snorting, shooting, popping, and I'd never know it. I could be too! I did feel that he and I had come to some understanding. We had firmed up a connection, that if he were thinking about using, he would come to me first. I guess this is trust. I trusted him to keep himself safe. I trusted him to make good decisions, or at least to want to make good decisions. We all make a bad decision here or there.

It was difficult for me to wave goodbye at the airport. I had the same feeling I got when I left my kids at camp or on their college campus for the first time. A bittersweet pang—more about me than them—because I knew my children were ready just as I knew Bobby was ready. Will felt it too: he looked into my eyes, and as we turned around together, he put his arm around me and gave me a supportive squeeze as we made our way to security.

I sent Bobby an encouraging email the night before we left on our trip:

From: Renée Hodges
Subject: Things to think about while we are gone
Date: Friday, August 2, 2013, at 11:31 p.m.
To: Bobby

My dear Bobby,

I am leaving you tomorrow for a week, and I wanted to write you this letter before I went to sleep. I like to put my thoughts on paper, and I tend to dramatize a bit while doing it! I do it to all my kids!!! Bear with me, please . . .

I know you are disappointed that you didn't pass the real estate test on the first attempt, but I have to think that if this is the worst thing that is happening to you right now, I am feeling pretty damn happy. You have had a few days to feel sorry for yourself and now I want you to pull yourself up and let it go. I think you are already doing just that, but in case you wanted to backslide once mean ole Aunt Née was out of the picture, I want to emphasize some things.

First, there is nothing you can do to change what has already happened. There is still today and tomorrow. So, now that I have said this, you need to make a plan of action for the next test. You have from now until you take the test the first week in October and you will work your butt off every day.

The most important thing I think is getting outside help. We can discuss this when I get back.

Study three to four hours a day. Not just for the test, but because you must be prepared with the knowledge for real-life situations. If you pass the test but barely understand the problems, what good is that?? I would rather you fail the test many times until you can say, "I know everything there is to know and I am confident I can use it in a real job."

Also, you are grown, but I am telling you that if you spend the rest of the day just sitting around and watching TV, you will not feel better about yourself.

When I get home from Wisconsin, I would like for you to have a plan or have something to do part-time for the next eight weeks. Volunteering each day, bagging at the grocery store, working for my friend at the sub shop, and lots of other ideas. Do not turn on the TV except for an hour or maybe two max each day; that is all, no more. Not because of the TV, but because you need to keep busy. Can you do it? Yes, you can.

After studying and working, you might also read a book, do the 12 steps, take a walk with the dogs, have dinner with a friend. I assure you, you will feel great about yourself if you keep busy, and I know you can do this.

We will be at Franklin's Lodge in upstate Wisconsin. You can call me anytime on my cell, but I only check it a few times a day. The resort will find me if you call their number and tell them it is important. Leave a message on my cell if it isn't important and I'll get back to you when I can.

This is a big week as you will be alone in the house in the evenings for the first time. Also you can do some things for me while I'm gone, please. Please use the alarm when you leave the house. Don't forget to feed the dogs and take out the trash and recycling. Have some friends over for dinner. Buy some burgers and grill. Leave me the bill by the telephone. I want you to use the house like you would your own home.

You are so, so close, Bobby! Please stay safe this week. Please call me if you feel unsafe. We are so proud of you and what you have accomplished. Let's finish the job. The sky's the limit!

Written with love, Aunt Née

———

From: Bobby Redford
Subject: Things to think about while we are gone
Date: Friday, August 2, 2013, at 11:59 p.m.
To: Renée Hodges

Thank you for thinking of me and everything you've done for me. Without you and Uncle Will, I would be lost. Love you!

———

From: Renée Hodges
Subject: Update to self
Date: Monday, August 12, 2013, at 10:38 a.m.
To: self

For the first time, Bobby stayed by himself while we were in Wisconsin for the week, and I think he did fine. What a huge step. He is still having intermittent nightmares, and he told me that he hates to be alone at night when he has one.

———

OUTSIDE HELP

In late August, we discussed a math problem he was struggling to understand. I was a stellar math student in high school and college, so I told Bobby what I thought was the right answer: multiply. I heard Will correct us from the other room: we had to divide. And Will was right. I was somewhat embarrassed to see my mental math memory had failed me, but it also gave me a great teaching point to pass on to Bobby.

I had been out of college for thirty-two years, and in that time I had used very little higher math, even though I'd been top of my class in high school. He had been out of high school for nearly ten years and didn't use math every day like his Uncle Will did. It was perfectly reasonable that he would need to brush up on his math skills for the real estate test; I should do the same if I was to be of any help to him.

I searched and found a young, cute girl around Bobby's age to tutor him twice a week. I never heard Bobby complain about being tutored, and, in fact, I believe he looked forward to these sessions.

SIX MONTHS TWO DAYS

September 5

DREAM SPECIALIST

Nightmares are a way to release anxiety that is too great to handle during waking hours; they are the way your mind self-protects. At least this is what Mary Costello once told me when I was having significant nightly disruptions. Both Bobby and I released our anxiety with nightmares.

Bobby had nightmares since his arrival. First, they were every night, eliciting high-pitched screams and garbled words that Will and I could hear downstairs and through our closed door. After a few weeks the nightmares became more sporadic, or I just didn't hear them, immune to them as I am to Will's snoring.

But Bobby continued to have one recurring nightmare that frightened him to the core, and, by the end of summer, I was racking my brain about how to help. We had never discussed the content of his nightmare, as I never wanted to discuss the content of mine. I am thankful he told me when it occurred.

I found it strangely coincidental that both Bobby and I suffered these frightening events in the dark of night. I understand how real they can be, how helpless you can feel, how the thoughts you most fear during the day—the ones that you push to the back of your mind so you can go about your daily activities—how these thoughts, like a bloodsucking vampire, only come out at night.

I understood how these sneaky, creepy, and frightening thoughts are played out in Technicolor. Some nights I would turn off the light, and my hand would linger for a split second as dread began to rise in my chest. On those nights, I would think: *Will I have one tonight? Will I wake screaming, flailing, crying, heart racing only to forget what I was dreaming about? Or will I remember? As I wake myself up, will I remember my most vivid nightmare, snakes encircling the children, losing a child, the blond hair slipping under the massive expanse of water, blue face and unseeing eyes, water appearing out of nowhere to separate us, snakes appearing everywhere, wrapping me like an Egyptian mummy? When I wake, will I remember that I try? I try hard to rescue them.* I scream their names in my nightmares. I sometimes scream them aloud, helpless and out of control.

My nightmares never end well. I might wake myself mid-stream before any finality, or Will wakes me if I am having an especially difficult night. I have had regular nightmares since my kids were born and my father died, nearly twenty-three years ago. I sometimes have two in one night; after the first nightmare I finally calm myself, steady my breathing, and doze off, only to awaken again in a cold sweat.

My nightmares took a hiatus for a short while, but they returned when Bobby came to live with us. In short spurts they would reappear, maybe several a week, and then they would take a month long vacation. Why? I don't know.

Now the nightmares come very infrequently. I still avoid snakes whenever possible. And my family, knowing the content of my nightmares, respects this phobia of mine.

I connected with Bobby because we had both been in the same foxhole, facing the same enemy. Early in his stay, when Bobby's terrors were at their worst, he asked me if Reverend Bowen would talk to him about his nightmares. As Bobby was weaned from most of the heavy-duty mood-altering drugs he'd been taking when he arrived, he was able to remember one particular recurring night terror, and he had trouble shaking his fear in the mornings.

This nightmare with demons felt so real to Bobby that he

was petrified to sleep at night for fear they would envelop him in the dark. Reverend Bowen came to the house and went straight up to Bobby's room. I again respected Bobby's privacy by not asking what the two of them talked about, trusting that if I needed to know something the Reverend would tell me. I was happy to see that their conversation seemed to calm Bobby for the moment.

In late August I told Mary Costello about Bobby's recurring nightmare and how much it affected him, how it took him hours sometimes to quell his shaking and get back to sleep. I wished he could find out why he was suffering.

Mary's sister, Dr. Claire, happened to be one of the foremost dream specialists in the country and would be visiting her soon. Coincidental? Of course. Providential? Absolutely! It was another way in which the people Bobby needed most came into his life at precisely the right time.

Mary described her sister to me as, "the bravest, most perceptive human I have ever known," saying that insight had been in her blood since she was young. If the glowing recommendation had come from anyone other than Mary, I'd think they were a bit biased.

As I left her office, I stopped and bought a lottery ticket. It so felt like my lucky day.

At my urging, Bobby contacted Dr. Claire. On his own initiative, he set up the appointment and worked out the logistics. In the meantime, his homework was to fill out a questionnaire and keep a journal of his dreams. He signed a privacy release, and Dr. Claire did her homework too by conferring with Jeff Georgi.

When Bobby returned from his appointment with Dr. Claire, I nearly tackled him at the door. "What did she say? What did you say? Did it help?"

"Aunt Née, it was amazing. She understood me. And she doesn't think I am crazy," Bobby declared.

Crazy? What?

"Aunt Née, I thought I must be crazy because my recurring dream is so real to me that I had a hard time believing it wasn't real. Dr. Claire taught me about dreams and nightmares and why we have them." Bobby animatedly described his session, in awe of Dr. Claire's wisdom. They had talked about how to manipulate dreams while in progress and how to force yourself to wake up.

Dr. Claire explained what the demons represented to him, and he felt comforted by this revelation. I think by voicing and understanding his nightmares, they lost their power over him. He spoke his fears aloud and learned from them. He was confronting and controlling something he feared and did not understand. By doing this, he owned his demons.

That was the end of any talk about dreams, nightmares, and craziness. I'm sure Bobby still has a bad dream or two, but I felt much peace after his session with the dream specialist and I know he did too. Maybe, one day, I'll have a session with Dr. Claire too, but for now my nightmares are getting farther apart and I am sleeping like a baby.

It wasn't until much later that I realized Will and I had been taking a holistic approach in our treatment of Bobby. Instead of just treating the symptoms of his addiction, we were treating Bobby's entire being, mind, body, and soul. From his weight to his physical appearance and ailments, even his dreams, we made sure everything was running smoothly. Looking back, supporting every part of Bobby's rehabilitation, no matter how small and insignificant it might have seemed, made a difference in Bobby's recovery.

SEVEN MONTHS

REAL ESTATE TEST II

For eight weeks Bobby prepared for the October 3 exam, attending real estate classes and meeting with a math tutor.

As October neared, both Will and I were pleased by the amount of effort he was putting into preparing for the exam. Meeting with his math tutor gave him a confidence I hadn't seen before the first test, and we were all optimistic.

The morning of the second test, Mr. Pig said: "Do your best. That is the best you can do."

Bobby filled his pockets with peppermints and set off.

Despite these efforts, he missed passing the exam by four points.

From: Renée Hodges
Subject: Bobby
Date: Thursday, October 10, 2013, at 9:17 p.m.
To: Jill Redford

Hey Jill and John,

Bobby found out he did not pass his test today. We will regroup here. We are already looking at when he can take it next. It may be near Elizabeth's wedding.

Please send me his plane schedule for the wedding so we can plan for the next real estate test.

Thanks, Renée

From: Jill Redford
Subject: Bobby
Date: Thursday, October 10, 2013, at 11:40 p.m.
To: Renée Hodges

I am so sad for Bobby. I sent Bobby's tickets for Elizabeth's wedding and a confirmation to you today. I will text him tomorrow.

Love you, Jill

———

From: Anne Howard
Subject: Bobby's test
Date: Sunday, October 13, 2013, at 9:11 p.m.
To: Renée Hodges

Hope he is doing okay. Think about him constantly. I talked to Reverend Bowen briefly after church and he said he saw Bobby there. Didn't see him. Was with my shepherding group down front. I love you and can only imagine what you live day to day. I did it and know what a toll it can take and I didn't even have a husband to consider. I hope Bobby got something from the sermon today. It applies to all of us not just him. I don't care how much money we have or anything else, we all still have hardships. Keep me posted.

Love, Anne

———

NEVER GIVE UP

We did not give up; we made a game plan. Rather than taking the class again, Bobby continued to work with the tutor and downloaded study aids and mock tests from the internet. We had six weeks before the next test.

In the meantime, he continued to work on himself—seeing Jeff Georgi and attending AA meetings, running errands and doing odd jobs for money, and continuing at the Duke Wellness Center to strengthen his back and keep himself physically healthy. He would take the test again in November and he would be fully prepared.

In the meantime we had his sister's wedding to look forward to in October.

EIGHT MONTHS

October

WEDDING PLANNING

Bobby had lived with us for eight months. At the beginning of Elizabeth and Charlie's wedding weekend, I had as much anxiety as the bride and groom. I had become the main spectator in a reality show starring Bobby. I knew he was not completely recovered as I saw his inner struggles every day. Where to find a date, how many AA meetings he should attend in order to control his urges or racing thoughts, whether to get out of bed or turn over, when to leave the dinner table or restaurant as he became anxious, and a fistful of other signs.

After eight months, he was finally making good decisions, healthy decisions, strengthening his resolve to succeed. Last March he was in a purgatory of stunted immaturity, stagnated at the age of twenty-one, the age he began to take OxyContin in college. I wasn't quite sure he would ever be able to handle "adult" responsibilities and emotions. But he had matured years in the past months, hopscotching into a gentle, sensitive, loving, and responsible young man of twenty-nine.

As I daily witnessed his emotional growth, I hadn't worried much about backsliding. Will and I protected him from life's hurts as best we could while he was healing, but we all knew our protection wasn't realistic or long term.

Bobby's attendance at his sister's wedding to his childhood best friend was an enormous goal that had been vaguely somewhere in our collective future, a milestone to strive for, something to hope to attend, but a nebulous event in our daily recovery routines.

Now it was here. The proverbial moment of truth, the test of whether or not he could rejoin his family and society.

I was filled with fear so deep and cold that I shivered uncontrollably when I thought of all that could go wrong, the largest of which was his insecurities becoming greater than his resolve to stay clean. For three days Bobby would face the demons that had ruled him for many years.

There would be alcohol and possibly recreational drugs, with music and laughter and a beach-party atmosphere. Bobby's father would be front and center to give away his only daughter—a daughter he adores and loves. John still grieved for the childhood time with her he drunkenly piddled away. Bobby's grandmother, my mother, would be there, someone Bobby idolized as only a lost child could. My mother loves grandly on her oldest grandson, maybe as silent compensation for his father's early neglect, or maybe from the shared commiseration of being raised by an alcoholic father.

Bobby's oldest friends and many of their parents would be in attendance at the wedding. They could say "I knew Bobby when . . ." if they cared to remember the old Bobby and not just the masochistic, haunted drug addict.

And his only sibling, Elizabeth, and her fiancé, Bobby's best friend from high school, would be there to vow to love and honor each other in sickness and health for as long as they both shall live. Before his move to Durham, Elizabeth and Charlie had severed ties with Bobby, frustrated, saddened, powerless to help him. The only way for them to protect themselves was to cut him out of their lives, block his phone, Facebook, and emails. The drug-addled Bobby was dead to them—and with good reason.

For Elizabeth and Charlie to invite Bobby to attend their wedding and ask him to be a groomsman was tantamount to a miracle. And the knowledge that Bobby received the thumbs-up from his drug counselor to take this airplane trip made me weak in the knees with joy.

Everyone that Bobby cared about in his lifetime would be here for this wedding weekend. I prayed to myself, *Lord, please. Please keep him safe.*

Okay, I'll admit it; I had one other big concern about this wedding. I was a cynic about a destination wedding at the beach in the middle of hurricane season. In October the odds were high that a hurricane or tropical storm could wipe out the whole three-day weekend. I was a doubting Thomas and I was wrong to be such a pessimist—and thrilled I was wrong. It turned out to be one of the most glorious weddings I have attended, and the weather could not have been more perfect. High white puffs of clouds against a brilliant baby blue sky so opaque it felt like the sky and ocean were one. And there was a breeze, not much, but just enough to keep the humidity to a minimum. The bugs must have been on vacation as nary a one was seen. Spirits were high; love abounded. The excitement was palpable. To me, the best thing about this magical weekend, other than the union of two young lovers, was clear: Bobby, the prodigal son, was returning.

The wedding was held on the glorious sand near my mother's beach house. Mom's home is beautiful, situated high on the top of a scruffy hill with vistas of green-blue water on three sides. A resort hotel lies at the foot of the hill tucked onto a miniature peninsula straddling a small bay and the Atlantic Ocean. At the White House, as Mom's house is affectionately called because it is, duh, white, the wind is constant, cooling, and keeps mosquitos at bay during the high season.

After my father died, Mom bought the house on a whim,

needing an adventure and a place to run away to. The White House has a special place in Elizabeth's memory as she spent many weeks of childhood vacation on that beach. Having her wedding there was a dream come true.

I flew in a week early to help Jill with last-minute chores and decisions, but there was no need as she had it under control. I mostly ran interference between her and my mom. When Jill is nervous or anxious, her obsessive cleaning kicks in—usually a great thing, but not so when she is staying in my mother's retreat.

Nearing eighty years of age, my mother is set in her ways. Her memory isn't as good as it once was (whose is?), and when something is not where she has had it for twenty years, it drives her crazy. And, yes, Jill can be crazy-making.

It is ironic that I was the peacemaker, the calm force, the soother the week before the big wedding event. My role in the family is usually as the confronter, the face-the-nation, the let's-get-it-all-out-on-the-table. Jill and Mom are the if-I-don't-think-about-it-or-say-anything-then-it-never-happened, head-in-the-sand type.

I was masterful in my arbitration between the two. I would take Mom aside and say, "Mom, Jill is about to host a wedding. She needs all the latitude you can give."

And to Jill I would say, "Yes, if you need to clean that cupboard out for the third time today, I'll keep Mom busy."

I was glad I came early if only to be with Jill. We ran errands, went to the grocery and wine stores, and made sure the resort staff had everything in check. We laughed and told old stories. We kept it light and upbeat and I relaxed. I missed Jill in my life and this was fun.

We talked about Bobby, not too much, but just enough. The decision to let him attend the wedding was not mine. It was made between Jeff and Bobby. I would facilitate it, but I could not make this call for him. It was a monumental decision.

Even so, although I could not stop thinking about all the things that could go wrong, I was determined to not show a crack to Jill and John. I put on my best confident suit when I left Durham and wore it every day we were at the beach.

In the weeks leading up to that weekend, I prepared Bobby as well as I could, detouring and rerouting to make sure he kept on the straight and narrow path while at the wedding. I stipulated that Bobby stay with my immediate family in a condo and not in the White House where his father, mother, sister, and grandmother were staying. With the nervousness of the wedding, emotions would be running high and offhand comments might be misconstrued more easily. I felt that separating Bobby from the root of his anxiety would lessen the anxiety for everyone, including myself.

Rachel and Katherine were unable to attend the wedding. Will, William, Bobby, and I would stay down the hill from my mom's house in a beautiful villa right off the white sand beach where we could easily dip our bare feet into the warm, salty water. We would have just enough distance for Bobby to keep himself safe and have a place to retire if things became overwhelming, and this proved to be a very healthy idea.

No unnecessary chances taken. Bobby understood the risks, especially the unseen ones, but I believed if we could do this right, his reward would be impossible to measure—truly priceless.

There were a little over one hundred guests in all, mostly family, the bridal party, and a few close friends. Because Elizabeth was marrying Bobby's longtime friend, Bobby knew and felt comfortable with most everyone in attendance. And all the guests went out of their way to revel in his sobriety. There was a great buzz around him, questions asked and answered and much curiosity over his lost years. I was so happy that he and I had discussed what he would say when uncomfortable questions were asked.

One of the questions that worried him was what he was doing in Durham. "When someone asks what you are doing, you might tell them this: 'I have moved to Durham to get a new start, and I have been studying to get my commercial real estate license as I have been offered a job after I pass the test.' That says all you need to say."

There were other questions that worried him, mostly recovery questions. I told him that showing was better than telling. The moment people saw him and talked with him, there wouldn't be any more questions. The old Bobby could shine through; his new, safe behavior would say it all.

And he was so handsome, having been on a high-protein diet and working out at the gym several days a week for the last eight months. Friend after friend slapped him five and hugged his neck, and I could see his apprehension dissolve into the briny air. He visibly stood up straighter, his back releasing anxiety. He smiled so widely and for so long that I was afraid his jaw muscles would hurt later that first night.

Throughout the weekend I stayed close: overprotective, invisibly wrapping him in my arms and daring someone to hurt him. I grilled him about his thoughts, his emotional state, his urges. Without a cell phone it was not very easy to find out where and with whom he was hanging out, but Bobby had proven himself that week we were in Wisconsin. He could handle this on his own and I needed to let him. I was a wreck but I was a good wreck. I beamed. For the first time it started to sink in that he was healing, his body and mind emotionally stronger, both in maturity and humility.

On Friday morning I broached the topic of a toast at the rehearsal dinner. Bobby is a great speaker, and I didn't know if he had considered a toast to Elizabeth and Charlie.

"You don't have to give a toast. No one will think twice. But if you are thinking of giving one, I suggest you write it out and practice it. Whatever you say just say it from the heart. Mean it. Own it. If you do that, you cannot go wrong."

He surprised me with his enthusiasm, and I could see his mind kick into gear. He worked most of the day on the toast. He closed himself off in his room for the early morning hours, and several times during the day I found him with pen and paper in hand, diligently scratching through an unwanted line or chewing the end of the pen, which was neatly parked between his lips as he thoughtfully created his speech. I inquired several times if he would like to practice in front of me, but he declined with a wink and a grin, saying I would hear it when everyone else did.

Later in the day, I was getting dressed for the rehearsal dinner and putting on makeup, chatting excitedly with my husband. I stopped mid-sentence. "What is that, Will? Listen."

We strained to catch the sound. It was muffled and unintelligible but it was clearly Bobby. He was in the shower practicing his toast.

———

REHEARSAL DINNER

A golf cart dropped us on the beach, the sun perched and waiting for us to arrive before it began its slow descent into the sea. A magnificent setup, the rehearsal dinner was a beach barbecue, complete with flip-flops handed out upon arrival. I ditched my heels, happily donning the rubber flats and sinking into the gentle tract of still-warm sand.

Set up on the nearly secluded side of the cove, the rehearsal dinner was going to be a shindig. The bonfire was soon lit, golden-red flames shooting ten to fifteen feet high, sparks like fireworks against a backdrop of glass-like bay. On one side the four large open kettle grills were being stoked as the cooks waited for the coals to burn down to just the right temperature to grill the lobster, shrimp, fish, oysters, and assorted meats to perfection.

A small dance floor was set on the sand, interlocking wood squares making a sturdy platform and piquing our anticipation of the events of the evening. An exotic-flavored steel drum band stood behind the dance floor, beating out melodic rhythms with the heels and palms of their hands.

A dozen round tables and one long main table separated the grills and music from the canvas half tent that was housing the remaining food, a literal smorgasbord of vegetables, fruits, and desserts.

Torches were lit for ambience and votives adorned every table. Even when the sun set, there was enough light from the moon and from the strings of small bare lightbulbs strung around the perimeter to illuminate the entire area.

Will and I located our table, mere feet from the dance floor. Bobby and William had been seated at a table with other young folk.

I tried to keep an eye on the boys early in the evening but abandoned the effort as I was caught up in the mingling and meeting of Charlie's family and friends.

One advantage of having a destination beach wedding, other than the tan, is that the guests are together 24/7, which bonds everyone immediately. After the "Meet and Greet" the previous evening, the small wedding group continued to celebrate down at the resort. And, this morning, we break-fasted, then sunbathed, beach volleyballed, and lunched—if not together, in the same vicinity. The cute young adults were engaging and respectful, conversing with the older adults—myself included—and making us feel light and youth-ful. A destination wedding makes for grand intimacy.

When the time came for the toasts to begin at the re-hearsal dinner, I was jumpy. I searched the crowd, but the light was dim and my eyesight is not so good at night. I could not distinguish where Bobby was sitting.

Every time someone finished a toast and there was a lull of anticipation, I held my breath.

The toasts were lovely, not the immature and embarrass-ing toasts made at some rehearsal dinners, but the beautiful, heartfelt good wishes of Elizabeth's and Charlie's families and close friends. Each speech was special and each guest was drawn even more into this amazing circle of love.

As the toasts came to an end, I saw Elizabeth give Charlie the signal to stand and close it out.

Come on, come on, I thought. I was strung so tightly that it was hard to stay seated in my chair.

Charlie picked up his champagne flute and began to rise. Then I heard Bobby announce, "I have something to say."

I saw him as he rose above the seated guests. He stood tall. If I hadn't watched his transformation firsthand, I would find it hard to believe this was the same kid who tried to kill himself in March. His newly cut hair was brushed back and gelled. I couldn't see his blue eyes, but I knew he was holding back tears. I was also pretty sure the new tan on his face was complementing his gigantic smile.

Will reached underneath the tablecloth and took my

hand to give it a squeeze. I didn't take my eyes off Bobby, but I gave Will's hand a good squeeze back in appreciation. I saw Elizabeth take Charlie's hand as well.

I heard a few murmurs in the crowd and the sound of bodies swiveling to get a good look at Bobby. There was a feeling of nervousness in the air, of not knowing what would come out of his mouth. Would it be appropriate? Would it be emotional? Where did the relationship between Elizabeth, Charlie, and Bobby stand at this moment? I slid closer to the edge of my seat as I imagined half the guests did too.

He waited just long enough for there to be slight discomfort and uncertainty, scanning the crowd, peering into faces, a joyous look at this perfect setting. Then, he unfolded several pieces of crumpled paper from his back pocket and began.

First he praised and thanked Charlie's family for being the hosts of this beautiful party. Then he squinted at his piece of paper and told a funny story about Charlie in high school, directly following it with a pseudo-embarrassing story about Elizabeth that only a brother could tell. He set everyone at ease and his delivery had guests laughing out loud. There was an air of approval, of lightness now, exhalation and happiness from the spectators. Several people nodded their affirmations; everyone smiled in complicity.

Bobby was oblivious to anything going on around him as he regaled us with his stories, obviously enjoying himself immensely. He had been holding his written notes in his hand, but at some point he put them down. He shifted his weight back and forth unconsciously. Then the funny stories stopped. He stopped speaking and stood completely still, looking down at his shoes, unsure how to continue—a pregnant pause. The crowd was so quiet I could hear the seawater gently lapping the shore.

My heart was beating a million times a minute. I watched

as several in the crowd leaned over and whispered to their partners; others fidgeted uncomfortably. Some might be thinking that he would not be able to finish the toast; that it was too soon, too heavy, too much. They worried he would choke up or revisit past hurts. Or possibly show anger—anger at how Charlie and Elizabeth had cut him out of their lives. Surely, Bobby had a well of anger that had not been tapped.

He was on his way to a full recovery, but might this family function send him into a tailspin? It must be so difficult to be estranged from your whole family, from all your close friends, estranged from your past life, and then one day step back into it like it was all a bad dream, a nightmarish agony of wanting—needing—to use drugs so badly that you gave it all up for the stick of the needle, the pop of the pill.

Because Bobby truly gave up everything for the drug: he lost his acceptance, reputation, dignity. He lost his friends, his family, his home. Could he begin to gain some of it back tonight?

I closed my eyes and urged him on, *you can do it, you can do it.* I whispered it over and over to myself, digging my fingernails into Will's palm. *Come on. Come on, Bobby.*

And he did. I opened my eyes as he raised his head and looked directly at the wedding couple, penetrating and non-blinking, decisive. There was a hush, a few *shhhh's*, a finger to the lips of several guests in silent gesture. The pop and ping of the bonfire was the only sound heard as he began to talk from someplace that had been closed and locked for many years: his heart.

He began by telling Charlie that he was and would always be his best friend along with his other best friend, Elizabeth. He congratulated Charlie, saying how happy he was that Charlie was marrying Elizabeth and would become the brother Bobby has never had. He talked about love, his deep love for both of them, and his wish for their future happiness. He was grateful for the invitation to be in the wedding, the chance to share it all with them and to honor them. He ended his toast by telling them again how much he loved them.

It took a moment. The clap started out slowly, like you would see in a movie, the slow clap of one person and then another and another until the momentum built. This is how I remember it anyway. There were no shouts or cheers, no raucousness. The emotion was contained because no words were needed. Everything that needed to be said was felt in the clapping of their hands.

I think it was Charlie and Elizabeth who stood up first, but by the end everyone was on their feet and clapping, a standing vote of approval, an ovation of acceptance and love for Bobby and his long, arduous journey home.

PART THREE

OxyContin and heroin are chemically similar, they are equally addictive, and heroin and OxyContin are considered very difficult to withdraw from.

—Novus Medical Detox Center

On May 5, 2009, the FDA invited Novus to provide testimony before a special FDA committee that was investigating what Risk Evaluation Mitigation Strategies (REMS) to impose on dangerous prescription narcotics like OxyContin.

The testimony (condensed) stated that this is known about heroin and OxyContin:

- Heroin was initially advertised as being less addictive than morphine and widely promoted in the United States for the treatment of pain and respiratory problems.

- Because of its addictive qualities, heroin was made illegal in 1914.

- OxyContin was released to the public in 1995 by Purdue Pharma.

- Heroin and OxyContin are molecularly almost identical.

- Heroin and OxyContin operate in the same manner in the body.

- Heroin and OxyContin are interchangeable and addicts regularly use the one that is available.

- OxyContin is easily obtained from a number of doctors who prescribe it for any excuse as long as the patient can pay for the office visit.

—OxyContin and Heroin Facts, FDA Testimony,
http://novusdetox.com/oxycontin-heroin-facts.php

NINE MONTHS

November

WHEN A DOOR CLOSES

The wedding seemed like a dream once we returned home, far away and distant, but there were small reminders that would bring a smile to my face, like finding a bit of sand in my shoes or Bobby showing me beaming pictures of himself that friends had posted on Facebook.

The several weeks after we returned to real life were big ones for our household. I underwent my third knee surgery, the second one on my right knee. It was just a cleanup job—arthoscopic—but it was much needed.

I made up my mind to try not to use pain pills (except for Advil, of which I should have bought stock in the company), as I was so much more aware of the pitfalls of prescription opioids, such as Oxy, Lortab, Percocet, or Vicodin. I wanted to set a good example for Bobby, but more than that, I am fearful to use them, even short-term. FACT: opioids are highly addictive.

Bobby was retaking the real estate exam for the third and hopefully last time. I knew how nervous he was because I was just as nervous. If it weren't for my postsurgical knee pain to take my mind off the test, I would have been even more of a wreck.

The real estate exam day came and went in a blur sometime in early November as I daily convalesced on the family room sofa. Several days after taking the exam, Bobby came to my side and plopped down into his overstuffed chair. He announced in a resigned, monotone voice that he had once again failed the test.

The mood around the house was bleak. Bobby was beside himself, made more miserable that he had failed his third try by only one measly point. One point! Cruel and unusual punishment and bitter, bitter disappointment. I was unable to think about how much it hurt and how helpless I was to change it without feeling a crushing weight on my chest.

A few days passed as we all grappled with the new realization that real estate might not be in Bobby's future.

Late one afternoon I felt so overwhelmed with discouragement that I crawled into bed and fell asleep for several hours. When I woke up, I suddenly knew what we were going to do, and I hurriedly grabbed my crutches and three-legged my way as fast as I could to the bottom of the stairs. I don't know how I came up with this idea, whether I read it somewhere or it came to me in a dream. It doesn't matter. It was one of the most useful tools we used for Bobby, and we employed it in the nick of time. I called him downstairs.

First I gave him the ole pep talk to soften him up. I told him that I knew he was dejected that he hadn't been able to pass the real estate test. But I encouraged him to look at the failure from a different angle. It was not wasted energy or wasted time. He had learned things he would use the rest of his life, important worldly knowledge. No, this experience was not a zero, and in fact, he'd learned a lot of information all people should know. When he went to buy his first home, or invest in a piece of land, he would look back and be thankful for the time he spent learning real estate laws.

I also told him I would much rather he fail the real estate test ten times over than pass the test and not really know or understand the material. This was the real world now, and he couldn't bluff his way through on his good looks and charisma.

He was shaking his head, and I couldn't tell if it was in agreement or because he thought I had cracked.

I continued, telling him that Will and I always believed that there is some purpose for each of us that we must find. I reluctantly admitted that Will and I never thought real estate was his purpose, but that we didn't want to speak up since he wanted it so badly and was working so hard.

Failing this latest test had given us a grand opportunity! Will and I had been feeling a bit neglectful that Bobby hadn't had the chance to investigate many avenues of jobs and careers, but now he had the opportunity.

I was up on my feet now, hobbling back and forth, crutches clanking each time they struck the wood floor, gathering steam. It was time for my big idea.

"I want you to do something for me. Humor me, please. Here is a pad of paper. I want you to write down things you think you are good at or things you love to do but may not be the best at and things people think you are good at or compliment you on. I am talking about everything. If you love walking the dogs, write it down. If you love working with the elderly or you love eating watermelon or throwing darts, write it down. If people think you are good at poetry, a snazzy dresser, or a great massage giver, write it down. Then come find me."

That was just what he did. He spent the rest of the evening and the next morning on the task before he brought me the multiple pages of scrawl.

The first few items he wrote down made me think he hadn't taken me very seriously. Under "things I am good at or love to do," he wrote:

Knowledgeable about rehab and rehab centers.
Know a lot about addiction and alcoholism.
Know a lot about helping others that are addicted.

The next few lines were about hunting and guns.

Love to hunt.
Knowledgeable about most guns and ammunition.
Good shot.

And then he wrote about his love of automobiles and his RC car hobby.

The second page was full, and I was excited to see he had taken time and dug deep.

Things other people think I am good at:
Good with people.
Good public speaker.
Funny.
Good with cars.

And much more.

When we spread all of the pages out on the kitchen table, we had a wealth of information.

"Bobby, is this list pretty complete? You gave it a lot of thought? You can't think of anything else?"

"No, I don't think so."

I smacked my hand down on the hard marble with a new realization. "Bobby, you did not mention one thing here about real estate. Nothing. Nothing remotely close."

I then pulled out a red pen and started grouping items that went well together. The outdoors-hunting group was large, as was the automotive group and the group dealing with addiction, rehab, and working with or helping others.

"What could you do with the hunting category?" I asked him.

"Shooting range. Law enforcement. Security guard. Gun-smithing."

"What about automotives?"

Bobby didn't hesitate. "Mechanic. Welding. Radio controlled race track owner."

"What about this last big grouping? The one about how you are knowledgeable about addiction? Let's talk about this one." I realized quickly that he hadn't listed these talents as a joke.

We began a thirty-minute discussion about the skills he'd acquired during his rehabilitation. Bobby *is* knowledgeable. And he has had the opportunity to help many others through the process when he could. At that very moment he was mentoring a childhood friend who was struggling with alcoholism. He talked to him long-distance every day and whenever his friend felt the urge to drink. Like Bill W. of Alcoholics Anonymous, his friend would reach out to Bobby for support to weather his craving. Bobby gathered encouraging books and cards, sending them to his buddy. I realized that his recovering friend depended on Bobby for emotional support and accountability.

I asked him if he enjoyed helping this pal. He looked at me like I was a Martian with two heads. "Of course. I feel I have to help him. And I want to."

"One option you might consider is becoming a counselor. A licensed therapist. Or a social worker. You would have to go back to school, but you are exactly the right age to go back to school. Graduate schools want students who are a little older these days."

He was visibly excited about this option, but fearful that he was getting too old to begin a new career, especially one that might take several years of schooling. On the other hand, the economy was in a deep recession, and most kids coming out of undergraduate programs were having a terrible time landing a job—any job—much less one that was in their chosen career field. So it was a good time to be in school.

Once again, Bobby peeled himself up off the floor, and for the rest of November he researched different areas of interest. He looked into gunsmithing school and—egads!—it was a two-year wait to get into the class. He researched RC tracks and traveled the state to talk to the owners of these tracks. He looked up requirements for law enforcement and security guards. We did not discount any idea—big or small—that he suggested.

After several weeks of research, he came down the stairs one day and announced that he wanted to go back to graduate school to get a Master of Social Work to possibly become a substance abuse counselor. He had been talking to Jeff Georgi, and the two of them felt it was a good fit. I smiled broadly and clapped him on the back. I had always thought he would make a good social worker or licensed therapist. He is gifted with people, and he has a deeply empathetic nature, not to mention life experience. To me, a substance abuse counselor was a bull's-eye.

Bobby's eyes lit up while he continued talking. Animatedly he described the path he wanted to take and how, in his experience, addicts want to talk to somebody who has been in their shoes—who has gone to hell and come back.

If that was one of the qualifications for a good substance abuse counselor, he would be perfect for the job.

From: Renée Hodges
Subject: Request
Date: Tuesday, November 19, 2013, at 4:55 p.m.
To: BS

Dear Bible Study friends,

I have a prayer request: please pray for Bobby. He has decided that real estate/automotives, etc. was not something he could get excited about. But what he decided he can get excited about and what he wants to do with the rest of his life is to become a social worker and possibly an addiction counselor.

He has an appointment with the dean of our local university graduate program to discuss admissions requirements for a Master of Social Work degree tomorrow night at six. If you know Bobby, you know that this is exactly what he should be doing with his life. He will help so many people. Please pray that the dean will see the benefit of guiding Bobby, and helping him to get into this program. I think this will be a life-changing event for him if he gets in.

Loved being with you all today!

Love to all, Renée

DICK'S SPORTING GOODS

Bobby decided that he could not wait any longer. He needed to be making money with a "real" job instead of doing the odd errand here and there while writing applications and holding out hope for admittance to a Master of Social Work program at a local university.

He sent his resume to random places. He stopped by several auto repair shops and an oil change franchise, thinking he would enjoy working with cars. He found the pay lousy, the hours long, and that he wouldn't be doing much more than answering the phone. He persevered and widened his search.

When Dick's Sporting Goods interviewed him mid-November, he was offered a job on the spot because of his expertise with guns and hunting equipment.

Even though Will and I knew the position was a stopgap measure, we also recognized it as a major breakthrough. Bobby had found a job on his own. Yippee! He was demonstrating ambition and drive, something we couldn't help him with, and showing us that he was working toward a future, a future he could see. We saw hunger and restlessness in him, and I felt him champing at the bit as Will and I still held tightly to the reins. This was a good change.

He was beginning to feel and act more like a grown man. As he put distance between his checkered past, time between his last usage of alcohol and drugs, and work into understanding the emotions he battled, he matured before our eyes, growing up and bridging the stagnant period of his lost years.

Alcoholics and drug users remain stunted at the age they begin using, which meant that Bobby's maturity level when he came to live with us was that of a much younger man. His wanting and seeking a job and the desire to be self-sufficient were all indicators of healing.

Dick's hired him as a part-time employee to assist during the holiday rush that begins the week before Thanksgiving and lasts through the New Year. He worked three to four days part-time per week the first few weeks and filled in when called upon. He was so reliable and knowledgeable in the gun department that after the third week he was hired as a full-time employee in December.

The Hodges household was bustling with excitement on Bobby's first day of work as a full-time employee. It reminded me of my kids' first days of school and I almost took a picture of him, but I didn't. Annie Walters, our housekeeper, came in early and fixed him a special breakfast, but he was too anxious to eat and stirred his food around on his plate. I fixed him lunch because he never had time to eat on the job when he was part-time, and Annie and I hovered around him like lionesses with their pride, fiercely protective and proud.

Late into his shift on his first full day, I decided to drop in to Dick's and surprise him. The gun department was located in the farthest left-hand corner of the store, past the workout clothes, shoes, and sports equipment. I was off my crutches but still limping and very slow, which gave me time to wistfully bemoan my lack of agility as I passed a cute tennis outfit.

I rounded the corner and scanned the hunting department. Not seeing him, I searched each aisle, up and down, and only then began to panic. I hobbled up to the gun counter and waved down the lone employee. "Umm, I'm looking for Bobby Redford. Is he working today?"

Just as I was inquiring, I saw the door to the stockroom open. It was Bobby. He saw me and a big, proud grin appeared. He scurried over to me and asked in his most professional voice, "Ma'am, can I help you?" Then, under his breath, "I'll be finished with this customer in a few minutes. Can you wait?"

Enjoying the joke, I loudly declared, "I need a knife as a Christmas present. I'll just look around until you can help me, young man." I returned his smile.

He worked eight-hour-plus shifts and his schedule was

random, so he never knew which hours he would be working. He could be called in at any time, and I began to feel his manager equated working many hours with being a successful worker. Bobby was willing to work any and all number of hours because he wanted and needed to prove himself to everyone—including himself.

By the end of his first month as a full-time employee, he was awarded his first "Employee of the Week."

During the Christmas rush, Bobby came home one afternoon all aglow. A customer he had waited on had written a long email to the national office of Dick's commending him for going out of his way to help her. She reported that Bobby was courteous, knowledgeable, and helpful, and she felt he had gone above and beyond in his capacity as a salesman. The Dick's Sporting Goods national headquarters sent a team to take Bobby's picture and write a feature about him for the employee magazine. Sadly, the manager in charge of his store quit before it was submitted, and the story fell between the cracks and wasn't published. But I knew and Bobby knew. He was being recognized for doing something good! Excelling! Achieving! Will and I took him to dinner to celebrate. Sparkling water all around!

Despite the successes he was experiencing in this position, Will and I were concerned that he was taking on too much, not advocating for himself and working too-long hours, including many twelve-hour shifts. Employee morale was low during this holiday time as the store was going through managerial upheaval and high employee turnover. Bobby would find himself regularly responsible for half the store, and the pay was lower than what he had been paid to dog walk. Still, Will and I could see the enormous benefits he was getting from the self-esteem boost.

NINE MONTHS TWENTY-TWO DAYS

Christmas 2013

It wasn't until mid-December that Will and I realized that because Bobby was a full-time employee, and a very valued one, he would not get much time off work for Christmas, the high season in retail.

After talking to Jeff Georgi, we invited Jill and John to come spend Christmas with us, with Bobby. After reuniting at the wedding, Bobby was excited by this idea and his parents were delighted to make the trip north. I began to plan.

Jill and I decided on a price limit for gifts, and I begged her to stay within the parameters. I can safely say that I always adhere to the limit and Jill and John do not. I am always a conflicted beneficiary.

Bobby saw the busyness of the season all around him and began to fret about what to get his parents for Christmas. He asked his sister for suggestions, and she kindly said he could split the cost of a piece of pricey luggage that she was getting for their mom. Although Elizabeth could afford to buy the luggage, he and I both realized that splitting the cost was unrealistic as the brand she was buying made a very beautiful, but high-end product.

I finally sat him down and had a heart-to-heart.

"Are you making a lot of money? Do your parents know how much you are making?"

"I'm making minimum wage, barely enough to put gas in my truck."

"Yep. And your mom and dad know this, right?" He nodded as I continued, "What do you think they would think if you went out and bought them each a very expensive present for Christmas? What would you think?"

Bobby fidgeted. "They would be mad. They wouldn't want me to do that." He sighed, dejected. "But, Aunt Née, I want to get them something nice. I want them to know how much I love them and appreciate all they've done for me."

We sat quietly in the kitchen with our dilemma.

"I have an idea. It is only because it would be what I would want for Christmas. I wouldn't want you to spend money on me either. So, for your dad, why not get him a sleeve of really nice golf balls, especially since you have an employee discount? And for your mom, maybe a beautiful scarf from Target or T.J. Maxx?"

He didn't look too thrilled, so I kept talking. "And then," I said, pausing for effect, "I would give them the best present of all. I would write them each a love letter from your heart. Tell them how much you appreciate them. How much they mean to you. How much you love them. That would be more priceless than gold."

And that was just what he did the Christmas of 2013.

When I opened up my present from Bobby, a brand-new can of tennis balls with a sealed note taped to the top of the can, I swelled with emotion. I looked around at my beautiful husband and kids, my healthy and happy brother and sister-in-law, and dear, sweet, Bobby, who is a shared gift for sure.

I silently bowed my head and thanked God for all the many blessings I had in my life. Merry Christmas, indeed.

TEN MONTHS

January 2014

From: Renée Hodges
Subject: Winnie the Pooh
Date: January 6, 2014, at 9:04 p.m.
To: Bobby

"You are BRAVER than you believe,

STRONGER than you seem, and

SMARTER than you think."

~ A.A. Milne ~ (Christopher Robin to Winnie the Pooh)

The past year witnessed so many changes in Bobby's life and in mine. Physically Bobby was as healthy as he had been in the last nine years. He was free of illegal drugs. He was off all but a minimal dose of prescription medication. Gone were all the mood-altering, high-potency drugs that turned him into the perfect cast member for *Return of the Zombies*. Bobby was able to feel and to care again.

The excess weight he had carried as a side effect from medication had melted away. He was lean and trim.

He was keeping his hair out of his eyes and in some semblance of a hairstyle; he was able to look directly in someone's eyes and hold their gaze, and to interact and connect.

After Thanksgiving he spent several weeks after work writing his application essay for the Master of Social Work program he wanted to pursue. He'd met with the admissions director of a local university and had been led to believe that he would not need the GRE to be accepted, which was good because he had missed the deadline to take the test.

I had called upon my close friend, Dee, an English major and former teacher, to help Bobby with his essay and his confidence, as it had been a decade since he'd last applied to a school.

After several back and forths to Dee and his mother, Jill, for proofreading, Bobby submitted his application to just the one university in the beginning of January, and we began the long, agonizing wait.

ELEVEN MONTHS

February

PHILIP SEYMOUR HOFFMAN

I was walking through the family room to get to the kitchen, beginning to think about what to cook for dinner. The TV was on and Bobby, home from work, was sprawled in his adopted chair, watching a program.

"Aunt Née, look at this."

Concerned by the alarmed tone of his voice, I quickly took a seat next to him. He was intently staring at the screen where a breaking-news alert showed pictures of a flashing ambulance being loaded with a covered body on a stretcher.

The Academy Award–winning actor Philip Seymour Hoffman had been found dead in his apartment with a needle sticking out of his arm. The New York City medical examiner officially ruled it an accident, but the mix of heroin, cocaine, benzodiazepines, and amphetamines just seemed like a recipe for suicide. Hoffman, a former heroin addict who had been clean for nearly twenty years, had recently relapsed and it had taken his life.

I was on the edge of the couch, unconsciously biting my fingernails. Bobby was quiet, unnervingly quiet. I glanced at him every so often, but he seemed unaware of my presence. We were immersed in a stranger's death, bound up by the tragedy because we silently knew how close this story hit to home.

God, I thought, *please give me a reason for this senseless heartbreak. Why, why, why?* The question most asked by the helpless.

We stayed this way for many minutes as we watched the full report—the esteemed and incredibly talented actor's accomplishments, the partner and young children he'd left behind, his early struggles with drugs, his recovery, his final day.

I was still engrossed when I realized Bobby had gotten up from his chair. He mechanically headed to the back door leading to the screened porch. I knew where he was going; he was going outdoors to smoke. And to reflect.

God, I wanted a cigarette so badly I could taste it, damn it.

We never ever talked about Philip Seymour Hoffman again except for a short conversation when Bobby knowingly told me, "Sometimes, after an addict has quit for a while and then relapses, they will use the same amount of heroin they were using before they quit, thinking they will get the same high. Their tolerance is down. And you never really know how much is too much."

Bam.

———

SPIRALING

February

January came and went. Happily, I was able to get away to be with my mother for a few weeks, and Will was able to meet me, although he only stayed a few days.

Bobby had become reliable and responsible, two traits that I believe he had always inherently possessed, but somehow lost in the haze of addiction. Throughout January he shone at work, and although fatigued, he was happy to be making money and be employed.

He was consistently named employee of the week at Dick's and had now been awarded employee of the month as well. This was mostly due to his great work ethic but also partly due to the fact that many of the part-time employees had quit and there was still turmoil in management.

By late January, Bobby was again covering several departments and working long hours. It was when Dick's started scheduling him to regularly work the truck shift, 4:00 a.m. to 2:00 p.m., that his sleeping and eating patterns became erratic and he became cranky and exhausted all the time.

I believed he was still working hours that would kill a horse at Dick's because he was willing to work anytime. His long and late hours made it difficult for me to keep up with him. When he worked the graveyard shift, he came home while I was winding down for the afternoon. He slept the rest of the day or spent it lethargic and uncommunicative. He was not routinely working out or going to AA meetings now because his schedule didn't allow for it. This worried me.

He wanted to go home for his thirtieth birthday on February 28. He hadn't been back to his hometown by himself for a year. He was feeling the pull of family as we all do at those times in our lives where we need a little shot of home. After talking to Jeff, he asked for a week off from work and made plans to drive to Louisiana.

I could feel Bobby withdrawing from us, detaching emotionally. I thought I knew what he was thinking. In the back of his head I thought he was realizing that working at Dick's was not a long-term option for him. His wage wouldn't allow for him to pay rent on an apartment and put gas in his truck to get to work. The reality was stark and painful, making him all the more nervous and anxious that he had not heard from the one graduate school he had applied. He was weary. We were all weary.

So too did I notice he was losing too much weight; he was only eating Honey Nut Cheerios with extra sugar and was back to drinking liters of Diet Coke. When he did sit down to eat dinner or lunch with us, he left for the restroom immediately afterward. I inquired about it and he said he sometimes threw up because of the anxiety. He said he couldn't cook his food because of the nausea and so he ate the Cheerios.

He might have been sinking into a depression, feeling the emotional fatigue of his year-long efforts. He was starting to regress, to act as he'd acted when he first came to North Carolina: head down, not meeting eyes, spending most of his time in the bedroom instead of interacting. He was aloof and hangdog looking. He turned down all forms of invitations. Dinner out, Duke basketball games, free theater tickets, walks, just about anything he was offered he declined, preferring to stay home and watch TV. He wanted a connection, a friend/girlfriend so badly, but didn't know how to have or keep a relationship.

I needed some advice before he left for Louisiana. I was concerned because of his change in demeanor, the pulling away from us, and I emailed Jeff with my concerns. It was not lost on me that the one-year anniversary of his near-fatal trip and arrival in Durham was next week. Bobby should be ready both physically and emotionally to make the long road trip, but I was hesitant to let him go while he was so dejected.

Maybe I was contributing to his downward spiral? I could see a marked difference in the household as winter was ending. Will was chafing to have Bobby begin his life, his new path, in his own apartment. He was a grown man and it was time. I knew it was time, Will knew it, and Bobby knew it.

My whole body stayed tense and jittery. I now understood the phrase, "jumping out of my skin." I became fearful to turn on the car radio, as music seemed to cause an involuntary tearful release. And, Lordy, going to the grocery store where soft contemporary music was piped into each row, soothing and encouraging the harried shopper so as to enhance the shopping experience—well, the grocery store downright made me weep into the collard greens.

I did what I could and talked, talked, talked to Bobby—that is, when I could nail him down for a minute or two. I think he was avoiding me. He must have found it confusing when I told him to plan for the future but live for today, and I knew I drove him absolutely nuts with all my talk about hoping for the best and planning for the worst, my standard head cheerleader line. I did feel Bobby needed to be planning right then, in case he didn't get into the Master of Social Work program in the fall. It was like he was paralyzed though and could not think about another step forward, not because he wanted to do nothing but because the effort was bloody heavy, and he could not bear the weight. It was as if by making a contingency plan he was sealing his fate.

I was relieved that Bobby was going home to his parents for the week. It shifted the burden of planning for the better or the worse to his mother and father.

From: Renée Hodges
Subject: Bobby's trip to Louisiana
Date: Sunday, February 23, 2014, at 10:25 a.m.
To: John Redford, Jill Redford

Hi Jill and John,

Bobby left in his truck yesterday morning and was as upbeat and excited as I have seen him in weeks. He was "giddy" with anticipation.

We discussed his trip and went over what he needs to do to keep himself safe. He promised he would watch his diet. He has planned on discussing his transition with you. He may hear about his application to the local university on March 1 (he thinks) by email. Would be nice if he would call and find out the exact date, but then again he may already know and just be hesitant to tell us.

Have a wonderful time with him on his birthday. Don't hesitate to call me if you have questions. I will check in and you can leave a message on my cell.

Love, Renée

Text from Jill Redford to Renée on Sunday, February 23, 2014:

Bobby made it in this afternoon! We were so happy to see him. John cooked and we had a nice Sunday supper. I will keep you in the loop.

Love you,
Jill

For Bobby's birthday, I asked those closest to him to write a personal happy birthday letter of encouragement, and I put them in a box, specially wrapped, to be opened in Louisiana on the actual day. This was my contribution:

Friday, February 28, 2014

Dearest Bobby,

HAPPY BIRTHDAY! You have made me so, so, proud. You have done so much in one year that I am proud of and I hope you are too. You are clean. You are aware of what you eat (good and bad) and changing bad habits one at a time. You are working . . . working hard. You are clear headed . . . enough so that you have formulated a path for yourself. You have melded into our family so seamlessly that I selfishly count my blessings that you came my way. You are keeping a schedule, taking control of your life, cutting the umbilical cord, making some good decisions . . . and some not so good . . . and this will be for the rest of your life. Just remember, we all make mistakes and it is only when we don't learn from that mistake that it is really a mistake!

You are transitioning now; getting ready to launch. No matter if you get into school or don't get into school, you must be patient and kind to yourself. You have grown immensely in one year. I can't wait to see where you are next year at this time.

Remember, you will always be considered part of our immediate family. We want you to come on trips, spend holidays, count on us. You are blessed to have two families that love you and want you. All families are dysfunctional in their own way, but real love is an unconditional love, a love-the-whole-person-warts-and-all kind of love. We hope you love all our warts!!!

Lastly:

I wish you happiness.

I wish you strength.

I wish you courage.

I wish you great faith.

I wish you humbleness.

I wish you joy.

But, most of all, I wish you love, the greatest of all.

With love, Aunt Née

———

From Anne Howard:

Friday, February 28, 2014

Dear Bobby,

A little birdie alerted me to the fact that you have a big birthday! What a milestone. And look how far you have come in the last year!

It's hard to believe you arrived here at the same time Thomas died. I can't believe March 1 it will be a year. I hope Thomas's death has some impact on you to steer you in the right direction. I'd hate to think his death was in vain.

I love you so much, Bobby, and have been praying for you along the way. I know it's not easy. You have made such great strides and look how far you have come. You're such a wonderful person and so full of love. Your day is coming. I know it. You have so much to offer to this world and God has put you here for a reason.

We don't always know God's ways, but I believe you and I both will discover what it is. I still don't know what I'm to do when I grow up. I have felt so lost without Thomas, but my many friends continue to lift me up. I keep praying for you and know you can do it. Please don't end up like Thomas. What a waste!

I love you, my sweet son. If you ever need anyone to talk to, I'm always here. I don't judge, I just want to help. In the end, it's up to you. What a wonderful life you have to look forward to. Thirty years, you're a baby! I wish I were thirty. I'd be chasing you around in circles!

Your third mom, Anne Howard

From Will:

Bobby:

First, Happy Birthday!

It's hard to believe you have been a Duke-cheering Durhamite for almost a year. Both Renée and I have loved having you as part of our lives. I realize you may not be where you want to be. But I am impressed with your progress in the past year. I'm not sure you can remember the first few weeks here. You were struggling on a number of levels. Slowly you started getting traction with both your mental and physical self. For us it was an incredible transformation to witness.

We loved sharing your successes and milestones. Our talk the day you came home with an AA sober days token and did not share it with us is a memory I'll always have. Partly because at the time you were hesitant to share the accomplishment with us and partly because at the time you didn't want to share it with your AA group.

I remember us talking about how important it is in life to celebrate our successes with those whom we love and how important it is to give others in AA hope by showing you accomplished it. We all need people with whom we can share success and failure. They are what keep us going. I loved sharing your growth and successes.

You never know where life will take you. I am thankful for at least this part: it brought you to us. Someone pointed out that "there is a reason your windshield is so much larger than your rearview mirror." It represents the possibilities and expanse of your future compared to the past. Still we need the rearview mirror to remind us where we came from and how we got to where we are. There are no assurances in life. As you go forward, do so unafraid and embrace the possibilities. I hope it takes you on a journey full of peace and happiness. We'll always be here for you.

Love you,

Uncle Will

———

From Annie Walters:

Hi Bobby,

What can I say without getting emotional? I know this has not been an easy journey for you, but you are doing it with great hope. I am so proud of you, Bobby. I have watched you over the past year just finding your way, and you are doing a great job. I want you to know that I am here for you. I am glad God put you in our lives. He knew I needed someone else to help take care of besides Roux and Saint . . . LOL! I am going to end with one of my favorite scriptures:

Isaiah 41:10

Fear not, for I am with you; be not dismayed for I am God; I will strengthen you, I will help you, I will uphold you with my righteous right hand.

Have a safe trip home, Bobby, and always keep God first. Xoxoxoxoxo

Love u,

Annie Walters

PS. Have a Happy, Happy Birthday and remember life is filled with special gifts, moments, and people to appreciate. So when life gives you lemons, make lemonade.

ONE YEAR

ANNIVERSARY OF THOMAS HOWARD'S OVERDOSE

From: Renée Hodges
Subject: Sad Reminder
Date: Friday, February 28, 2014, at 7:34 p.m.
To: BS friends

Dear Bible Study friends,

Just wanted to remind you that tomorrow is the one-year anniversary of Thomas's death. Anne is already struggling, so all prayers are welcomed and needed.

Tomorrow is also Bobby's thirtieth birthday, leap year baby! And the one-year anniversary of when Bobby began his journey to Durham. Surely, God has a plan!?

xo Renée

———

From: Anne Howard
Subject: Thomas
Date: Friday, February 28, 2014, at 9:08 p.m.
To: Renée Hodges

A toast to Thomas tomorrow afternoon at five in his room. That's when I found him. Love you.

———

From: Renée Hodges
Subject: Thomas
Date: Friday, February 28, 2014, at 9:28 p.m.
To: Anne Howard

Yes, a toast. He was a good son and he is at peace. Thomas is with God right now and together they will watch over you tomorrow.

Love, Renée

On Saturday, March 1, 2014, at precisely 5:30 p.m., Anne and I released several dozen white balloons into the early evening sky in front of her home, watching, watching, arms intertwined, straining our necks and eyesight until the very last balloon disappeared into the heavens.

———

WILL AND BOBBY

When Bobby returned from his birthday trip to Louisiana, I was attending the wedding of the daughter of a close college friend. Will did not attend the wedding and was home when Bobby arrived back in Durham. He sent the following email to me with an update.

From: Will
Subject: News on Bobby
Date: Friday, March 7, 2014, at 10:22 a.m.
To: Renée

Dear Renée,

Bobby came back to Durham from his week in Louisiana with a positive outlook. I don't think we realized how depressed he was/is before he left—e.g., no friends, no prospects. He came back with these goals: doing something for himself once a week, get back in meetings, get involved in church again, get out and meet people, move out within three months, figure out what he wants to do, possibly get back in summer school until he can go full-time, and either get the full promotion or cut back to part-time with Dick's Sporting Goods.

He sat down with me for almost forty-five minutes and we talked. He has been very depressed (eating, sleeping). When he has gone to "run his RC cars," he just leaves and sits in his truck and cries.

Will

When I returned, Will decided he needed to have another man-to-man talk with Bobby.

"Your work hours are insane. We know you feel like Dick's is taking advantage of you, and you tell us you are unhappy. But you have never told them you don't want to work the graveyard shift. Maybe you are given these hours because you always say yes. With employee turnover so high and your record of impeccable service, you are in a position to negotiate. The lesson here is that you must advocate for yourself. No one else will advocate for you. And if you don't ask for what you need, you will never know if it is available to you. No one can take advantage of you without your permission."

Bobby told me later that it made an impact that his uncle Will was willing to sit down and listen to him. Because I know how difficult it was for Will initially, when I think of this conversation and of Will listening and giving Bobby advice, I find it hard not to choke up.

After their manly talk Bobby had a sit-down with the

new store manager. He told his manager he needed more income and stable hours. He stood up for himself for maybe the first time in his life. The manager listened and offered him the position of certified fitness trainer, which came with a raise, better hours, and defined responsibility.

Working at Dick's Sporting Goods taught Bobby about work vs. career, responsibility and reliability, being proactive vs. complaining. In the end, Dick's gave him a glowing personal recommendation for graduate school and a recommendation that would get him a job at any other store.

I still frequent Dick's.

Will's update on Bobby was a major surprise to me, as I had not realized he was so defeated and that I had been missing the warning signs. Was I too close to the situation, seeing trees but not the forest? Even though Will's email was a bucket of ice water, I couldn't help but feel warm inside picturing Bobby sitting at the kitchen table confiding in Will and Will listening with care.

I can't pinpoint the exact time that Will bought into my plan of helping Bobby because it wasn't an "oh snap" moment. It happened gradually over the year, as Bobby slowly became a person again, able to think and feel for himself. I could see it happening as Will and Bobby started bonding over small things. A sprinkler head would break and I'd hear Will explaining to Bobby how to fix it. There would be a rattle in an old car we owned and I would overhear their contemplations of the different possible ailments. I would have a meeting or a tennis match and find Bobby and Will out for lunch together upon my return.

They both had something to give each other besides companionship and mentorship. Will is an especially good conversationalist and loves an eager audience. Bobby is a great listener.

As the months slipped away and a year was marked, I was so thankful for both these wonderful men and knew that they had helped each other grow, Bobby in his quest for peace, and Will in opening up and giving more of himself to someone in need.

———

DISEMBARKING, AGAIN

March 23

Could it be over a year since Will and I had disembarked a catamaran in the British Virgin Isles on a beautiful day in the beginning of March? Invited for the second year in a row, I took a moment on the bow of the boat on our last morning to contemplate nothing in particular, relishing the sense of openness the sea emanated, giving me a gift of emotional clarity and receptiveness, a feeling that a binding had been released, my breath no longer restrictive, my nervous system at peace.

I relied on the iron mast to help pull me upright, and standing with both hands on my hips, I looked up at the tall pole listing in the wind and thought how both of us were teeming with purpose, swaying with contentment.

Okay, I was ready. I hopped off the sailboat, landing with a strong thud onto the well-worn wooden pier, wincing at the flashback, a raw déjà-vu moment as I switched on my iPhone.

———

WHAT IF?

Even though March started off on an upward trajectory, Bobby had been in the dumps since returning from Louisiana in early March. He hadn't heard boo from the graduate school, even after calling, and he didn't have any other options as he had put all his eggs in the proverbial one basket: one application to one graduate program. He hadn't taken the GRE, nor had he applied to summer school, and independent living wasn't even a bullet point yet. He was setting himself up for disaster. And, to add insult to injury, Dick's didn't seem to be working out as the newest manager did not want Bobby as a full-time employee and was scheduling him just shy of full-time hours.

I was worried about the what-if's. What if Bobby didn't get into graduate school (and it was looking like he wouldn't)? What if he wasn't prepared and ready for yet another disappointment? What if Will felt it was time for Bobby to be on his own? Bobby had no contingency plan.

I recruited Jill to help in his contingency planning. We communicated back and forth by email, racking our brains on how to keep Bobby engaged in this process and to come up with some action measures. Bobby is very close to his mother and her nagging would probably be a nice change from my nagging.

Still it seemed Bobby was moving at a snail's pace. Will had stressed over and over that he needed to look at his career search like a shot from a shotgun, hitting a big range, spreading out, attacking a bigger target area, and not like a rifle shot, accurate but only hitting one point. A great analogy and one which Bobby, the marksman, could and should understand well.

The beginning of April I decided to bring out the Tommy Gun and send Bobby an email, nag that I am.

From: Renée Hodges
Subject: Plan
Date: Saturday, April 5, 2014, at 9:18 a.m.
To: Bobby

Bobby,

I am so proud of you and I don't want to ride you, but you really need a plan of action. Right now. There are many things you can be doing. As I've said before, you are NOT on vacation and I don't want you to get used to all this free time. If Dick's isn't giving you enough hours, let's put in another part-time application somewhere. You should be working full-time until you decide if you are taking the GRE, going to summer school, or going another path.

I know you put in an application at the Auto Store today. Put in ten more at other places this weekend.

Also, applications for the fall are due at any and all graduate schools right now.

I looked up the GRE information and the next class starts in May. You should definitely know by then whether you got into grad school. You cannot afford to count on going to this one school for the fall if you haven't heard from them by now.

Let's get going. I'll help you but you have to kick-start it.

Love, Aunt Née

—————

CRISIS: BOILING POINT

The stress was enormous. Bobby should have heard something by now, even if he had been placed on a waiting list. Daily I asked if he had heard anything and always received a negative headshake.

There was an undercurrent of anxiety in the house, and it was seeping into all our relationships. Will and I argued over minute and inconsequential things, keeping tucked away the conversation about Bobby that neither of us wanted to have. I didn't want to have it because I felt we were so close to finding a path for him and I believed we had too much invested to not see him through to the end. Will was avoiding it because we were so far away from finding a path for Bobby. Will was ready for the bird to find another nest. He felt that Bobby's living arrangement with us was doing Bobby a disservice and might in fact be hurting his self-esteem.

—————

NOOOOOOOOOOOOOOOOOOOOOOOOOOOOO!

In the end, Bobby was not the one to tell us. I guess he couldn't face us with the news.

From: Renée Hodges
Subject: He did not get in. Jill told me.
Date: Monday, April 7, 2014, at 5:19 p.m.
To: Will Hodges

—————

From: Renée Hodges
Subject: What do we do now?
Date: Tuesday, April 8, 2014, at 10:37 a.m.
To: Jeff Georgi

Hi Jeff,

I thought I'd check in with you to get some advice on what I should be doing at this point with Bobby. I would like to please come in for fifteen minutes with or without him.

Here is an update:

He seems to be transitioning but to what, I am not sure. If he is going to meetings, they are during the day. I can't speak to his attendance.

Most days he is tinkering or playing with his cars. For hours. Or he is watching television with a computer in his lap.

He has gone back to his old appearance from when he first came here: hair long and unkempt, baggy athletic shorts, baseball cap turned backward. I don't really care what his choices are so much as if he is choosing for a reason.

On his own he has made a reservation to go to Louisiana for Easter for a week. I was hoping he would have a job, a plan, something to show before he took another week's vacation.

He seems, I think, to be content with doing nothing. But Will and I are at the launching stage and I can't quite get him to launch. We are at a loss as to what to do.

What I have written isn't so much a complaint as what I am seeing.

Thank you, Renée

———

From: Jeff Georgi
Subject: What do we do now?
Date: Tuesday, April 8, 2014, at 8:18 p.m.
To: Renée Hodges

Renée,

What you are describing is worrisome and what I feared could happen if we did not have a tight transition plan. He has worked very hard, as have you and Will. I would hate to see this damn disease reach out and grab him after the effort all have committed to his recovery.

If we can, let's get together with Bobby. I need to see him this week. Lunchtime is an option on Wednesday or Thursday.

If we simply cannot set up a face-to-face visit, can you please coordinate a phone call between Bobby and me?

Thanks, Jeff

———

From: Renée Hodges
Subject: Bobby
Date: Sunday, April 27, 2014, at 6:38 p.m.
To: BS Friends

Dear Bible Study friends,

Here is the quick update you asked me for . . .

Bobby did not get into school because they filled their class with kids that had taken the GRE after all. He actually never had a chance at admittance. He is going to take the GRE this summer and bolster his transcript with several summer school classes as well. He is still working part-time at Dick's and is meeting with the

*regional manager to talk about his potential for management. He
went home for Easter and came back with a stronger and more
determined than ever attitude to become a substance abuse
counselor, and I could not be more proud of him if he were my
own. I guess I could use your prayers too, to keep me positive and
upbeat, to not give up, to have God overcome this weariness I feel.*

*Fun news: Bobby has met a young lady from Baton Rouge, and
they have been having a good time going to Bulls' games,
restaurants, and taking long walks. We are planning his move to
his own apartment, hopefully by the end of the summer.*

*Please continue to pray for him and for me as I continue to balance
Will and Bobby in my life.*

Love, Renée

There is something to daylight savings time in the spring.
The longer evening sunlight generates surplus energy, and
the household becomes like a giant solar panel, soaking and
radiating, and for me, hope for Bobby became visible again.

From: Renée Hodges
Subject: Website to help you find smaller schools
Date: Friday, May 3, 2014, at 9:43 a.m.
To: Bobby

http://www.petersons.com/graduate-schools

*This is a wealth of information. If you find a school you are inter-
ested in, call their admissions department.*

After I sent this and several other reference emails to Bobby
with information on graduate schools, he holed up in his
bedroom for two days straight.

One afternoon he wandered into the kitchen with a ream of paper under his arm. He pulled it from his pit and dropped it on the counter with a loud thunk. On this pile of paper Bobby had printed every graduate school in every state and every admission requirement and due date. Large schools, small schools, urban, rural, he wasn't selective. He had begun calling and talking to the admissions departments of all grad schools that had a Master of Social Work program whose requirements fit his GPA, telling his story, probing for a way to become their newest student in the fall.

He had circled a small school in western North Carolina, a traditionally African American university.

"Aunt Née, I talked for thirty minutes with a dean, and they have a brand-new program they are implementing next fall. She asked if I could drive down on Monday and speak to her in person."

His eyes visibly sparkled, and as I jumped up and whooped and high-fived him, I said to myself what I imagined Louis Zamperini from the book *Unbroken* said to himself every time he endured and survived another catastrophe: "This has got to be the last time. It just has to be."

From: Renée Hodges
Subject: Secret of Living Well
Date: Wednesday, May 7, 2014, at 8:39 a.m.
To: Mary Costello

M—

I found these passages from Rachel Naomi Remen, and I am feeling compelled to share. :) I love the healing vs. cure stuff, and I particularly love, love this first passage from her website!

"Perhaps the secret of living well is not in having all the answers, but in pursuing unanswerable questions in good company."⁵

And I love this excerpt too!

"A place to meet together to explore healing; your own and other people's. Healing is not a work of perfection or expertise. We are all healers. We heal with our wholeness, our humanity, all of our life experience, even our wounds. Our own wounds make us gentle with the wounds of others and able to trust the mystery of healing, not as a theory but from lived experience. Our vulnerability connects us to the vulnerability in others in compassionate and loving ways.

"Healing is actually a worldview, a cosmology. . . . For a healer, the world is not broken and in need of fixing . . . the world is hidden. Everything and everyone has in themselves a hidden wholeness, a potential for growth, a dream of themselves. A healer reminds people. A healer befriends dreams. A healer is a feeder of dreams."⁶

—Rachel Naomi Remen

Dang Mary. The more I see, the more my eyes are opened.

PS. If I get to be a pain in your ass, just tell me. This new jumble of thought, connectedness, vulnerability, and yearning is all so new to me, I think I feel like Helen Keller must have felt at the water pump . . .

PPS. I sent Remen's quotes to Bobby. Perfect for him and I think he will like them!!

---

5 Rachel Naomi Remen, *My Grandfather's Blessings: Stories of Strength, Refuge, and Belonging*

6 http://www.rachelremen.com

ONE YEAR TWO MONTHS TWELVE DAYS

May 15

AT THE TAILOR'S

"Thanks so much. When can you have my dresses ready?" I was dropping off several outfits to be altered at the neighborhood alterations shop. Charlotte had been working with me for a long time, taking in and letting out clothes as my body did the middle-age swing. It was a small business, with barely enough room for the three tailors, the racks of clothes, and the counter I was leaning against.

I heard the bell ring at the front door, alerting us that someone had entered. I reflexively cut my eyes to the sound and then back to my checkbook. *Wait! Did I see who I think I saw?* I quickly turned back toward the door and, sure enough, Bobby was walking in, cell phone to his ear. His face was serious and he gave me a nod as he pointed to the phone.

My heart thudded. I hadn't told anyone I was coming to the tailor. He must have tracked me down. There must be something serious going on, and I thought it might be bad news. I worked myself up so quickly I thought I'd hyperventilate before he got off the phone.

I grabbed his free arm in a viselike grip, which got his attention. He looked up and I could see there was something going through his mind. I listened as he thanked whoever was on the other end of the call and clicked his phone off.

I couldn't keep the anxiety from my voice as I asked him how he knew to find me here at the tailor.

"Naw, Aunt Née, I wasn't looking for you. I'm here to pick up my alterations. I had to take in every single one of my dress pants because I couldn't hold them up, even with a belt."

The tension broken, I realized I was sweating through my cotton blouse. I began calming down, relaxing that it was just a coincidence that we were both in the same shop today. I smiled, proud that he was taking such responsibility for his appearance, something he never would have done when he first came to live with our family. But that would not be my best surprise of the day.

"Guess who just called me?" He didn't wait. "That was the dean of the school I met with last week, the one I told you about. She wanted to tell me personally that I have been accepted into their Master of Social Work graduate program for the fall semester. They are starting a new program, and I was told I am a good candidate to be in it." No one has ever grinned as widely as Bobby did at this moment. He was going to get his master's degree.

And what did I do? First, I was stunned into stone. I just stood there mute, not moving a muscle, trying to comprehend what he had announced. "What did you say?" I knew the answer; I just needed time to process.

"I'm starting school in the fall. I got in." He looked at me with concerned amusement as I began to stutter and repeat what he had just told me for the second time.

"Bobby, you are going to get your master's?" Duh. He'd told me twice, but he humored me and shook his head yes.

The three tailors in the shop had stopped their sewing machines and laid down their needles, watching this impromptu scene play out.

I looked at them and then back at Bobby. Then, like a sudden electrical shock, the enormity of it all hit me, and I broke down. Completely. All those months of hope, hard work, not giving up, and it all came down to a single phone call.

Like the tailoring of his clothes, Bobby had taken all that had been given him over the last fourteen months and was a changed man. And I had been incredibly changed too: cut, shaped, stitched, and finally altered—for the better.

I bawled like a big ole baby, elephant tears rolling down my cheeks, blurring my vision, nose running. I started jumping up and down and around and grabbed Bobby around the neck and gave him a good reason to revisit the Duke Spine Clinic. I high-fived everyone in the shop. I screamed with laughter and with tears. "Thank God, thank God," I repeated.

Euphoric with happiness, so proud of this beautiful young man next to me, I stood with my arm around his waist and in some unintelligible pig latin, tried to explain to Charlotte and the others why I was acting like I had just broken Michael Phelps's gold medal record.

Much later, I would shake my head with wonder when I thought about the great providence of Bobby being in the alterations shop at the same time he was getting the acceptance call from graduate school at the same time I was dropping off some clothes.

It was perfect. Just so perfect.

ONE YEAR THREE MONTHS
TWENTY-EIGHT DAYS

June 30

LAST DAY

I Dreaded this day coming. Yes, with a capital D. Not because I was having a total knee replacement the next day at 7:00 a.m. Yes, I dreaded that too. But what I was most nervous and scared about, what had kept me up at night and made my heart quiver like Jell-O, was that day would be Bobby's last day under our roof. When I got back from the hospital after my knee replacement, Bobby would be gone.

He was moving out, packing up his bedroom, cleaning every drawer and closet, taking his last RC car out of the mudroom and putting it in his truck bed. He had sold all but two of his beloved RC cars to help offset his living expenses, a testament to how much he had matured. He loaded his back seat with the hand-me-down tennis racquet I gave him and his attic finds: pictures, lamps, and old, forgotten, and discarded furniture covered in fifteen years of dust, items I was more than happy to pass on so he could furnish his new place.

He was upbeat, ready to sever the cord and get on with his life. He could barely contain his energy, and he hadn't been without a show-your-teeth smile all day. I stood back and looked at him, evaluating this new person, this transformation, this living, breathing, beautiful God's creature, and sighed. Bobby had lost massive amounts of weight, and with each pound he lost, he'd shed so much more. He no longer needed to hide behind physical things. He could and did meet you with both eyes trained on yours. He could confidently hold your gaze and let you look into his soul without flinching. His clothes and hair once literally and figuratively camouflaged him. He now dressed and groomed with self-esteem, putting his best foot forward every morning. Whatever shame he had brought with him to my home, I did not see it anymore. It might be there, would probably always be a part of him, but it was no longer a burden. He had set it down, released the torment, quieted his soul.

Bobby, with the help and openness of our community, accepts his past and old haunts and will not place blame on others. He is determined not to use ever again. Bobby is breaking the insidious cycle of addiction and enabling.

He was excited to begin his educational journey because of the knowledge he wanted to pass on to others who struggle as he did. He had hope and an openness bigger than the Grand Canyon. He was oozing love, acceptance, and pride from every pore and he didn't even know it. But I did, and I quickly wiped another tear from the corner of my eye before he caught me.

I was not ready to let go. Bobby had become another child of ours. I had the identical feeling as when my eleven-year-old William went off to summer camp. William solemnly took me aside and softly told me, "Mom, it is you that is not ready for me to go to summer camp. It is not me who is not ready. This is your problem and not mine. I am ready for summer camp and I want to go."

Damn, I was not ready to let Bobby go and it was my problem. I hadn't prepared for this graduation of sorts, and it had come so quickly, creeping up and taking me by surprise.

Surely it hadn't been sixteen months since Bobby came

into our lives, our home, our family. There was so much I wanted to tell him before he left, but as I scurried around, I couldn't put two words together. I was overwhelmed with my own feelings of self-pity, but, as with William and his camp, I knew deep down that he was ready and not only did he want to go to his next chapter but he needed to move on.

I had asked him to move out before I came home from the hospital, as I would be on pain medication for my knee replacement. He understood that he needed to keep himself safe and shouldn't stay in any household containing pain pills. *That was so very important*, I thought, as I taped another packed cardboard moving box shut.

The doorbell interrupted my thoughts. It was my young neighbor Linsey Hughes. I saw her through the multipaned glass door, a small potted plant in her hands, vibrant and green. It was a young plant, not quite filling the pot, giving it plenty of room for growth.

"What's this?" I asked.

"It's for Bobby." She grinned.

I called for Bobby and he rounded the corner, smiling as he sees Linsey.

He gave her a hug. "Did you come to say goodbye?"

Linsey gave the plant to Bobby.

"This is for you," she explained. "It is a cutting from the original Alcoholics Anonymous plant that Bill W. nurtured and cared for in the 1930s. I want you to have it."

I let out a gasp. The importance and symbolism of this plant was not lost on any of us.

Linsey continued, "I'm sure you know that Bill W. was the first patient of Alcoholics Anonymous. And Doc Silkworth, who helped cowrite the AA guidebook, was Duncan's great-great-granduncle. Bill and his wife lived in a house in the lower Hudson River Valley and were avid gardeners. It was part of his therapy and they took it very seriously. When Bill W. died, the NYC area AA group continued to help his wife in the garden. When she died, the house became somewhat of a museum that can be visited by appointment. Our plant came from their garden, given to Duncan's family by Bill W's wife, Lois."

"At the time of her death, it was fall, and all the helpers took the plants that would not survive the winter. Those plants are being shared all over the world as beautiful symbols of roots, life, and continuance. That is how we were blessed with one and now we would like to pass this on to you. Duncan's family has sent clippings to many—it is truly staggering to think of the widespread joy that has come from that special garden."

I was so moved by this gesture, filled with enormous wonder at how the original plant had been kept alive for all these years by cutting and re-rooting thousands, maybe hundreds of thousands of new lives, transplanted and transformed, giving hope and purpose to those recovering.

It is the perfect symbol—a supportive, caring community friend brings a gift, one of regrowth and life, cut from the mother plant to live on its own, to one day blossom and give to others. Yes, perfect.

Bobby stood dumbfounded in the entranceway, two hands clutching the plant like it was his first time holding a newborn baby, awed. He couldn't take his eyes off it, turning it one way and then another as if he wanted to make sure it was for real.

"Bobby, don't forget to pass it forward," Linsey instructed.

"I won't. I promise I won't forget."

This moment is seared into my memory. I remember all

the mornings Bobby came into the kitchen and headed straight to the Polly Pocket tomato seed plant, filled a cup full of tap water, and gingerly poured the liquid into the miniature terra-cotta pot.

This gift from Linsey and Duncan represented full circle for Bobby. Bobby was able to take care of something even on days he didn't want to take care of himself. He loved on another living, breathing thing, the master of its life, the architect of its growth, and he learned the valuable lesson that he could indeed take care of himself and take care of something else. His tomato plant is his past, long since transplanted to an outdoor planter, outgrowing its sacred place in the kitchen. This new potted plant from Linsey and Duncan, and Doc Silkworth and Bill W., and the innumerable people in between, was his future.

When Bobby texted me pictures of his new apartment, the first picture was this AA plant sitting proudly on the kitchen counter. Damn, I was so happy I cried my eyes out. This was truly the best feeling in the world.

———

HOSPITAL

July 1

I was in a dreamlike state. I could hear whispers and shuffling and beeps, but I couldn't wake up my brain. I slipped in and out of semi wakefulness.

Someone was calling my name, shaking my shoulder gently. "Renée, Renée. Can you wake up?"

It was Will. I slowly started to register where I was and what I had just been through. I struggled to open my eyes, and they flickered and fluttered and finally opened. It took a second to focus on Will's face.

"Renée, Bobby has come to say goodbye. He is packed and headed out right now and wanted to check on you before he leaves."

I tried to sit up, but I was tethered by lines and wires to the noisemaking culprits, vital signs–monitoring machines.

I rotated my head to the left, and Bobby was standing next to the hospital bed, both hands clenched on the bare bars of the engaged safety rail.

"Hi, Aunt Née." His voice was low and soft, soothing, like my ears might hurt if he spoke too loudly.

I was woozy. It had only been a few hours since my knee was replaced, and I had just been moved to a lovely, antiseptic hospital room.

I reached my hand up and Bobby took it. "How are you?" he queried.

"I don't have a leg to stand on." I smiled grimly.

Ironically I was maximum-dosed on OxyContin, and I was seduced by the floating, relaxed feeling. I was not hurting, but I was not thinking clearly. It took me a few moments, but it began to register that Bobby was leaving. He was leaving for good. Pow. The air was sucked from my chest, bushwhacked. I was too vulnerable to put perspective to the situation, remnants of anesthesia lingering, the toll on my body from a major surgery making me emotional.

My tongue was thick. How could I sum up all that we had been through the past sixteen months? Both of us fighting with all our might for just this outcome, this one moment in time when Bobby began his life's journey with a plan for his future and healthy as a horse.

Peering up, I knew I couldn't possibly tell him what a

gift he had been to me, to my family, to my little community of friends. My whole body ached to be able to express this before he left, but all I could do was squeeze his hand harder.

If I could have forced the words out, I would have told him this: we are all changed and there is no going back. Together, we have broken the cycle in our family. Together, we are taking opioid addiction out of its hiding place. We are opening the eyes of those we touch to the disease of addiction, to the epidemic abuse of prescription medicine and correlating heroin use.

Knowing Bobby's and Thomas's stories forces us to step away from the sidelines of naivety and ignorance and into a game we must win. That is why I have shared their stories with you—it's time to get off the sidelines. GAME ON!

A doctor entered behind Bobby to check my vitals and that was his cue to go.

"I love you, Aunt Née," he said as he turned to hug Will, Will's arm slung over Bobby's shoulder, the love and respect so apparent between the two.

As I watched Bobby's back go through the door, I started to weep, big wet tears welling and spilling down my pale cheeks, my shoulders shaking gently.

Will took Bobby's place and clasped my hand, grasping it warmly, silently meeting my eyes, and I felt his loss as well.

The doctor was a quiet spectator, diagnosing the situation in a heartbeat. He asked if Bobby was my son.

"Yes, yes, he is," I sniffled. The doctor then said the most encouraging thing. As he leaned over with a stethoscope, he whispered, "Ma'am, you gave him wings to fly and that is what he is doing. But those same wings will fly him back to you."

SIXTEEN MONTHS

GOODBYE LETTER

Written fifteen hours after surgery:

From: Renée Hodges
Subject: Missing you already!
Date: July 2, 2014, at 3:46 a.m.
To: Bobby

Dear Bobby,

As you know, I always like to write my children a note when they are going off somewhere, so here it is.

Sixteen months ago, I met a boy in trouble, down on his luck and digging a deep hole even deeper. Today, sixteen months later, I see a man who has fought hard to change. A man who trusts people again, who trusts life again. You have clawed your way out of this hole, sometimes sliding backward before hanging on and going forward again, but you kept climbing!

This is the making of a man, Bobby: it is how one deals with adversity and not how one deals with success. Sure, you must celebrate your successes, but there are far more mistakes and failures in life than successes. When you can say "I failed at this" or "I made a mistake" and then truly learn something from these trying times, that is where the rubber meets the road. That is where you become a man. Adversity will strengthen you. Never give up. Never, ever give up.

I also want you to remember that there is always going to be someone who is ahead of you in line and always someone behind. Your duty to yourself is to help those below you in life—and there are many. All peoples are deserving of respect. Do not judge. Instead, walk a mile in their shoes. And, for those ahead of you in line, if you choose wisely, you will find that there are many who are willing to build you up as well . . . they will mentor you. Don't be afraid to ask for help as you will learn a lot from those who are ahead of you.

You are blessed with great charisma and good looks, but this will only get you so far. It is what is in your heart that matters. I have never seen a face with a smile be called ugly. Even Miss America can be ugly without a smile.

Another take-home for you is that money can force power, but it cannot earn respect. As you become more successful, never forget this important concept.

Remember not to be too high maintenance. Girls don't want someone to take care of but someone who will take care of them. Eventually it becomes mutual caring for each other. You grew up with a family that shares every complaint, but it is really not natural to do. Complaints can become like the "The Boy Who Cried Wolf" story. The more you tell, the less likely people will listen. I must say that in the last six months you have really changed in this regard and should take pride in this. You went from being a whiney, complaining, depressed little boy to building a confident and strong foundation for the man you have become.

Remember to stay in touch with those you love and that are safe for you. I know you will build a support system in your new hometown as you have with us in Durham, but the best support will be from yourself. You can only be happy if you want to be happy. No one and nothing will make you happy if you don't want to be.

Remember to stay in touch with Jesus. He has a plan for you. I just know it!

Work hard. You now know what you want to be when you grow up. Many kids your age are still stuck in minimum wage jobs and have nowhere to go. You are blessed to be doing something that will get you out of bed in the morning, with the opportunity to do something you love and want to do. And you will be good at it.

Bobby, PLAY THE GAME. Always sit up front, never be late for class or skip class unless you are headed to the ER spurting blood. Make sure all your teachers know you by name by the end of the month. Lastly, the teacher is always right. You have a lot of street knowledge and experience in some things and might be asked to share, and debate is good, but when it comes down to it, the teachers will grade you on what they have taught you. It is the educational game, so play it well. Use all services the school and community has in tutoring, attending extra credit classes, and seeking help and explanations from the teaching assistants. Play the game.

And, for heaven's sake, always be truthful. Your words are your honor. Lies always are found out. Mature adults don't tell lies and if you are always truthful, you will never have to worry about anything you said. Ask yourself these questions before you open your mouth.

1. Is it truthful?

2. Is it nice?

3. Is it necessary?

And if the answer to any one of these is no, then don't say a word.

And lastly, you must eat a good breakfast every day. You must start eating healthier. And you know this. How can you be a role model for others if you don't live what you preach?

Please, please call me if you feel you need advice, help, money, but especially if you are thinking about using or drinking. For that especially, call me anytime - middle of the night too. Promise, promise me you will do this. Anytime. Just say you need me and I will be there for you.

We love you and you are immediate family now. We hope you will stay with us during any holidays, weekends, or just to get away. Keep your house key. It is yours always. This will always be your home and please use it as such.

I am expecting you to join us at the Hodges family reunion Easter 2015. We are in Louisiana for Thanksgiving and Christmas this year, and you may spend it with us or your family or both.

Look behind you one last time at the pit you have been climbing out of. Then never look back again unless you need a powerful reminder of your past. What happened behind you has shaped you and your future, and although you and I would never have wanted addiction in our family, we can and ARE breaking the generational cycle. We won't blame others anymore. We have the tools in our toolbox to move on. And we are breaking the cycle of silence and shame. Share your struggles; ask for help.

I hope you will save this letter and give in to some of my thoughts. But, as much as I am doling out advice, you are grown and you need to learn to take in lots of perspectives and choose the best ones for yourself. You will always be stuck with me giving you my thoughts, but that is all they are. It is your responsibility to weigh information and make adult decisions. Do not be indecisive. Stand up and lead by example, by your actions. This is what matters in the long run.

Like the doctor said to me right after you said goodbye today, "Ma'am, you have given the bird wings to fly away, but those same wings will fly him back to you!" Go now, but remember, family means sharing failures as well as successes. We love you unconditionally.

So use your wings to find me at any time.

Written with love for you, Bobby, soon to be MSW behind your name!! We are so proud of you.

Love, Aunt Née and Uncle Will—as I know he feels the same way.

******** DO YOUR BEST and that is all one can ask of oneself. You are the judge of this as you are the only one who will know.

SOJOURN

The addiction in my family has tormented me for almost twenty-five years. It is difficult living with the guilt of not having an addiction. You may think that it is only the addict or alcoholic who carries the burden, the shame, the guilt, but I am here to tell you that those left behind are every bit as scarred.

For over two decades I have felt guilt for being healthy and helpless to aid my loved ones. Guilty while watching them band together, whether to hide from or maybe to save themselves from my critical judgments, anger, and own shame. We really are so intertwined and tangled, aren't we?

Addiction is insidious in families and it takes no prisoners. I have felt anger, both warranted and not, isolation, and abandonment. I have drowned myself in pity and jealousy. I was insanely jealous of not being a part of the toxic chemistry. I just wanted a little attention too. And then there is the blame, enough blame to fill our liquor cabinet a thousand times over. I carried my cross for over two decades and, my God, I was tired. But I just couldn't put it down, so I kept dragging it, a sick type of addiction in its own way.

Helping Bobby through his journey forced me to finally and forever put my burden down, and face up to the fact that I have survivor's guilt in many ways and posttraumatic stress in others. In a surprising twist of fate, Bobby's addiction battle was my personal fight as well. Not everyone who helps an alcoholic or addict will discover the same cathartic ending I was most fortunate to find.

I know how Forrest Gump felt when he stopped dead in his tracks and said, "I'm pretty tired . . . I think I'll go home now." For me, the day Bobby came to live with me was the day I quit running from myself.

I never realized that inviting him to come stay with us while he received a medical evaluation would turn into an apocalyptic event.

What I imagined: Duke would help Bobby. His stay would be temporary, no more than the time it took for him to get a place to live. He could find a job or go back to school. I was capable of handling it all.

What I learned: Battling addiction is a war, long and devastating, fraught with peril and setbacks. It cannot be fought alone, and I needed all the help I could get.

At times I was arrogant and ignorant, innocent and an idealist. I do know this: there was something inside of me that wouldn't let him go, wouldn't give up, blind to the difficulties and effect it would have on me, my family, my friends.

I was a cheerleader every day. I was a guidance counselor, a dating coach, an honest and open sharer of my life and my own struggles.

I was lucky. I had the heart of a loving husband who, although he sometimes wanted to box my ears, stuck with me, loved me, let me ride his back through the river. All my children, especially the child living closest to home, Katherine, were supportive, always worried about how I was coping and if they could help hold the heavy part of the load I carried.

I had the hand of a wonderful psychologist who went above and beyond helping me cope, dishing out wisdom and comfort, knowledge and strength. Every woman needs a Mary in her life. I had the bond of friendship and family, both communities of love and extraordinary caring, holding Bobby, Will, and me up every single day. Through visits, emails, recommendations, advice, shoulders, prayers, love— always love—it took the whole team to win. What a sojourn, what a gift.

FINAL REMARKS

One never knows when one's life path will change, when something will send you veering off course, plunging you down a steep, rocky slope. For me, my course was forever altered by the death by overdose of my best friend's son and by choosing to take in and care for my opioid-addicted nephew. These two events set me on a path I never would have chosen for myself.

It was lonely at first, but over time I realized that I didn't have to travel this road alone. When I refused to hide in secrecy, opened up, and shared Bobby's situation, asking for support and understanding, others began not only helping, but began sharing their own stories.

It was staggering to discover how many people in my circle of friends, in my neighborhood and community, were on a parallel journey, dealing with addiction in their own families, and dealing alone.

I am not a licensed physician, social worker, or counselor. I am one of the millions of everyday people tragically affected by addiction. I began writing this story for my nephew, but in the end, I realized I was writing this story for myself and for all of us affected by the helplessness of addiction.

Addiction grows its power from secrecy and shaming; being honest and open brought a community together and saved a young man's life while opening our eyes wide to the scourge of this millennial generation: opioid and heroin addiction. This story isn't about shaming or parenting failures, or what we could have done differently; it is about answering the question: What can we do to help each other?

This widespread prescription-drug abuse has created an

epidemic which is affecting darn near all of us, and I see no reason why we shouldn't wage this battle together, leaning on and supporting each other as was done for Bobby and me by my community. This is Bobby's story, but it is also Thomas Howard's story and the story of so many others, most of whom are fighting for their lives in ashamed silence. But it is also my story and silence has never been my way.

AFTERWORD

by W. Hodges Davis, MD

Dr. Davis is an orthopedic surgeon, specializing in foot and ankle surgery. He serves as the medical director of the OrthoCarolina Foot & Ankle Institute. More importantly, he is the father of five boys.

Last week I volunteered to form and participate in a special committee at work. You should know that I hate committees. My experience is that for the most part they accomplish little, and as a surgeon I am used to making decisions after weighing my own data. The reason I formed this particular committee is I am scared. I am scared for my children and I am scared for my patients. After a thirty-year career as an orthopedic surgeon that has been laser-focused on helping people in pain, I am scared that my colleagues and I are the fuel of a much larger problem that is causing more pain than any orthopedic pathology I treat. The problem is scary because my profession is fueling the use and abuse of prescription opioid pain medicine.

The statistics are undeniable. The use of prescription opioids has risen 900 percent since 2002. The incidence of death by overdose from an opioid written by a licensed practitioner is more common than death from car crashes in the younger demographic. It was estimated by the CDC that in 2013, 1.9 million Americans abused or were dependent on prescription opioids. CDC Director Thomas Frieden summarized, "We know of no other medication routinely used for a nonfatal condition that kills patients so frequently." This is scary if that were the only problem with this drug class. I mentioned my children.

My greatest fear is for my children and their generation. As my kids reach college age, my frank discussions with them on this topic make me realize that my profession is helping my kids' generation become poorly trained pharmacists. I hear stories of "homework meds" and "chill meds." Meds that make the "pain" better and meds that help sleep come. They are all prescriptions for controlled meds that are first written by a doctor. "The meds must be fine because a doctor prescribed them. They are safe because my doctor gave them to me or my friend. If we mix the drugs, they take away the pain." I am scared for them.

I don't know when Americans became convinced that life should be pain-free, but my profession has fueled this misperception. The use of opioids allows us to truly help people cope with cancer or surgery, but the promise was never that all pain would be gone. Pain is part of the human experience. My role as a doctor is not to change the human experience, and my role as a parent is not to shield my children from all that is truly human. Pain is the gift no one wants, but the problems with no pain are clearly more deadly. Pain serves a purpose.

This uniquely American belief of the right to a "pain-free life" has become clear only recently as I started to refuse to refill my patients' opioid meds, when they were clearly past the reasonable time frame for the treatment of their postsurgical pain. Many have responded with anger and a sense of entitlement for the pain-free life that clearly reflects this shift. In this era of patient satisfaction being equated to quality of care, I give my profession a bit of a pass to go the easy route and refill. This does not make it right.

This is why I applaud the call to arms that is this book.

This may be the bravest book I have ever read. First, for Renée to face the realities of the family disease that is addiction. The brutal self-examination of that wonderful woman in her mirror is awe-inspiring. Second, the bravery of Bobby to choose to be human rather than pain-free. It is so much easier to choose the meds and the escape, but he chose to live. So hard to do but so important for physicians and patients to embrace as the better way, the road less traveled.

I am on this work committee because doctors are supposed to be part of the solution, not the first step in our patients' journey to addiction and even death. I need to believe that we can make this right. I applaud Renée and Bobby for their courage to tell their personal and painful story. The more voices raised to shine the light on this problem can only help. The voice raised in this book is loud and so very real. Thanks for helping me pick up the flashlight in my house.

EPILOGUE

Bobby graduated on May 15, 2016, with a Master of Social Work Degree. When I began writing this book, I never dared dream that this day would come, but it is here. It wasn't an easy two years for him, but it was exceptional. He graduated with a perfect 4.0, was inducted into the Phi-Alpha Honor Society, and was awarded Presidential Scholar for his academic achievements.

The director of the program, Jeanne F. Cook, emailed me with her thoughts:

> *Bobby has been an asset to our program. I remember the first time I spoke with him and talking with him now he shows such positive growth. He has taken his studies very seriously. His professors, field supervisors, and fellow students all speak positively of what he contributes. He will make us all proud to have known him.*

During graduate school he thrived at two internships, the first of which was a social worker assistant working with families fostering children in the Department of Social Services custody. I wasn't surprised when he was awarded Best Caseworker, Placement of the Year award in 2015. He has a unique gift of empathy, a selfless heart, and a yearning to give back.

His second internship was in a children's hospital where he worked in the Pediatric Oncology-Hematology and Bone Marrow Transplant area, providing services to children and families. Again, he was honored for his exceptional work by earning the Internship Spotlight Award in 2016 for identifying specific psychosocial needs within the hospital's patient-family population.

Bobby worked hard outside of school and in his internships but his first priority was always to himself and he did a fantastic job keeping himself safe.

He still keeps up with his counselor Jeff Georgi, and Jeff had lunch with Bobby graduation week.

So many people from Durham wanted to support Bobby when he graduated that we rented a large van to make the two-hour trip.

My youngest daughter, Katherine, graduated from college several weeks after Bobby, and he sat in the audience whooping it up as her name was called. Rachel and William are doing just fine. Mary Costello is still saving the world, one person at a time. My husband, Will, is enjoying his empty nest. And I am too.

John and Jill are celebrating their first grandchild. Elizabeth and Charlie delivered a baby girl on March 1, 2015. Timing was such that Bobby was on spring break, and he was able to be with his family throughout Elizabeth's labor, delivery, and trip home with their newest member. He sent me a picture, head propped up on a pillow with his new niece resting on his belly, a most loving smile on his face, his hands gently placed on her back. This newest member of the family will be well loved and taken care of by her Uncle Bobby.

Like many graduating students, Bobby is applying for jobs, hoping to pay off his student loans, find a soul mate, have children, and live a long and quiet life. He will have quite the story to tell his children, one that includes heartache and courage, perseverance and love.

I myself have gone back to a quiet life. These last few years feel like a dream but I know they were not. I hope

Bobby wasn't too embarrassed by his ole Aunt Née on graduation day because I just couldn't keep quiet; I loudly and proudly screamed with joy when his name was called.

And, just like Bobby, his AA plant is thriving!

———

If you would like for Bobby to speak to your group,
you can find him on Facebook at
Facebook.com/SpeakBobby

Special Discounts are available on quantity purchases by
corporations, associations, educators, and others.
Inquiries can be made at
ReneeHodgesAuthor@gmail.com.

ADDITIONAL NOTES

The Opiate Epidemic: How It Happened and How to Help

By Becky Georgi, MS, LPC, LCAS, CCS

Renée's story began as thousands of others have over the last decade. When her nephew Bobby was still in elementary school, long before he ever considered taking a drink or using a drug, decisions were made within the medical community that would profoundly impact his adolescence.

In 1995 the American Pain Society identified the negative impact of poorly managed pain on the overall health of our nation. Five years later, when Bobby was ten years old, the Joint Commission on Health Organization Accreditation added pain as the fifth vital sign. This meant that in addition to taking a patient's temperature, pulse, blood pressure, and breaths per minute during each visit, a patient was asked about pain. If pain was identified, physicians were instructed to reduce the pain level by the utilization of narcotic pain medications.

This decision, though well intended, may have opened the door for the opioid epidemic of the last decade. Within a short period of time, millions of patients were beginning to use opiate-based medications for even modest levels of discomfort.

Sadly, this decision convinced an entire generation of physicians and health-care professionals to overuse narcotics to cover up chronic pain rather than actually treat the pain itself. Not unlike Valium, which was never intended for prolonged use in its treatment of anxiety, narcotics, which are effective in acute pain management, became the medication of choice for chronic pain.

- Studies have shown that while cumulative pain levels remained constant among Americans, prescriptions for pain medications more than quadrupled between 1999 and 2010. [7]

- By 2013, hydrocodone was the most commonly prescribed drug in the United States. [8]

This well-meaning decision was an effort to help patients cope with all levels of pain, but it ended up challenging the most fundamental foundation of the Hippocratic Oath: do no harm.

Physicians began to view narcotic medications as safe and commonplace, becoming as comfortable with their use as if they were using aspirin, acetaminophen, or ibuprofen. Without addressing the historical hazards of addiction associated with these medications, young physicians continued to overestimate the effectiveness of narcotics for pain control and underestimate their risks. In their effort to help, driven by a policy they did not write, a public health crisis began brewing.

- In a relatively short period of time millions of patients in the United States were prescribed opioid therapy for chronic pain. In fact, 245 million prescriptions were filled for opioid pain relievers in the United States during 2014.[9]

---

7 See Center for Disease Control and Prevention, 2011.

8 See Mathews and Beck, 2015.

9 See Jones, 2015.

- This increase in opioid prescribing is also associated with increased opioid-related visits to the emergency department and deaths from drug overdose.[10]

- An individual who is prescribed opioids for the treatment of pain is three times more likely to develop an opioid addiction than an individual without an opioid prescription. Furthermore, individuals prescribed low-dose or high-dose chronic opioid therapy are 15 or 122 times more likely, respectively, to develop opioid addiction.[11]

- It is now estimated that approximately four out of ten patients on this medical regimen will abuse their medications.[12]

These policy changes led to increased use of Oxycodone, Percocet, and Vicodin, which created higher levels of addiction. Additional ramifications impacted an entire generation of emerging adults. It soon became clear that because their brains were still developing, they seemed more prone to dependency.

If their prescriptions for narcotics were interrupted for any reason, they were often driven to an even more powerful pain reliever—heroin.

- Heroin use more than doubled among young adults ages 18–25 from 2002 to 2013. [13]

---

10 See Dasgupta et al., 2006; Wisniewski, 2008; and Center for Disease Control and Prevention, 2011.

11 See Edlund et al., 2014.

12 See Beaudoin et al., 2014.

13 See Jones et al., 2015.

- Heroin use has increased across the United States among men and women, most age groups, and all income levels. Some of the greatest increases occurred in demographic groups with historically low rates of heroin use: women, the privately insured, and people with higher incomes. [14]

- Heroin overdose mortality has quadrupled.[15]

Bobby, like thousands of his generation, walked into the series of medical missteps which led to the heroin epidemic. There are any number of dazzling statistics that illustrate the impact that heroin and over-prescribed opioids have had on the emerging adult population. However, there are two statistics that scream louder than all the rest.

- Accidents are the primary cause of death for individuals aged 18 to 25 years. Historically, car accidents have represented the bulk of these fatal accidents. However, in 2009, more young people between the ages of 18 and 25 died from drug overdoses than from car accidents.[16]

- The United States represents 5 percent of the world's population yet consumes 75 percent of the world's prescription drugs. (In 2009 the United States consumed 99 percent of the world's hydrocodone, 60

---

14 See Center for Disease Control and Prevention, 2015; Rudd et al., 2014; and Compton et al., 2016.

15 See Rudd et al., 2014.

16 See Paulozzi et al., 2012.

percent of the world's hydromorphone, and 81 percent of the world's oxycodone). [17]

Every parent, physician, politician, health-care provider, and concerned family member should take a deep breath and allow these statistics to propel them into action. Tragically, young people are extremely capable of hiding their drug use until it truly spirals out of control. Even when their use becomes unmanageable, families often misunderstand what is going on or are paralyzed to act because of lack of information.

Even more destructive is the power of shame which may immobilize family members from intervening.

The shame and vulnerability research of Brené Brown, PhD, supports this. Dr. Brown says shame is the intensely painful feeling that we are unworthy of love and belonging. It is the internalized belief that "I am not good enough," "I don't measure up," "I'm not as smart as I should be," "I am not muscular enough," and/or "I can never seem to make my parents happy or live up to their expectations."

These voices of shame plague our young people and create an internal environment that makes it impossible for them to see their true value. Prescription opioids and particularly heroin can temporarily relieve the emotional agony experienced so often by our young people. The ultimate tragedy of heroin addiction is that it causes greater levels of shame, requiring more drug use each day just to keep going.

When families learn of a loved one with a heroin addiction, shame can bring about blindness. Just as the heroin addict temporarily relieves their own psychological pain with

---

17 See Manchikanti et al., 2010.

the drug, the family escapes their emotional pain by redefining the problem. Perhaps it is simply "hanging around the wrong crowd," "partying too much," or any number of other reasons. For almost any other illness—cancer, pneumonia, or depression—as soon as the family identifies the symptoms, they seek help from other family members or health-care professionals. Sadly, this is not so in the face of heroin addiction.

Addiction occupies space in the public mind as a failure of character rather than a medical affliction, a lack of willpower rather than a legitimate disease, a choice that's made rather than an illness that strikes. On an individual level, shame drives addictive illness and interferes with a family's ability to get help. On a much broader scale, the shame associated with heroin use carries such a powerful stigma that the culture itself interferes with family members supporting their loved one.

When family members see their loved one suffering, what can they do to stop the downward spiral of this insidious illness? The family must reach beyond the shame, talk to each other, and get help.

If you are concerned that your loved one is addicted to narcotic pain medication and/or heroin, search for the overdose reversal drug, naloxone (also known as Narcan), through your pharmacy or family physician. If naloxone is administered quickly, it can counter the overdose effects, usually within two minutes, allowing enough time for the EMS to arrive.

Once the individual has been stabilized, the first step is to get outside help. Treatment works, even though there may be a return of symptoms.

Finding a qualified professional to guide the family is of paramount importance. This is easier said than done and, like searching for the right doctor or therapist, a good fit is essential. During my time in this field, many families have asked me how best to find a professional with the necessary qualifications.

The chosen mental health professional must have specific training, certification, and licensure in substance abuse treatment. Academic degrees do not necessarily determine competency. I urge you to check on the qualifications in your state.

Professionals with degrees in Social Work, Counseling, Rehabilitation Counseling, and Psychology should have specialty training and/or certification in the area of substance abuse treatment. Many states now require the licensing of substance abuse professionals.

If you find a professional with the appropriate credentials, these are important issues to discuss:

- The professional must believe addiction is an illness and use language to support this belief, the language of the medical community. Use of the correct language validates it is an illness and supports recovery while helping to reduce shame.

- The professional must determine whether outpatient or inpatient (residential) services are required and should use American Society of Addiction Medicine Placement Criteria. A thorough assessment should determine the diagnosis and the diagnosis determines the appropriate level of treatment. Some addiction professionals are connected to different treatment centers, and they may use these. This is something families need to be aware of.

- It is important that the professional utilizes drug testing. Drug testing is an important step of recovery for many reasons: it provides accountability, patients get positive reinforcement when they test negative, and it's helpful to have a track record for future employment. If professionals do not regularly drug test their patients as a part of treatment, proceed with caution.

- The professional must have working knowledge of Alcoholics Anonymous, Ala-non, and Narcotics Anonymous.

- The professional must view recovery holistically, and encourage the use of other recovery aids such as psychotherapy and the integration of self-help groups (AA, NA, or others). It is important that they have familiarity with any AA and NA young people's meetings in their area.

- Determine how the provider or treatment team will respond to a relapse. This should be addressed in the beginning of treatment. Family members need to know that it is not expected and, if it occurs, they should be included. Having a signed release of information makes it possible for the supportive family members to work with the therapist to stabilize the patient before the relapse gains increased energy.

- Ask about interventions: the professional should not have a "confrontational and shame-based approach" to dealing with the addicted. The addicted young person is filled with self-loathing and is aware of the pain he has caused the family. It is important to maintain a loving approach to the discussion of treatment with clear and reasonable expectations. A family meeting with the patient should not be a surprise attack.

Finding an addiction specialist who fits your needs is a necessity, but there are also many other ways in which friends and family can support a loved one who may be struggling from an addiction. Many of these steps support work they are doing with the addiction specialist.

How Families Can Help:

- Create a low-stress alcohol-and-drug-free environment.

- Establish realistic expectations, especially related to alcohol and drug use.

- Reinforce small steps toward improvement.

- Be informed about effective use of medication in recovery.

- Work with the professional(s); work as a recovery team.

Important Components of Recovery:

- Abstinence with twelve-step involvement

- Establishing positive rewards and negative consequences
- Frequent drug testing to reinforce success
- The use of recovery mentors and/or coaches, positive role models
- Management of relapse, when or if it occurs
- Modified lifestyle to include a good sleep-wake cycle, healthy eating, exercise, and mindfulness
- Active and sustained monitoring for at least one year

In the face of addiction, it is important to ask for help and to use all the resources available. I recommend the following:

It Takes A Family: A Cooperative Approach to Lasting Sobriety, by Debra Jay.

"Dying to be Free," Huffington Post: http://projects. huffingtonpost.com/dying-to-be-free-heroin-treatment National Institute on Drug Abuse, The Science of Drug Abuse and Addiction: https://www.drugabuse.gov/ publications/media-guide/science-drug-abuse-addiction-basics

Becky Georgi, MS, LPC, LCAS, CCS, has invested over twenty-five years working with adolescents, young adults, and their families through substance abuse education, prevention, and treatment. She holds licenses as a clinical addiction specialist, a certified clinical supervisor, and a licensed professional counselor. Recently, Becky and her husband,

Jeff, cofounded Bluefield: A University Recovery Community in Durham, North Carolina, to serve students and their families who are committed to a path of recovery, self-discovery, and academic excellence after returning to university after substance abuse treatment. She is currently the director and owner of Georgi Educational & Counseling Services (GECS), providing substance abuse training and consultation for a statewide project in South Carolina, and is an adjunct associate in the Department of Psychiatry and Behavioral Sciences, Division on Addiction Research and Translation at Duke University Medical Center. She earned her BS and MS from Indiana University and completed a postgraduate certificate program in Family Therapy in South Bend, Indiana, through the Menniger Foundation.

WORKS CITED

Beaudoin, Francesca L., et al. "Prescription Opioid Misuse among ED Patients Discharged with Opioids." *American Journal of Emergency Medicine* 32.6 (2014): 580–585.

Centers for Disease Control and Prevention (CDC). "Vital Signs: Overdoses of Prescription Opioid Pain Relievers—United States, 1999–2008." *Morbidity and Mortality Weekly Report* (MMWR) 60.43 (2011): 1487.

Centers for Disease Control and Prevention. "Vital Signs: Today's Heroin Epidemic—More People at Risk, Multiple Drugs Abused." Centers for Disease Control and Prevention (2015).

Compton, Wilson M., Christopher M. Jones, and Grant T. Baldwin. "Relationship between Nonmedical Prescription-Opioid Use and Heroin Use." *New England Journal of Medicine* 2016.374 (2016): 154–163.

Dasgupta, Nabarun, et al. "Association between Non-Medical and Prescriptive Usage of Opioids." *Drug and Alcohol Dependence* 82.2 (2006): 135–142.

Edlund, MJ, et al. "The Role of Prescription in Incident Opioid Abuse and Dependence among Individuals with Chronic Noncancer Pain: The Role of Opioid Prescription. *Clinical Journal of Pain* 30.7 (2014): 557–564.

Jones, Christopher M., et al. "Vital Signs: Demographic and Substance Use Trends among Heroin Users—United States, 2002–2013." *Morbidity and Mortality Weekly Report* (MMWR) 64.26 (2015): 719–725.

Jones, Christopher M. "The Latest Prescription Trends for Controlled Prescription Drugs." National Institute on Drug Abuse, https://d14rmgtrwzf5a.cloudfront.net/sites/default/files/cjonesnid a-bhccprescriptiontrendsslides.pdf. Accessed August 4, 2017.

Manchikanti, Laxmaiah, Bert Fellows, Hary Ailinani, and Vidyasagar Pampati. "Therapeutic Use, Abuse, and Nonmedical Use of Opioids: A Ten-Year Perspective." *Pain Physician* 13 (2010): 401–435.

Mathews, Anna W. and Melinda Beck. "Generic Vicodin Was a Top Medicare Drug in 2013, Data Shows." *Wall Street Journal*, https://www.wsj.com/articles/generic-vicodin-was-a-top-medicar e-drug-in-2013-data-shows-1430 697811?mg=prod/accounts-wsj. Accessed August 4, 2017.

Paulozzi, Leonard J. "Prescription Drug Overdoses: A Review." *Journal of Safety Research* 43.4 (2012): 283–289.

Rudd, Rose A., et al. "Increases in Drug and Opioid-Involved Overdose Deaths—United States, 2010–2015." *Morbidity and Mortality Weekly Report* (MMWR) 65 (2016).

Wisniewski, Angela M., Christopher H. Purdy, and Richard D. Blondell. "The Epidemiologic Association between Opioid Prescribing, Non-medical Use, and Emergency Department Visits." *Journal of Addictive Diseases* 27.1 (2008): 1–11.

ACKNOWLEDGMENTS

Thanks to our many supportive friends and family; because of you, Bobby was able to save himself. It truly takes a village/community/tribe. It takes us all.

To Bobby, my beautiful nephew, for letting me share his story. You will change the world.

Thanks to my family, Will, Rachel, Sam, William, and Katherine, always.

To the Redford family for your courage and support, Annie Wright for your love and encouragement, and to the whole Hodges clan, you are an inspiration.

To Joy and Lucy Hodges; Matty, John, Madeleine, and Hamilton Sateri; Jane Scott and Philip Hodges; Anne and Thomas; Mary Beth Arciuolo; Linda Sue Satterfield; Mary LaScala; Jeff and Becky Georgi; and Mary Dodge, my other Mary.

Thanks to Hodges Davis, my best cheerleader, and all the boys—West, Will, Henry, Jake, and Sammy. To my sailing buddies: Leslie and Kirk Kirkland, Page and George Littlewood, Anna and Bob Whalen, and Anne and Jess Eberdt, and to my Pennyfeather sisters: Kaye Amick, Barbara Garmon, Dee Mason, Joy Long, and Anne Long.

To Lee and David Bowen, Peace! To Kappy and Perry Black, Laura Shaffer and Doug Henley, Lee and Tom Wollman, Laurie and Colin Myer, Theky and Ted Pappas, Carolyn and Steve Sloate, Lucy and Al Martindale, Meredith Martindale, Beth and Mike Sholtz and family, Ann Blackwell, Deborah Welch, Tee Zimmerman, Maureen Spencer, Peggy and Walker Harris, Denise Carr, Maricela Cooperberg, Beth and Kevin Reeves, Connie and Phil Kearney, Larke and Ray Wheeler, Colleen and Marty Buehler, Amy and Mike Russell, Linda Ho, Annegret Tree and Paulene Stone, Susan and Jeff Hamill, Shari and Usher Winslett, Pamela and John Northington,

Karen Daly, Kyle Drerup, Kit McLean, Gigi Pierce, Kay Peters, Janet Hawkins, Nancy Roberts and my small group, Lynne and T Moorman, Linsey and Duncan Hughes, Laura Branton, Holly Broughton, Joanne and Rodger Liddle, Susan and Dave Cator, Ruth Caccavale, Nancy Pike, Mimi Hanson, Carolyn Davidson, Charlotte Jones, Marjorie Pierson, Della and Steve McDowell, Virginia Dirschl, Shelayne Sutton, Margaret Conrad, Elizabeth Moshier, Monica Jenkins, Kate Shults, Dana Lange, Andrea Leidolf, Mark Bonner, Kennon, Holly, and Aerin Borden, Nan and Britt Galloway, Louise Tranchin, Olivia Shelton, Elise Tyler, Claire Costello, Dorothy Rogers, Kim Leversedge, Leslie Garrison, Tracy Landi, Jeanne Cook, Ellen Lenghi, Kristine and Jack Hodges Jr., Kylie Harris, Amanda Davison, Mary McLean, Gail Obenour, Liz and Murray Garrott, Bette Powell, Michele Smith, Janie Wagstaff, Leslie Bovay, Margaret Watson, Rob Bickham, Ann Colgin, Elizabeth McDonald, Helen Smith, Betsy Brittain, Chris Brooks, Susan Wilkerson, Kaylen James, Caroline Faught, Heather Alexander, Karen Lamont, Katie Corley, Christy Bowman, Donna Tyler, Roger Peterson, Mary Jo Hendrickson, Carey Brittain, Barbara Boatwright, Carol Shepard, Paula Pink, Bria and Torsie Judkins, Michael Ulku-Steiner, Robert and April Rayborn, Lisa Nichols, and Mimi Prioleau.

To my Bench: Becky and Henry Wood, Mary Hamilton, Patricia Johnson, Joy Dunlap, Debbie White, Malissa Kilpatrick, Sharon Baxter, Lynne Moorman, Susan Ruch, De Cutshaw, Desiree Denton, Beth Sholtz and Theky Pappas.

To Grace Turner, who touched me deeply with her generosity. I have paid it forward.

To Brightleaf Book Club, Bull City Book Club, Jane Friedman, Andi Cumbo-Floyd, Libby Jordan, Madeline Hopkins, Elisabeth Kauffman, and Pamela Long.

To Kaye and Deesie for having the last word.

Special thanks to these brilliant women and their help in bringing life to this project: my book coach, Allison Kirkland, who believed in me, Brooke Warner and Lauren Wise and She Writes Press, and Caitlin Hamilton Marketing.

From Bobby on his graduation day:

Remembering Time

I remember a time when I lived in a village. I remember living one day at a time. I remember the good times and bad times, both leading to where I stand today. I remember my family. I remember Mom, Dad, Elizabeth, Aunt Née, and Uncle Will. I remember cousins Rachel, William, and Katherine. I remember Ms. Annie and Ms. Anne. I remember Roux and Saint. I remember meeting new people and making new friends. I remember these friends with open arms; I remember these friends believing in me after open arms part. I remember these friends making me their family; I remember my time with this extended family. I remember how lost I felt and I remember the village that found me. I remember finding my way. I remember doing the next right thing. I remember how to believe in myself once again and I remember those who never stopped believing in me. I remember a village that took a chance. I remember a village that raised me. I remember that village in Durham and Chapel Hill.

Bobby

May 2016

ABOUT THE AUTHOR

Although her Louisiana roots run deep, Renée Hodges and her husband have called North Carolina home for the past thirty years. Hodges has worked as a campaign manager for a candidate for the Texas State House of Representatives (she won); front deskperson at a ski resort; and volunteer recruiter and registration head during a presidential campaign in New York City. She also cowrote and self-published the Best Kept Secrets series of guides in the 1980s. Settling into motherhood and raising a family has been her most satisfying work, however, and today she is a wife, mother of three, writer, investor, community volunteer, and avid tennis player. Learn more at www.ReneeHodgesAuthor.com.

BOOK
CLUB
QUESTIONS

1. What is the significance of the title? Would you have given the book a different title? If yes, what is your title? How does the cover art make you feel?

2. Would you have done what Renée and Will did, taking in a relative who is in recovery? Why or why not?

3. Do you think Bobby would have been successful if they had not taken him in? Did it surprise you how much effort it took to get Bobby back into a normal day-to-day lifestyle?

4. Do you think the situation for Bobby would have been different if Renée and Will were not of some financial means? How much do financial realities affect recovery success? How does family support affect recovery success?

5. What was your favorite passage? What scene was the most pivotal for the book? How do you think the story would have changed had that scene not taken place?

6. Renée believes that the shame of addiction causes families to hide it, and that this shame and secrecy hinder recovery. How did feeling ashamed affect Bobby? Affect Renée? How important to Bobby's success was Renée's openness with family and friends?

7. Renée shares emails and journal entries in her book. What effect does this have on the telling?

8. Were there any moments where you disagreed with the choices of any of the people? What would you have done differently?

9. Bobby needs a community to hold him up. So does Renée. Discuss.

10. Do you believe certain cultures make it easy for people to overindulge?

11. How did you feel when reading about the amount of prescription drugs that Bobby had been prescribed while in rehab?

12. The Hodges approached addiction recovery holistically. Why?

13. This book is informative, at times heartbreaking, and also inspirational. Do you feel differently about tackling problems in general, having read it?

14. What role does faith play in this book?

15. How do you feel the experience of caring for Bobby has affected Renée, Renée and Will, her relationship with her brother, and the larger community? Does it change your views on addiction and recovery, especially knowing how big a problem opioid addiction has become?

16. What does this memoir say about failure? What does it say about success?

17. What do you hope for Bobby?

18. An orthopedic surgeon writes in the afterword, "Pain is the gift no one wants, but the problems with no pain are clearly more deadly. Pain serves a purpose." Discuss this statement. How did having the afterword enhance your reading of this memoir?

19. There are lots of headlines lately that address urgent, pressing concerns. Were you aware of the news about the widespread opioid addiction in this country? Did you learn anything new about opioids and addiction reading this book?

20. Why do you read memoirs? What do they provide as a reading experience that general nonfiction or novels do not?

SELECTED TITLES FROM SHE WRITES PRESS

She Writes Press is an independent publishing company
founded to serve women writers everywhere.
Visit us at www.shewritespress.com.

Blinded by Hope: One Mother's Journey Through Her Son's Bipolar Illness and Addiction by Meg McGuire. $16.95, 978-1-63152-125-6. A fiercely candid memoir about one mother's roller coaster ride through doubt and denial as she attempts to save her son from substance abuse and bipolar illness.

Searching for Normal: The Story of a Girl Gone Too Soon by Karen Meadows. $16.95, 978-1-63152-137-9. Karen Meadows intertwines her own story with excerpts from her daughter Sadie's journals to describes their roller coaster ride through Sadie's depression and a maze of inadequate mental health treatment and services—one that ended with Sadie's suicide at age eighteen.

Warrior Mother: A Memoir of Fierce Love, Unbearable Loss, and Rituals that Heal by Sheila K. Collins, PhD. $16.95, 978-1-938314-46-9. The story of the lengths one mother goes to when two of her three adult children are diagnosed with potentially terminal diseases.

Rethinking Possible: A Memoir of Resilience by Rebecca Faye Smith Galli. $16.95, 978-1-63152-220-8. After her brother's devastatingly young death tears her world apart, Becky Galli embarks upon a quest to recreate the sense of family she's lost—and learns about healing and the transformational power of love over loss along the way.

Don't Leave Yet: How My Mother's Alzheimer's Opened My Heart by Constance Hanstedt. $16.95, 978-1-63152-952-8. The chronicle of Hanstedt's journey toward independence, self-assurance, and connectedness as she cares for her mother, who is rapidly losing her own identity to the early stage of Alzheimer's.

The Longest Mile: A Doctor, a Food Fight, and the Footrace that Rallied a Community Against Cancer by Christine Meyer, MD. $16.95, 978-1-63152-043-3. In a moment of desperation, after seeing too many patients and loved ones battle cancer, a doctor starts a running team— never dreaming what a positive impact it will have on her community.